# NUGGETS

## OF

# GENUINE

# GOLD

# OTHER TITLES BY PAUL L. KING

### Finding Your Niche: 12 Keys to Opening God's Doors for Your Life

Universal biblical principles from more than 35 years of ministry experience for unlocking the gateways to your assignment from God and encountering new vistas of God's purposes for your life and calling. Discussion and study questions included.

ISBN 10: 0-9785352-8-6 Paperback

ISBN 13: 978-0-9785352-8-5

### Moving Mountains: Lessons in Bold Faith from Great Evangelical Leaders

Amazing stories and teachings of bold, wise faith from George Müller, Hudson Taylor, Charles Spurgeon, Andrew Murray, A.B. Simpson, Hannah Whitall Smith, Oswald Chambers, E.M. Bounds, Amy Carmichael, A.W. Tozer, and more! Study guide included. *"Feast on wind and fire!"—Calvin Miller*

ISBN 0-8007-9375-7 Paperback

### A Believer with Authority: The Life and Message of John A. MacMillan

The ground-breaking biography and teachings of the Christian and Missionary Alliance missionary and professor who was a trailblazing pioneer in spiritual warfare and the seminal writer on the authority of the believer. *Endorsed by Jack Hayford and Neil Anderson.*

ISBN 0-87509-917-3 Paperback

### Genuine Gold: The Cautiously Charismatic Story of the Early Christian and Missionary Alliance

The rediscovered and fully-documented history of the supernatural in the C&MA, featuring first-hand testimonies of early Alliance charismatic experiences (even before Azusa Street), relationships between the C&MA and the early Pentecostal movement, and evidences of historical drift and recovery. *"[A] valuable book. . . . King's research is impressive."—Pneuma: The Journal of the Society for Pentecostal Studies*

ISBN 0-9785352-0-0 Paperback

### Binding and Loosing: Exercising Authority over the Dark Powers (co-authored with K. Neill Foster)

Understanding properly the biblical and theological concept and sound practice of combating the powers that war against Christ and His Church through binding and loosing according to Matthew 16:19—when it is appropriate, when it works and when it does not. Illustrated from real life experiences. Study guide included.

ISBN 0-87509-852-5 Paperback

### Only Believe: Examining the Origin and Development of Classic and Contemporary Word of Faith Theologies

"The definitive, comprehensive study of the teachings and practices of faith throughout church history. Thoroughly documented with classic and contemporary citations, it breaks new ground, uncovers new historical and theological information about the origins of faith teaching and practice; corrects inaccurate information and misinterpretations; discerns healthy and unhealthy teachings and practices in today's Word of Faith movement; and provides sound counsel for walking by faith . . . at once scholarly, accessible, and practical."—Mark E. Roberts, Ph.D.

ISBN 978-0-9785352-6-1 Paperback

### Anointed Women: The Rich Heritage of Women in Ministry in The Christian and Missionary Alliance

The remarkable stories of women used by God in amazing ways, documenting hundreds of women who served as Alliance pastors, evangelists, and teachers, planted hundreds of churches, and led thousands of people to salvation in Christ, healing, and a deeper Christian life.

ISBN 978-0-9819526-7-3 Paperback

To order copies see www.higherlifeministries.com or e-mail pking@higherlifeministries.com.

# NUGGETS
## OF
# GENUINE
# GOLD

SIMPSON, TOZER, JAFFRAY, AND OTHER
CHRISTIAN & MISSIONARY ALLIANCE LEADERS ON
## EXPERIENCING THE SPIRIT-EMPOWERED LIFE

*A Treasury of Testimony and Teaching*

COMPILED BY

## Paul L. King, D.Min., Th.D.

WORD & SPIRIT PRESS
TULSA

*Nuggets of Genuine Gold: Simpson, Tozer, Jaffray, and Other Christian & Missionary Alliance Leaders on Experiencing the Spirit-Empowered Life*

Copyright 2010 by Paul L. King <pking@higherlifeministries.com>

The author and publisher believe that excerpts from copyrighted works used in this work fall within the fair use provision of copyright law. Copyright owners claiming otherwise should contact publisher permissions at WordSP@gmail.com. Complete publication information occurs in the endnote to the first use of each work.

The author gratefully acknowledges permission by Wingspread Publishers, Camp Hill, PA, for use of excerpts from the following: *Born after Midnight*, 1959, 1987 renewal by the Children of A. W. Tozer; *Tragedy in the Church: The Missing Gifts*, 1990; *God Tells the Man Who Cares*, 1993; *Days of Heaven on Earth*, 1897, revised edition 1984.

ISBN 978-0-9819526-6-6 (pbk. : alk. paper)

Published by Word & Spirit Press, Tulsa, Oklahoma.
http://WandSP.com ; <WordSP@gmail.com>

Designed and composed by Booksetters. <Booksetters121@aol.com>

Quotations marked NASB are from the New American Standard Bible®, Copyright © 1960, 1962, 1963, 1968, 1971, 1972, 1973, 1975, 1977, 1995 by The Lockman Foundation. Used by permission. (www.Lockman.org)
Quotations marked NKJV are from the New King James Version. Copyright © 1982 by Thomas Nelson, Inc. Used by permission. All rights reserved.
Quotations marked KJV are from the Holy Bible, King James Version.

Manufactured in the United States of America if purchased in North America, in the United Kingdom if purchased in Europe.

# Contents

What Does the Alliance Believe about the Supernatural?

Are the Supernatural Spiritual Gifts Operative Today?

Why Don't We See More of the Supernatural Today?

Should We Expect Power Encounters or Power Evangelism?

Does the Alliance Believe in Restoring the New Testament Church Today?

What Is the Full Gospel? Is the Alliance a Full Gospel Church?

What Is the Latter Rain? Should We Expect It Today?

How Has the Latter Rain Fallen on the Alliance?

Is the Kingdom of God Here Now or Future?

What Does the Alliance Believe about the Baptism in the Spirit?

But Isn't the Baptism in the Spirit the Same as the New Birth?

Doesn't 1 Corinthians 12:13 Teach Baptism in the Spirit at Salvation?

Why Is the Baptism in the Spirit Important?

Are There Other Terms for the Baptism in the Spirit?

How Can I Know I Am Filled with the Spirit?

# CONTENTS

# CONTENTS

# CONTENTS

# CONTENTS

# Introduction

One of the chief core values of The Christian and Missionary Alliance is: "Without Holy Spirit Empowerment, We Can Do Nothing." This book explains and encourages this Alliance core value from the words of the founders and historic leaders of the Alliance themselves.

Ever since my book *Genuine Gold: The Cautiously Charismatic Story of the Early Christian and Missionary Alliance* was published, people have been suggesting to me that I compile a "Reader's Digest Condensed Version," or "nuggets of genuine gold," as it were, for use in local church Bible studies and training.

As a sequel and supplement to *Genuine Gold*, this book is a collection of quotes, nuggets of genuine gold, from A.B. Simpson and a variety of leaders of the Christian and Missionary Alliance throughout its history regarding various aspects of the Holy Spirit and the Spirit-filled and empowered life. This collection by no means comprehensive, but is a compendium of writings to get a feel for historic Alliance positions that relate to the beliefs and practices of the modern-day charismatic movement. Its format is as a primer or catechism, asking a question and letting Alliance leaders speak for themselves in answering the question. In addition to founder Dr. A.B. Simpson, Alliance leaders cited are:

- **Dr. Keith Bailey**—former Vice President of Church Ministries of the C&MA
- **Dr. J. Hudson Ballard**—early C&MA Board of Managers member and Secretary of Education
- **Fred F. Bosworth**—C&MA healing evangelist and pastor, author of *Christ the Healer*, which was for many years required reading for C&MA Ordination studies
- **Warren A. Cramer**—C&MA pastor
- **Dr. V. Raymond Edman**—C&MA missionary, President of Wheaton College; editor of *The Alliance Witness*
- **Mrs. Mary Gainforth**—C&MA Pastor, friend of A.B. Simpson
- **Dr. A.J. Gordon**—Simpson associate, C&MA convention speaker, Nyack Missionary Training Institute instructor, and famed Baptist pastor and founder of Gordon College and Gordon-Conwell Seminary
- **Dr. Robert Jaffray**—C&MA missionary statesman to China, Indochina, and Indonesia, former Foreign Secretary of the C&MA
- **E.O. Jago**—C&MA missionary and district superintendent

- **William T. MacArthur**—associate pastor of Simpson's church and a Vice President of the C&MA whose wife received the gift of tongues
- **Kenneth MacKenzie**—associate of A.B. Simpson
- **John A. MacMillan**—C&MA missionary, Nyack professor, *Alliance Weekly* editor
- **F.E. Marsh**—British associate of A.B. Simpson
- **Dr. T.J. McCrossan**—C&MA pastor and Simpson Bible College president, who was a former Presbyterian professor of Greek, and whose books *Speaking in Other Tongues: Sign or Gift Which?* and *Bodily Healing and the Atonement* were widely circulated in C&MA circles.
- **Carrie Judd Montgomery**—long-time friend and associate of A.B. Simpson, who served as a member of the Board of Managers and an early Vice President of the C&MA. Her husband George served as an honorary Vice President of the C&MA until his death in 1930.
- **David Wesley Myland**—C&MA pastor, Columbus, Ohio, and District Evangelist
- **Watchman Nee**—Son-in-law of Chinese C&MA pastor, influenced by A.B. Simpson
- **George B. Peck**—early Alliance Vice President
- **A.T. Pierson**—friend and associate of A.B. Simpson
- **Paul Rader**— C&MA President following Simpson, pastor of Moody Church in Chicago
- **Paris Reidhead**—former Sudan Interior missionary, C&MA pastor, friend of A.W. Tozer
- **John Salmon**—C&MA Vice President and pastor
- **William C. Stevens**—early Alliance leader and Nyack Missionary Training Institute dean
- **Dr. A.W. Tozer**—C&MA pastor, former Vice President of the C&MA and Editor of *Alliance Life* magazine
- **Mrs. Etta Wurmser**—C&MA pastor, church planter, Bible School teacher and director
- **L.H. Ziemer**—C&MA pastor

These and others were all leaders of The Christian and Missionary Alliance from the past, well-respected in their time, as well as friends of A.B. Simpson and the early C&MA who taught in Alliance gatherings and wrote in Alliance periodicals (such as A.J. Gordon, S.D. Gordon, Andrew Murray, A.T. Pierson, J. Hudson Taylor, and others) and a few more recent significant Alliance leaders. Their teachings, testimonies and experiences were accepted and regarded highly. They have much sound counsel to give today to C&MA and both the charismatic and non-charismatic Christian communities in the 21st century.

For easier reading language has been updated for 21ˢᵗ century readers (e.g., "Holy Ghost" is translated as "Holy Spirit," "Thee" and "Thou" as "You," etc.). Likewise, where the King James Version was cited by earlier writers, the New King James Version (NKJV) has been used here, unless otherwise indicated. Further, it was common a century ago for writers not to refer to themselves in the first person singular (I, me, my), but rather in the third person (he, she, his, her, the writer) or in the editorial first person plural (we, our). For greater clarity and a more personal touch, in some places a writer's testimony in the third person or the editorial "we" has been changed to the first person singular.

I have included additional resources for study, using Alliance sources when possible, or sources outside of the Alliance that would be similar in teaching to the early Alliance belief and practice in these areas.

## ABBREVIATIONS

AW          *The Alliance Weekly*

CAMW        *The Christian Alliance and Missionary Weekly*

CITB        *Christ in the Bible*

CMAW        *The Christian and Missionary Alliance Weekly*

SSQ         *The Full Gospel Sunday School Quarterly*

WWW         *The Work, the Work, and the World*

# CHAPTER 1

## The Alliance and the Supernatural

### WHAT DOES THE ALLIANCE BELIEVE ABOUT THE SUPERNATURAL?

*The Alliance Stands Preeminently for the Supernatural.* "The Alliance stands for an absolute faith in supernatural things and a supernatural God."—A.B. Simpson[1]

"This movement [the C&MA] stands preeminently for the supernatural."—A.B. Simpson[2]

*Supernatural Power—Most Needed.* "A supernatural gospel is meant to accomplish supernatural results, and needs a supernatural power behind it and its messengers."—A.T. Pierson, friend and associate of A.B. Simpson, published by the C&MA[3]

*Supernatural Power—Most Lacking.* "Power, supernatural power. This is perhaps the most unique and impressive feature of the Gospel and is the element most lacking in the average life of the Christian and the Church."—A.B. Simpson[4]

*We Live By the Supernatural.* "We are a supernatural people born again by a supernatural birth, kept by a supernatural power, sustained on supernatural food, taught by a supernatural Teacher from a supernatural Book. We are led by a supernatural Captain in right paths to assured victories."—J. Hudson Taylor, quoted in the *C&MA Weekly*[5]

*We Are Supernatural or Nothing.* "Christianity is supernatural or nothing. . . ."—A.B. Simpson[6]

"The Alliance is supernatural or it is nothing. . . . One thing that is certain as regards the work of the Alliance, modern innovations accomplish no permanent good, and

I do not believe that anything but the Master's methods can adv. . . . ance the interests of our work. . . . It is not so much a matter of method as of the underlying principle or rule of action—doing what He saw the Father doing and adopting the method best suited to the occasion or the task."—William T. MacArthur[7]

*We Have a Supernatural Message.* "I know no movement that has so glorious a message to give to people today—a message of salvation, a message of deeper, fuller, victorious life, a message of Christ sufficient for the body and the temporal needs of Christians, a message of the blessed hope that He is coming, coming soon, a message of service, soul-winning, a message that is full of power, a message that is steeped in the Holy Spirit, a message that leads men and women to seek the fulness of the Spirit without exaggeration, without fanaticism, without unscripturalness of any kind, all that power can be and yet all with the spirit of a sound mind. I know no message so complete, so tested, and so fitted for these times as that which God has given to us."—A.B. Simpson[8]

*At the Heart of Our Faith Are Miracles.* "All that is worthwhile in Christianity is a miracle! Actually, I can get along nicely without the outward dressings of Christianity—the trappings and the exterior paraphernalia. I can get along without them because at the heart of our faith are the miracles that throb and beat within the revealed message of God and within the beings of those who truly believe—and that's about all there is to the Christian faith! As far as I am concerned, I believe that supernatural grace has been the teaching and the experience of the Christian church from Pentecost to the present hour!"—A.W. Tozer[9]

*We Do What We See the Father Doing.* "It is not so much a matter of method as of the underlying principle or rule of action—doing what He saw the Father doing and adopting the method best suited to the occasion or the task."—William T. MacArthur[10]

## ARE THE SUPERNATURAL SPIRITUAL GIFTS OPERATIVE TODAY?

*Jesus Christ Is the Same Yesterday, Today, and Forever.* "In view of much of today's dispensational teaching about Bible interpretation, the apostles, miracles of God, and the fullness of the Spirit, I must remind you that the Lord Jesus Christ is the same yesterday, today and forever. . . . There is nothing that Jesus has ever done for any of His disciples that He will not do for any other of His disciples! Where did the 'dividers-of-the-Word-of-Truth' get their teaching that all the gifts of the Spirit ended when the last apostle died? . . . When some men beat the cover off their Bible to demonstrate how they stand by the Word of God, they should be reminded that they are only standing by their own interpretation of the Word."—A.W. Tozer[11]

*The Christianity of Christ Is the Same Yesterday, Today, and Forever.* "In every age it ought still to be true, God also bearing them witness both with signs and wonders and with diverse miracles and gifts of the Holy Spirit according to His own will. If the Christ of Christianity is the same yesterday, today and forever, the Christianity of Christ ought also to be the same yesterday, today, and forever."—A.B. Simpson[12]

*We Believe in All of the Charismata.* "A common objection is observed in this way—Christ's last promise in Mark embraces much more than healing; but if you claim one, you must claim all. If you expect healing of the sick, you must include the gift of tongues and the power to overcome malignant poisons; and if the gift of tongues has ceased, so in the same way has the power over disease. We cheerfully accept the severe logic, we cannot afford to give up one of the promises. We admit our belief in the presence of the Healer in all the charismata of the Pentecostal church."—A.B. Simpson[13]

*All Gifts Are Still Needed Today.* "Were these [supernatural gifts] meant merely to be transitory and special and temporary signs in connection with the introduction of Christianity into the world? Or were they part of the permanent enduement of the church? Does not the apostle tell us that these gifts and ministries were bestowed 'till we all come into the unity of the faith and the knowledge of the Son of God unto a perfect man, unto the measure of the stature of the fulness of Christ'? Certainly the church has not yet reached that maturity and if these gifts were need then they are needed still."—A.B. Simpson[14]

*The Alliance Stands for All Biblical Pentecostal Manifestations of the Spirit.* "The Alliance Movement stands for all the scriptural manifestations of the Holy Spirit since Pentecost. Its peculiar testimony has ever been for the supernatural. Because we seek to guard against wild-fire and fanaticism, and against handing over our meetings to leaders of doubtful character and scenes of disorder and confusion, is no evidence of antagonism to any and all the operations of the Spirit of Pentecost. That Spirit Himself has bidden us 'try the spirits whether they be of God,' and has given us as tests of His true working, decency, order, self-control, soberness, edification, and above all else, love. Give us these and then welcome to all the dynamite of God."—A.B. Simpson[15]

*Missing Gifts Are a Tragedy in the Church.* "A tragedy in the church—the missing gifts. . . . Much of the religious activity we see in the churches is not the eternal working of the Eternal Spirit, but the mortal working of man's mortal mind—and that is a raw tragedy! . . . About ninety percent of the religious work carried on in the churches is being done by ungifted members. . . . There has never been a time in the history of the Christian church that some of the gifts were not present and effective. Sometimes they functioned among those who did not understand or perhaps did not believe in the same way that we think Christians should believe."—A.W. Tozer[16]

## WHY DON'T WE SEE MORE OF THE SUPERNATURAL TODAY?

*Compromise.* "There is no truth that has more need of emphasis in these days of compromise than the supernatural character and destiny of the church of the Lord Jesus."—A.B. Simpson[17]

*Unbelief.* "What right have we to go to the unbelieving world and demand their acceptance of our message without these signs following? . . . No, Christ did give them, and they did follow as long as Christians continued to 'believe' and expect them. . . . The signs shall correspond to the extent of their faith."—A.B. Simpson[18]

"The signs of healing do not follow all believers, but they follow those who believe for the signs."—A.B. Simpson[19]

"Faith for healing cannot rise above the general level of the Church's faith."—A.J. Gordon, Simpson associate[20]

"An unbelieving church has said, 'They belong to the apostolic age; they are no longer necessary; they were only for the establishing of the church; miracles are not to be expected in these days.' The true answer lies in the saying, 'According to your faith be it unto you.'"—William C. Stevens[21]

*Dispensationalizing Away the Power of the Holy Spirit.* "Those who taught us the combination key [of dispensationalism] say, 'God doesn't do those things now. God doesn't work like that any more.'. . . Dispensationalism does not open the book of Acts and the power of God; it closes them. . . . it is arbitrarily super-imposed by man. . . . Wherever dispensationalism gets in, it kills the deep spirit of prayer and revival. . . . But how bracing in this day of need to know that we are still in the dispensation of the Holy Spirit just as in the Acts, and that God can baptize and fill believers with His Spirit, set churches on fire, and through them bring sinner to repentance and to Christ. . . . For neither the promise of the Holy Spirit nor the promised Holy Spirit has been withdrawn, except where men no longer want Him as the first Christians did."—Armin Gesswein, C&MA evangelist[22]

*When the Body of Christ Is Unhealthy, The Spirit Cannot Flow.* "The Church of Christ is broken to pieces. . . . The whole body is mutilated and severed, so that it is not possible for the Spirit to flow with undivided and unhindered fullness through the whole. . . . The body is carrying around with it diseased and lacerated members."—A.B. Simpson[23]

*Scarecrows.* "For years the adversary of our Lord Jesus Christ and the enemy of our souls has been putting every possible means to keep the Church, the body of the Lord Jesus Christ, from its resources, tools, and weapons which would make her invincible in her warfare and task. How much longer can earnest, sincere, honest-minded evangelicals let scarecrows keep them from that which is rightfully their inheritance in our Lord Jesus Christ?"—Paris Reidhead, C&MA pastor[24]

## SHOULD WE EXPECT POWER ENCOUNTERS OR POWER EVANGELISM?

*Don't Emphasize the Signs, But Expect Them.* "We are not to go abroad to preach the signs, nor to begin with the signs, nor to produce the signs ourselves. Our business is not to work miracles and wait until we can do so before telling the story of Jesus. Our work is to tell the simple story of His life and death and resurrection, and to preach the Gospel in its purity. But we are to do it expecting the Lord to prove the reality of His power, and to give the signs which His has promised."—A.B. Simpson[25]

*Supernatural Ministry Is Essential to Preaching and Teaching.* "An unmutilated gospel ministry is two-fold—the supernatural in word and deed, preaching and teaching and healing through the power of the Holy Spirit. Supernatural works were the handmaid of preaching and teaching with Jesus. There is no better advertisement today. People can generally be reached quickest on the side of physical need; and the ministry to this need is as divine and spiritual as the ministry of the Word. But Jesus healed not as an advertisement, but as an essential ministry."—William C. Stevens[26]

*The Supernatural Is Necessary for the Mission Field.* "I care not what society a man belongs to. I simply want to know if he is filled with the Holy Spirit and has sufficient ability to master a foreign language. . . . In these days the supernatural must take place in the foreign field, especially among the Mohammedans, and we need men filled with the Holy Spirit."—E.O. Jago, Field Director of C&MA Missions, Palestine, speaking in a Pentecostal church in 1913[27]

*Most Conversions from Islam Are Preceded by Visions.* "Nearly every case of conversion among [Moslems] was preceded by a vision of Christ."—Laura Beecroft, C&MA missionary to Palestinians, regarding revival in Palestine[28]

*No Other Way to Show Moslems the Truth.* "We have come to feel so strongly that we need such 'signs and wonders' in the name of the Lord Jesus to attest the Message of the Gospel here in Makassar. It seems as though in no other way can we demonstrate to hardhearted Moslems . . . that Jesus Christ is verily the Son of God, and that He alone has power on earth to forgive sin, and to save their souls."—Robert Jaffray, C&MA missionary statesman[29]

*What Can Jesus Do That Mohammed Can't?* "For five long years my Islamic friend's question, 'What can your living Jesus do that my dead Mohammed can't?', has been a sword behind me driving me to the Bible to read, study search and believe God's Word. . . . Can we blame the Moslem if he asks for a sign before submitting to baptism, when he knows full well that such a step means almost inevitable death? Can we blame the Chinese coolie if he demands a miracle before burn his idols, when he remembers that the last man in his village thus to declare war on the demons was smitten with blindness on the second day?—Paris Reidhead, Sudan Interior Mission missionary and later C&MA pastor[30]

## ADDITIONAL RESOURCES

Deere, Jack. *Surprised by the Power of the Spirit*. Grand Rapids: Zondervan, 1993. Although not an Alliance source, Jack Deere affirms the continuing operation of the supernatural today similar to the C&MA. Deere, a former professor at Dallas Theological Seminary (and a former cessationist—one who does not believe in the supernatural gifts today) tells his theological and spiritual discovery of the reality of the supernatural today.

King, Paul L. *Genuine Gold: The Cautiously Charismatic Story of the Early Christian and Missionary Alliance*. Tulsa, OK: Word and Spirit Press, 2006.

Simpson, A.B. *The Supernatural*. Camp Hill, PA: Wingspread.

"Spiritual Gifts: Expectation without Agenda," C&MA position paper, C&MA website, www.cmalliance.org

## FOR REFLECTION AND DISCUSSION

1.  Read Zechariah 4:6 and 1 Corinthians 2:4-5. Do you agree with A.B. Simpson that supernatural power is the most unique and impressive feature of the Gospel and is the element most lacking in the average life of the Christian and the Church? Why or why not? How do we get that supernatural power back in our life and our church?

2.  Read John 5:19-20. William MacArthur said that we are to do what we see

the Father doing? What do you see the Father doing in the New Testament? What do you see the Father doing in the Church at large today? How can we do what we see the Father doing?

3. Read the Alliance position paper "Spiritual Gifts: Expectation without Agenda" (see C&MA website). What does it mean to expect the supernatural without agenda?

4. Have you been expecting the supernatural in your life and church? If not, why not? If so, what supernatural things have you seen happening?

5. If you have not been seeing much of the supernatural, what might be the reasons?

6. Read *Genuine Gold* by Paul L. King, Chapters 1 and Chapter 20. Describe the charismatic theology of A.B. Simpson and the early C&MA.

CHAPTER 2

———◆◆◆———

# The Latter Rain— Restoration and Increase of Apostolic Church Power

*He has poured down for you the rain, The early and the latter rain as before . . . .I will pour out My Spirit on all mankind . . . (Joel 2:23, 28).*

## DOES THE ALLIANCE BELIEVE IN RESTORING THE NEW TESTAMENT CHURCH TODAY?

*The Alliance Is to Be an Attested Copy of the Apostolic Church.* "The Holy Spirit originated the Alliance in order to produce in modern times an attested copy of the Church of apostolic times. The modern Church is far away from the original pattern. The popular Church is not the Church of Pentecost. . . . At whatever cost we must hold to the original type of this movement as revealed by the Spirit through the Word. . . . Only He who gave us the pattern, the blessed Holy Spirit, can keep us true to that pattern. I have written frankly out of my heart, for I greatly desire to see the Alliance preserved in an increasing and sustained vitality of spiritual life, an efficiency of ministry and scripturalness of statement until Jesus comes."—A.B. Simpson[31]

*A Primitive Piety—Back to Christ and Pentecost.* "We simply aim to help God's people back to primitive piety back to Christ and to Pentecost. We have no fads, no mysteries, no complex systems. We do not deal in fanciful interpretations, fanatical notions nor sensational novelties. We emphasize scriptural simplicity in life, doctrine and worldwide evangelization."—A.B. Simpson[32]

*We Are Still in the Apostolic Dispensation of Acts.* "To express the deepest desire and the most urgent request of our hearts, we would say, we desire your prayers, that we may be fully yielded to God, so that we may see His Acts as

— 23 —

they were manifested in the Apostolic dispensation following Pentecost. We are still living in the day and dispensation called The Acts, and it is our privilege to see the mighty working of God among the people. Ours should be a day of constant miracles, the mighty Acts of the Holy Spirit, so that we might continually exclaim, WHAT GOD HAS WROUGHT!"—Robert A. Jaffray, C&MA Missionary Statesman[33]

*Restoration of Healing Will Bring Restoration of All Gifts in Logical Order.* "The re-installment of healing would doubtless open the door for the return of all the operations of the Spirit . . . the outward miraculous manifestations. . . . Is it not probable that a church which stumbles through unbelief at this, loses all which follows in logical order, and that a church which by faith revived this gifts would go on to revive the rest?"—William C. Stevens, writing prophetically in 1891[34]

## WHAT IS THE FULL GOSPEL? IS THE ALLIANCE A FULL GOSPEL CHURCH?

*It Is the Higher Christian Life of the Baptism in the Spirit.* "The higher Christian life . . . full trust and full salvation . . . a deeper life attained after conversion. . . . the *full gospel*. . . . the baptism of the Holy Spirit is a reality and a more glorious one."—William E. Boardman, in *The Higher Christian Life*, the book that greatly impacted A.B. Simpson[35] (Note: Boardman may have been the first to use the terms "full gospel" and "higher Christian life.")

*It Is a Gospel of Full Salvation for Body, Soul, and Spirit.* "This glorious gospel of full salvation. . . . Jesus, a complete Savior for body, soul and spirit."—A.B. Simpson[36]

*It Is the Supernatural, Consecrated, Overflowing Life.* "The Highest Christian Life is the supernatural life . . . the consecrated life . . . the overflowing life of love and service."—A.B. Simpson[37]

*It Is the Full Restoration of Holy Spirit Power in the Latter Days.* "Just as the coming of Jesus brought the Holy Spirit, so the coming of the Holy Spirit in the fullness of His power will bring the second coming of Christ; and as that advent approaches, His power will be more gloriously manifested."—A.B. Simpson, 1895[38]

*The Full Gospel Is a Fourfold Gospel.* "What do we mean by the four-fold gospel? . . . . In one sense it is a manifold gospel with countless blessings and ever higher and higher stages of spiritual privileges and attainment. . . . There are four messages in the gospel that sum up in a very complete way the blessings which Christ has to offer us: Jesus Christ as Savior, Sanctifier, Healer, and Coming King. . . . Is not this great blessing of the *full gospel* worth believing, receiving and telling?"—A.B. Simpson[39]

"The Alliance has a Distinctive Testimony which from the beginning of its organization has been called The Fourfold Gospel—Jesus our Savior, Sanctifier, Healer, and Coming Lord. . . . George Mueller . . . told Dr. Simpson that this arrangement of truth was most evidently 'of the Lord' and suggested that he never change its mold."[40]

*The Alliance Was Founded as a Full Gospel Movement.* "The time has come and the way is clear for a simple, spiritual and undenominational movement to send the *full gospel* . . . to the neglected millions of heathen lands. . . Is it not fitting that the great multitude whom the Holy Spirit has called in these days into a closer union with Jesus, and a deeper revelation of His fullness, should unite in some work for the evangelization of others which would be a worthy expression of their gratitude and love, and in turn a bond of delightful union and a means of yet higher blessing to their own soul."—A.B. Simpson in 1887, announcing plans to found the Alliance[41]

*The Full Gospel Is the Message and Ministry of the Alliance.* "We believe it is in God's great heart of love to make the Christian Alliance a mighty and worldwide movement for Christ and the *fullness of the gospel* . . . the Alliance has a broader basis, and, while it includes the work of salvation, and has now entered upon it with definite and far-reaching plans through its Mission work, it also aims to accomplish an equally important work for the promotion of a higher Christian life and full salvation for both soul and body, and the evangelization of the world and its preparation for the Master's coming. Surely this is a plan wide and glorious enough to enlist the full interest of both earth and heaven. God help us to be faithful to this great trust. We owe it to the truth, we owe it to the work, we owe it to the world, we owe it to the Lord, to devote our highest energies and resources to the work in which we ourselves have been so blessed, and to give to all mankind the bread that has nourished and satisfies our once famishing but now rejoicing hearts."—A.B. Simpson[42]

## WHAT IS THE LATTER RAIN? SHOULD WE EXPECT IT TODAY?

The Alliance taught on Peter's quotation and application of Joel's prophecy to the outpouring of the Holy Spirit on Pentecost (Joel 2:23, 28-32; Acts 2:16-21). The Alliance, as did many evangelical leaders of that day, extended the application to the former and latter rains mentioned in the preceding verses in Joel 2:23-27, as a further fulfillment of the New Testament church age. Alliance leaders taught a form of "Latter Rain" theology, that God was pouring out a greater latter or end time rain before the Second Coming of Christ. The C&MA affirmed that the Latter Rain was falling, but did not accept all Latter Rain teaching, which they believed sometimes went beyond the clear teaching of Scripture. (Note that this is not in reference to the Latter Rain Movement of 1948 and following, originating in Canada.)

*Wonderful Exhibition of the Spirit in the Last Days.* "The last days of the age are not only to be characterized by increase of wickedness and wrong, but are also to be characterized by the wonderful exhibition of the Spirit of God and the fruit of the Spirit. . . . May we realize that, while the evil world, in its commercial and class conditions even, is startlingly presenting the foretold signs of the lasts days, we may and should be as strikingly revealing the spiritual signs in the return of Pentecostal godliness, faith, exploits of divine power and aggressiveness on the entire world with the Gospel of Christ and the Apostles."—William C. Stevens, 1899[43]

*Latter Rain Reappearance of Mighty Manifestations.* "In the former rain at Pentecost and after, these gifts included visible tongues of flame on the heads of the disciples, the power to speak in new tongues and mighty manifestations of God's healing and miraculous power as well as the more quiet, yet not less valuable enduements of wisdom, knowledge, faith and spiritual discernment. We may therefore, expect that, in the latter day manifestations of the Holy Spirit, all of these will reappear with equal, if not greater, power than of the days of old."—A.B. Simpson, 1907[44]

*May God Grant Us the Outpouring Once Again.* "'For the promise is unto you, and to your children, and to all that are afar off. . .' Which promise? The one spoken by the prophet Joel: 'And it shall come to pass in the last days, saith God, I will pour out of my Spirit upon all flesh: and your sons and your daughters shall prophesy, and your young men shall see visions, and your old men shall dream dreams, . . .' (Joel 2:28, 29; Acts 2:17, 18). God grant us the transforming wonder of our churches once more on fire for God and lost humanity."—Armin Gesswein[45]

*It Is Imperative to Seek Our Own Latter Rain.* "It is imperative that in these momentous days of opportunity we all become acknowledged seekers for our personal portion of the latter rain."—William C. Stevens[46]

*We Should Expect a Great Outpouring.* "We are to expect a great outpouring of the Holy Spirit in connection with the second coming of Christ and one as much greater than the Pentecostal effusion of the Spirit as the rains of autumn were greater than the showers of spring. There is no reason whatever to suppose that the great prophecy of Joel was fulfilled in any complete measure by the out-pouring of the Holy Spirit on the day of Pentecost and in Apostolic times. . . . We are in the time . . . when we may expect this latter rain."—A.B. Simpson[47]

### Pray for the Latter Rain

> Oh, I'm glad the promised Pentecost has come,
> And the "Latter Rain" is falling now on some;
> Pour it out in floods, Lord, on the parched ground,
> Till it reaches all the earth around.

> —David Wesley Myland, Alliance Pastor, Columbus, Ohio,
> and District Evangelist[48]

## HOW HAS THE LATTER RAIN FALLEN ON THE ALLIANCE?

*It Is the Time of the Latter Rain—At the Beulah Beach Convention.* "God poured out His Spirit . . . so that they spoke in tongues and magnified God. The sick were healed and demons expelled. The hosts of darkness which gathered about the camp of the saints were repulsed and driven back, and the glory of the Lord shown out of His temples. . . . It was a Pentecostal convention. . . . It is the time of the latter rain."—*C&MA Weekly,* 1907[49]

*The Latter Rain Was Poured Out at the Rocky Springs Eastern District Convention.* "A score or more received a special anointing of the Holy Spirit. Several received gifts of the Spirit and spoke with new tongues. The Latter Rain was poured out and the promise of the Father was realized in many hearts."—*C&MA Weekly,* 1907[50]

*These Are the Days of the Latter Rain!* "Often as the altar was made ready the people would rise almost en masse and press forward and there remain for hours. God was pleased to manifest Himself to many in much power, prostrating them with joy and glory. . . . these are the days of 'the latter rain.'"—*C&MA Weekly,* 1907[51]

*Alliance Affirms Joel's Latter Rain Prophecy Is Coming True.* "Bursting out in song, prayer or sermon, in languages entirely distinct, yet all unknown to the speakers or their hearers, even the most skeptical and hardened have yielded before the strange manifestation of what seems certainly divine power, and turned in terror from their sins.

People of all denominations attracted by the manifestations are flocking to the Alliance Hall. Clergymen have witnessed the demonstrations and come away profoundly impressed. Scores entering out of curiosity or to laugh and scoff have come away awed and unable to explain the manifestations, except as the Alliance people assert, that the prophecy of Joel is coming true and that in the latter days many shall speak with tongues."—F.E. Marsh, associate of A.B. Simpson[52]

*Nearly All Missionaries in India Have Spoken in Tongues of the Latter Rain.* "We are seeing the mighty workings of the Spirit here, in the gracious outpouring of the 'Latter Rain,' and are being so burdened for souls that the other things seem of small moment. Nearly all the missionaries at Dholka have received the baptism of the Spirit, new tongues being given." Many native Christians were also baptized in the Spirit, speaking in tongues, with some interpreting.—Alfred Snead, C&MA Foreign Secretary[53]

*The Church Is Being Lifted to a Pentecostal Plain.* "We praise Him for a clearer vision and conception of a Pentecostal plain to which His church is being lifted.... Praise God for the 'Latter Rain' Pentecost with signs and wonders following."—Samuel M. Gerow, Akron Alliance pastor, mentor of A.W. Tozer[54]

## IS THE KINGDOM OF GOD HERE NOW OR FUTURE?

*Preparing the End-Time Army and Bride of Christ.* "There are three great wings in the army of the Advent. One is . . . certain prophecies had to be fulfilled before Christ could come . . . . That wing of the army of the Advent has reached the point of junction. There is a second wing, and that is the preparation of the Bride of Christ, the purifying and perfecting of the followers of the Lamb so that they shall be ready to meet Him with the wedding robe. Surely that has been the great movement of our time. Surely for half a century the Holy Spirit has been getting His people ready for the coming Christ. Perhaps that movement is almost complete. But there is a third wing, and that is the missionary advance, for He said that the gospel must be proclaimed as a witness to all the nations before He came.... Surely it should stir our hearts as we realize that this one thing perhaps is keeping back the coming of our King."—A.B. Simpson[55]

*The Overlapping of the Ages.* "As in the past God was always overlapping the coming age, so is He today overlapping the next age. . . . The coming of the Lord is to bring the resurrection of these mortal bodies. Surely we may expect some earnests in the last days. . . . Healing of the body is an actual earnest and first-fruit of the future resurrection. . . . The healing of disease through the indwelling life of Christ is simply the beginning of the resurrection. . . .

The vision of prophecy seems to intimate that just prior to the Lord's return there will be a great and wonderful revival of salvation and 'whosoever shall call upon the Lord shall be saved.' Surely today we are witnessing something like the realization of this glorious overflow of grace and salvation. It is also most distinctly predicted that world-wide evangelism will reach a sudden and wide expansion just before the end. . . .

The past half century has been specially characterized in modern religious life by a revival of personal holiness and a new emphasis upon the baptism of the Holy Spirit. All this is the overlapping of the millennial day. . . . We shall find nothing awaiting us yonder that we have not begun to find in our experience here."—A.B. Simpson[56]

*Living Under the Powers of the Age to Come—The Border Zone.* "Just as these ancient saints looked forward, and overlapped and got into the age to come in some measure by their faith, so God permits us to live under the powers of the age to come, and come into the border zone, where our feet are yet on earth, and our heads, our eyes, and our hearts are in the coming kingdom. Divine healing is one of the overlappings of this coming age."—A.B. Simpson[57]

*A Millennium for the Soul Now.* "There is a sense in which His coming to each heart will bring a millennial blessing to that heart. There is a millennium for the soul as well as for the Church. There is a kingdom of peace and righteousness and glory into which, in a limited sense, we can enter with Him here. There is a Kingdom of God which is within us."—A.B. Simpson[58]

"We may press forward to His coming . . . by anticipating already in some measure the millennial life. Even here and now we may receive a foretaste of the coming kingdom."—A.B. Simpson[59]

"Let us begin the millennial life here if we expect to enjoy it by and by."—A.B. Simpson[60]

*A Kingdom for You Now.* "To each of us, like Esther, God has given a kingdom of influence and power, and has in His providence placed in us times and circumstances best adapted for the exercise of the power entrusted to us. . . . Our spiritual experiences constitute a still higher kingdom. . . . Our spiritual endowments and privileges constitute a still higher kingdom. . . . Our king has given to each of us a trust to occupy. . . . Have you claimed all your kingdom?"—A.B. Simpson[61]

*We Reign Now Through Christ.* "Christ's saints now reign *through* Him as an earnest of their reigning *with* Him."—George B. Peck, early Alliance Vice President[62]

***An Increasing Supernatural Presence.*** "The practiced sailor knows by the signs in the air and by the very breath he inhales that he draws near the shore. And spiritual intuition is feeling the nearness of the Parousia, and the signs and wonders that lead up to the coming of the Lord are beginning to appear. I like to think that that word *Parousia* does not absolutely describe a clear-cut event that is marked by the limits of chronology. It literally means *"presence."* The Parousia is the *presence* of the Lord. I cannot help thinking that the Lord's Parousia will approach us gradually and that nearer and nearer His longing heart, His magnetic touch will come to this old world to which He is looking so lovingly and longingly. As He gets nearer, the very air will seem to be alive with the thrill of a supernatural presence."—A.B. Simpson[63]

***Drawn Like a Magnet toward His Coming.*** "Did you ever see a great magnet held over a little box of sawdust and steel filings? As it came within a certain range, the very air seemed magnetized and the little particles of steel got restless, and movement passed through them, and they vibrated and trembled. There was some strange power possessing them and attracting them. As it came nearer and nearer, at last they began to rise, and suddenly, clinging together, they sprang up and attached themselves to the magnet. So as this divine attraction comes nearer and nearer, our hearts are strangely thrilled, and we are looking for and hasting unto the coming of the Lord. A heavenly presence and a divine atmosphere are abroad. It is gathering day by day, and week by week, and month by month. The mighty attraction is coming nearer; the Parousia is in the air, and our hearts are responding. Some day soon the attraction will be so supreme that we shall be caught up, and the gravitation of earth will be counterbalanced, and we shall be with Him in the air. . . . It is on the way, and though it may seem yet a little way off, we run forward to meet it, and He will meet us more than half way."—A.B. Simpson[64]

***Kingdom Work Requires Kingdom Power—Hasten the Kingdom by Exercising It.*** "Kingdom work requires kingdom power; and as this is given us by our gracious Lord in abundant supply. Why do we not exercise it more earnestly that the kingdom of God may be hastened?"—Warren A. Cramer, C&MA pastor[65]

## ADDITIONAL RESOURCES

King, Paul L. *Genuine Gold: The Cautiously Charismatic Story of the Early Christian and Missionary Alliance.* Tulsa, OK: Word and Spirit Press, 2006, especially chapters 6-9.

## FOR REFLECTION AND DISCUSSION

1. Read Acts 1:5-8 and Acts 2. How can the Alliance as a whole and your church be, as Simpson put, "a church of Pentecost" and "an attested copy of the Apostolic church" today?

2. Read Romans 15:18-19. Paul says that he had "fully preached the gospel" (or "preached the full gospel") in "word, and deed, and signs and wonders in the power of the Holy Spirit." How are these three elements of the full gospel—word, deed, and signs and wonders—a part of the full gospel message and ministry of the Alliance as a whole? For your church? For your life?

3. Read Joel 2:28-32; Acts 2:16-21. What does the latter rain mean to you? For the Church as a whole? For The Christian and Missionary Alliance? For your church?

4. What is the meaning of Simpson's three wings of the end-time army? How do you see this being fulfilled in the church today?

5. What does it mean to say that the kingdom of God is here now and not yet? That there is an overlapping of the ages? How is the kingdom here now in your life and church?

6. What is God's kingdom for you? How can you have a millennium in your soul now?

7. What are some of the signs that the coming of the Lord is near?

8. Read *Genuine Gold*, Chapters 6-9. Describe some of the signs of the Latter Rain in the C&MA revival of 1906-1909. Do we see those signs today?

CHAPTER 3

# The Baptism in the Spirit

## WHAT DOES THE ALLIANCE BELIEVE ABOUT THE BAPTISM IN THE SPIRIT?

*It Is a Second Blessing—A Distinct Experience.* "A definite second blessing, distinct in nature, though not necessarily far removed in time from the experience of conversion; . . . the baptism of the Holy Spirit as a distinct experience not merely for power for service, but for personal holiness and victory over the world and sin."—1906 C&MA Board of Managers Document

*It Is a Sanctifying Baptism.* "The Alliance accepts without question . . . The Sanctifying Baptism with the Holy Spirit."—W.M. Turnbull and C.H. Chrisman, Board of Managers, 1927, *Alliance Weekly*, 1932[66] (See the next chapter for a fuller explanation of the baptism in the Spirit as a sanctifying experience.)

*It Is a Crisis and Progressive Experience Subsequent to Conversion.* "It is the will of God that each believer should be filled with the Holy Spirit and be sanctified wholly, being separated from sin and the world and fully dedicated to the will of God, thereby receiving power for holy living and effective service. This is both a crisis and a progressive experience wrought in the life of the believer subsequent to conversion."—1965 C&MA Statement of Faith, Article 7

*It Is Immersion—Immersion in God.* "It is immersion in God. It is a covering or burial in God, of the child of God. . . . What is its object? To change our character into the likeness of our Lord"—Edgar E. Sellow, Alliance pastor[67]

## BUT ISN'T THE BAPTISM IN THE SPIRIT THE SAME AS THE NEW BIRTH?

*Different in Nature—Not Necessarily Long in Time.* "The difference is one in the nature of things rather than in the order of time. The early Christians were expected to pass quickly into the baptism of the Holy Spirit and the fulness of their life in Christ."—A.B. Simpson[68]

"We are willing . . . to concede that the baptism of the Holy Spirit may be received at the very same time a soul is converted. We have known a sinner to be converted, sanctified, and saved all within a single hour, and yet each experience was different in its nature and was received in proper order and by a definite faith for that particular blessing, and this involves the crisis: a full surrender and an explicit preparation of the promise of God by faith."—A.B. Simpson[69]

*A Copious Outpouring Beyond Conversion.* "Every Christian can have a copious outpouring of the Holy Spirit in a measure far beyond that received at conversion, and I might also say, far beyond that enjoyed by the rank and file of orthodox believers today."—A.W. Tozer[70]

*Wrong Teaching Has Robbed Millions of a Victorious Christian Life.* "I believe that the greatest blow the Devil ever gave the Church was when he got the ministers to teaching that all men are baptized with the Holy Spirit at the time of regeneration—or that receiving Christ is synonymous with receiving His successor, the Holy Spirit. The tragic absence of clear Scriptural teaching on this point has robbed millions of Christian of a joyful attractive, useful, and victorious Christian life. . . . It has been the defeat of thousands of churches. . . . It has robbed thousands of Christians of the supernatural gifts of the Holy Spirit, and has kept them from finding their place in the body of Christ."—F.F. Bosworth, Alliance Publishing House[71]

## DOESN'T 1 CORINTHIANS 12:13 TEACH BAPTISM IN THE SPIRIT AT SALVATION?

*For by one Spirit we were all baptized into one body* (1 Cor. 12:13).

Is this not the same as the baptism in the Holy Spirit, some may ask? Early Alliance leaders did not believe so. Rather, they believed in a three-fold baptism, closely interconnected but distinct: baptism by the Spirit into the Body of Christ (1 Cor. 12:13); baptism by a believer into water (Acts 2:38); and baptism by Jesus in the Holy Spirit and fire (Luke 3:16-17).[72]

*Baptism by the Spirit Not the Same as Baptism with the Spirit.* "The passage in 1 Cor. 12:13 is best understood as referring, not to the second crisis of the Christian life, the baptism or filling with the Holy Spirit, but rather to the operation of the Holy Spirit by which men and women are baptized into Christ when they first believe on Him, that is, spiritually joined to Christ, being born again by the

Spirit. This understanding of the passage leaves no conflict with the other obvious New Testament teaching concerning the necessity of a crisis experience after conversion."—Dr. J. Hudson Ballard, C&MA Board of Managers[73]

*The Difference Between Baptism "By" and "With" the Spirit.* "We come now to the distinction between the Baptism 'by' and 'with' the Spirit. . . . 1 Cor. 12:13: 'For by one Spirit we were all baptized into one body.'. . . This is not the Baptism 'with' the Spirit; it is clearly the Baptism 'by' the Spirit. . . . turn to Matt. 3:11 . . . 'He shall baptize you with the Holy Spirit and with fire.' Here we have the Baptism not 'by' but 'with' the Spirit."—Oswald J. Smith, C&MA pastor[74]

*Don't Confuse the Sanctifying Baptism with Baptism "by" the Spirit.* "Ephesians 5:18 is not speaking of the work of the Holy Spirit in regeneration whereby the believing sinner is born again. Rather, the experience referred to is the work of the Spirit in sanctifying power in the life of the Christian. This sanctifying, satisfying, stabilizing work is an experience in addition to conversion and should not be confused with the believer being baptized by the Spirit into the Body of Christ (1 Cor. 12:13)."—Jasper W. Smoak, C&MA evangelist[75]

*Baptism "By" the Spirit Is Union with His Body.* "The church . . . is an organic life; it is a living body constituted by the Holy Spirit. . . . So the Church is taken out of Christ by the Holy Spirit, and then given back to Him in divine union, as His glorious Bride. . . . The union must be vital; the work must be divine. It is called a baptism. This word expresses the deep truth of death and resurrection. It is by death of our natural life and the resurrection life of the Lord Jesus Christ, that we become incorporated into His glorious body and united with His life as the great Head of the Church."—A.B. Simpson[76]

"The Church is made by the Holy Spirit. 'For by one Spirit are we all baptized into one Body.'"—Dr. Ira David, C&MA pastor and professor[77]

*Baptism <u>By</u> the Spirit Is the Pauline Expression of New Birth.* "Let John McNeill (*Spirit-filled Life*) answer this. He says, 'This is the Pauline way of stating the being born again of John 3:7.' So say D.L. Moody, A.J. Gordon, A.T. Pierson, Andrew Murray, A.B. Simpson, Dr. Torrey, F.B. Meyer and many others."—Dr. T.J. McCrossan, C&MA pastor, professor, and Greek scholar[78]

*Immersed in the Ocean vs. Drinking of the Ocean.* "'We have all been made to drink into that one Spirit.' It is one thing to be baptized into the body, it is another thing to drink of the ocean into which we have been plunged. . . . This is the secret of being filled with the Spirit."—A.B. Simpson[79]

*Closely Connected, But Distinct.* "In the experience of the Apostolic Church, as recorded in the book of Acts, there were three things that were closely connected, namely: conversion, baptism and the reception of the Holy Spirit. . . . [They] are three separate and distinct things. . . . These three things, while separate and distinct, are yet closely related both as doctrines and experiences. . . . When a sinner is converted, he should seek [water] baptism as the open confession of his faith. . . . Then he should definitely receive the Holy Spirit."—Dr. George P. Pardington[80]

*The Double Baptism of Water and Spirit.* "The water and the Spirit were inseparably linked. The outward baptism was but a stepping stone to the higher baptism of the Holy Spirit, and they were all expected to enter into both, as though neither were complete without the other. . . . Baptism was much more than initiation into the Christian church. . . . It was the symbol of . . . profoundly earnest surrender of our life in self-crucifixion, . . . and entering into a new world of life through the resurrection of Jesus Christ . . . this was to be sealed by the actual descent and infilling of the Holy Spirit. . . . Indeed there was but one baptism, for the water and Spirit were each part of a greater whole . . ., one as the sign and the other as the divine reality."[81]

*Difference Between Holy Spirit With, In, and Upon.* "May it not be that there is such a thing as the Holy Spirit with, the Holy Spirit in, and the Holy Spirit upon?"—A.B. Simpson[82]

"For by one Spirit we were all baptized into (*eis*) one body. . . . The baptism with the Spirit is always the Spirit 'coming upon' (*epi*), 'descending upon' (*epi*), 'poured out upon' (*epi*), or 'falling upon' (*epi*), and never, never, never the Spirit coming into (*eis*) us."— Greek scholar Dr. T.J. McCrossan[83]

## WHY IS THE BAPTISM IN THE SPIRIT IMPORTANT?

*Every Believer Needs It.* "No man is fitted for the humblest service in the church of God until he receives the divine baptism of the Holy Spirit. The mother needs it in the nursery, the Sunday school teacher in his class, the preacher in his pulpit, the soul winner in his dealings with the inquirer and the saint in his ministry of prayer in the secret closet."—A.B. Simpson[84]

*Human Self-Sufficiency Is Not Enough.* "There is no truth that needs to be more emphasized in this age of smartness and human self-sufficiency than the imperative necessity of the baptism of the Holy Spirit as the condition of all effective Christian work."—A.B. Simpson[85]

*More in Touch with God's Thoughts.* "When our whole physical being is permeated with the presence of God and the baptism of the Holy Spirit, we are in more distinct touch with God's thoughts, influence and suggestions."—A.B. Simpson[86]

*Nothing Can Take Its Place.* "Modern schools, medical missions, industrial teaching, and a thousand other things can never take the place of the baptism of the Holy Spirit."—A.B. Simpson[87]

*Elevator to the Higher Life.* "The gift of the Holy Spirit . . . is God's great Elevated Railway, . . . borne along on His Ascension pathway by His own Almighty impulse. It is God's great Elevator, carrying us up to the higher chambers of His palace without our laborious efforts. . . . lifting us into a supernatural life in all respects. . ."—A.B. Simpson[88]

*Loosens and Sets on Fire for God.* "They then had a collective Baptism of the Spirit, one that loosens all tongues and sets them all on fire for God at once. Each assembly needs a collective baptism of the Spirit."—Dr. Ira David, Toccoa Falls College[89]

*Greater Results in One Day Than in Years of Christian Living.* "Since being baptized with the Holy Spirit I have seen greater results in one service than during eleven years between the time of my conversion and my baptism with the Holy Spirit."—F.F. Bosworth[90]

*It Is Our Only Source of Energy, Fervor, Efficiency and Glory.* "Its chief purpose is to fit us for Christian service as witnesses for Christ. It gives personal courage, boldness and faith in witnessing for God and testifying to men. It gives love for souls and holy tact and wisdom to win them. It gives effectiveness to our message and convicts the world through us of sin, righteousness and judgment. It not only works in the preacher, giving unction and power to His message, but works distinctly in the heart of the hearer, producing divine impression, conviction, persuasion, faith, and salvation. It equips us for our special ministries as evangelists, teachers, rulers, comforters, pastors, helpers. It gives wisdom for the emergencies which we are called to meet. It gives special faith for particular needs and exigencies and accompanies the workers with such special gifts of the Spirit, whether in healing the sick, or even sometimes miraculous answers to prayer as God sees best fit to bear witness to His Word and His worker. It is especially manifest in the ministry of intercession and becomes the spirit of intense prevailing prayer. Sometimes it is manifest in ecstatic tongues of praise and special messages of prophetic appropriateness in testimony, warning, comfort or encouragement. It is the spirit of revival coming down, not only upon individuals, but upon multitudes in mighty floods of Pentecostal blessing and leading men and women to cry, 'What must we do to be saved?' This blessed power is the heritage of the New Testament church. It is ours for the asking and receiving. It is the only power that can give energy, fervor, efficiency and glory to our work."—A.B. Simpson[91]

*There Is Much More Than Initial Salvation.* "It is a great thing to be saved. But salvation is only the letter A of the alphabet of the Christian experience."—George P. Pardington[92]

## ARE THERE OTHER TERMS FOR THE BAPTISM IN THE SPIRIT?

"Call it by whatever name you please—sanctification, the second blessing, the higher Christian life, the baptism of the Holy Spirit, entire consecration—it is the call of God today to His own people."—A.B. Simpson[93]

"Several statements refer to the same event: (1) receive (John 7:39); (2) endued (R.V., clothed) with (Luke 24:49); (3) baptized with (Acts 1:5); (4) come upon (Acts 1:8); (5) filled with (Acts 2:4); (6) poured out (Acts 2:16, 17); (7) shed forth (Acts 2:33; 'poured forth' in R.V. and Greek; same as in 2:17); (8) fell on, 'as on us' (Acts 11:15); (9) given 'even as he did unto us' (Acts 15:8). These nine (in reality eight) terms refer to the same event, the filling (Acts 2:1-4). Let us not, therefore, quarrel over terms, since one is as Scriptural as another. What we mean is receiving Him in His fullness, or being filled."—*The Alliance Weekly*, 1919[94]

## HOW CAN I KNOW I AM FILLED WITH THE SPIRIT?

*You Will Know—By a Witness of the Spirit.* "True faith brings a witness. . . . Neither in the Old Testament nor in the New, nor in Christian teaching as found in the writing of the saints as far as my knowledge goes, was any believer ever filled with the Holy Spirit who did not know he had been filled. Neither was anyone filled who did not know when he was filled. And no one was ever filled gradually. . . . The man who does not know when he was filled was never filled (though of course it is possible to forget the date). And the man who hopes to be filled gradually will never be filled at all."—A.W. Tozer[95]

*God's Fullness Will Produce Some Kind of Manifestation.* "Inadequate pneumatology [doctrine of the Holy Spirit] has left the church divided and many Christians spiritually impotent. By settling for a 'just-take-it-by-faith' pneumatology, we are depriving our children and ourselves of part of the glorious heritage of followers of Christ. . . . When you are baptized with the Holy Spirit, God's fullness will produce some kind of a manifestation. It may not happen instantly. You may need to tarry, to keep praying and seeking—to keep believing and expecting."—David E. Schroeder, president emeritus, Nyack College and Alliance Theological Seminary[96]

"When the Holy Spirit falls upon God's people . . . there will be supernatural accompaniments of some kind, though it be no more than an overwhelming sense of the divine Presence. We cannot and we must not stipulate what particular form such outward expressions will take in any given case, but one thing is sure, that each one upon whom the Holy Spirit falls *will unfailingly know it.*"—Watchman Nee, son-in-law of a Chinese Alliance pastor[97]

## WHAT ARE THE EVIDENCES OF THE BAPTISM WITH THE HOLY SPIRIT?

*The Clear Immediate Evidence—Power—Over Sin and for Service.* "The great question is: Have I power, power over sin, and power in service? If I have then I am living the Spirit-filled life, and if not then I do not know this experience. It matters not what my gifts may be, what success I attain, or what spiritual manifestations I have. Unless I have power over sin, and power in service, I am not living the Spirit-filled life. This and this alone is the evidence. Now of course there are many other results. . . ."—Oswald J. Smith, C&MA pastor[98]

*The Abiding Evidence—The Fruit of the Spirit.* "May I deviate for a moment from the Baptism as a crisis and speak about the evidence as a life that follows? . . . Look at the fruit. . . . This is the unmistakable evidence. When the Holy Spirit fills a man he immediately begins to bear fruit. . . . He may have many of the gifts, including tongues, but if he does not produce the fruit he is not filled with the Spirit. This is the abiding evidence."—Oswald J. Smith[99]

*"Faith Is the Evidence" (Heb. 12:1).* "The Apostle distinctly states that faith is the evidence."—Fred F. Bosworth[100]

## IS SPEAKING IN TONGUES THE INITIAL EVIDENCE OF THE BAPTISM IN THE SPIRIT?

*Spiritual Gifts Are the Full Equipment, But Not Essential Evidences.* "We do not for a moment believe that these special enduements [spiritual gifts] are really essential to the baptism of the Holy Spirit. That we may have without any of the supernatural gifts of power. These are additions to our special enduement for service, and we are encouraged to 'covet earnestly the best gifts,' our full equipment for the ministry of Christ . . . an additional experience, or a special ministry."—A.B. Simpson[101]

*Tongues Usually Comes First—But Not Always.* "It should never be forgotten that while last in the Epistle it is the first in order of experience in the Acts. May it not be that the Spirit usually gives the 'tongues' first to test us and see whether or not we may be trusted with greater gifts of the Spirit which may be indeed of more value in the Christian ministry."—Robert Jaffray[102]

*Thousands Have Received Tongues with Their Baptism—But Many Do Not.* "Many thousands have spoken in supernatural tongues as on the Day of Pentecost, as a result of the same mighty Baptism that came upon that waiting company in the upper room. . . . After some time in the work on Pentecostal lines (during which it has been my privilege to see thousands receive the precious baptism in the Holy Spirit) I am certain that many who receive the most powerful Baptisms for service do not receive the manifestation of speaking in tongues. And I am just as certain that many who seemingly speak in tongues are not, or ever have been Baptized in the Spirit"—Fred F. Bosworth[103]

*Some Receive Tongues Later, But Not at the Time of Their Baptism.* "We have known several saints who, at the time of their baptism, did not receive the gift of tongues, who today have that gift; but they all knew well that their baptism really occurred without tongues."—T.J. McCrossan[104]

*Tongues May Be* **an** *Evidence, But Not Necessarily* **the** *Evidence.* "To say that the gift of tongues is the only proper evidence of having been baptized with the Holy Spirit is rash and wholly unscriptural, and places a mere manifestation of the Holy Spirit above His higher ministry of grace. Love, which is simply a grace of the Spirit, is placed above any of the gifts, and this love will surely keep us from judging one another."—A.B. Simpson[105]

*Seeking Anything Less Than God Himself Will Miss God's Highest.* "One of these greatest errors is a disposition to make special manifestations an evidence of the baptism of the Holy Spirit, giving to them the name of Pentecost, as though none had received the Spirit of Pentecost but those who had the power to speak in tongues, thus leading many sincere Christians to cast away their confidence, plunging them in perplexity and darkness or causing them to seek after special manifestations of other than God Himself. . . . When we seek anything less than God, we are sure to miss His highest blessing and likely to fall into side issues and serious errors."—A.B. Simpson, May 1908 Annual Report

*Many Great Spirit-Filled Leaders Did Not Speak in Tongues.* "If we are not filled with the Spirit unless we have the evidence of tongues, then Augustine, Bernard, Thomas a Kempis, Frederick Faber, Charles Finney, David Livingstone, Charles Spurgeon, and George Mueller weren't filled with the Holy Spirit.... Can we say they wrought their mighty, world-changing deeds in the power of the flesh?"—A.W. Tozer[106]

## CAN OTHER GIFTS BE EVIDENCES OF THE BAPTISM IN THE SPIRIT?

*Interpretation of Tongues.* "I have known some to receive the gift of interpretation when they were Baptized in the Spirit who did not receive the gift of tongues."—F.F. Bosworth[107]

*Prophecy—The Most Prominent Result.* "Prophecy, which Joel said would be the most prominent result of the Baptism in the Spirit (Joel 2:28), and which Paul taught was the most valuable 'manifestation of the Spirit,' is not sought in many Pentecostal meetings nor even recognized as an evidence of the Baptism where it is already manifested."—F.F. Bosworth[108]

*A Wide Variety of Gifts—Healing, Interpretation, Wisdom, Tongues, Prophecy.* "A great part of the flocks [Alliance branches]... received the baptism in the Holy Spirit with signs following...., one would have the gift of healing, another the gift of interpretation, and we would be amazed at the wisdom given. Children began to open the Scriptures and old men and old women received the Holy Spirit."—Mrs. Etta Wurmser, Alliance pastor and Bible Institute Superintendent[109]

*And Still More!—Wisdom, Special Faith, Ministry of Intercession, Prophecy, Tongues.* "It gives wisdom for the emergencies which we are called to meet. It gives special faith for particular needs and exigencies and accompanies the workers with such special gifts of the Spirit, whether in healing the sick, or even sometimes miraculous answers to prayer as God sees best fit to bear witness to His Word and His worker. It is especially manifest in the ministry of intercession and becomes the spirit of intense prevailing prayer. Sometimes it is manifest in ecstatic tongues of praise and special messages of prophetic appropriateness in testimony, warning, comfort or encouragement."—A.B. Simpson[110]

*Holy Laughter.* "Oh, glorious rapture of the soul! I arose, shouted, and sang, and laughed in the Spirit until I cried for very joy as the flood-tide of God's grace rolled in over my soul again and again with purifying and cleansing power. I felt the holy fire of God burning in my soul.... The Lord Jesus Christ was baptizing me with the Holy Spirit according to His Word and power."—Rev. L.H. Ziemer[111]

Ziemer was Lutheran pastor who was fired as a result of his experience and ministry in the Spirit, then became a C&MA pastor.

## ADDITIONAL RESOURCES

Edman, V. Raymond. *They Found the Secret*. Grand Rapids: Zondervan, 1960.

Gilbertson, Richard. *The Baptism of the Holy Spirit: The Views of A.B. Simpson and His Contemporaries* (Camp Hill, PA: Christian Publications, 1993).

Lawson, James Gilchrist. *Deeper Experiences of Famous Christians*. Anderson, IN: Warner Press, 1911, 1960.

Lloyd-Jones, David Martyn. *Joy Unspeakable*. David Cook Dist. Kingsway, 2008. (Lloyd-Jones was a Reformed pastor and theologian whose view of the baptism in the Spirit was similar to the Alliance, except that he believed that sanctification was a result of the baptism of the Spirit, rather than a sanctifying experience itself. See the next chapter for the Alliance explanation of the baptism in the Spirit as a sanctifying experience).

Schroeder, David E. *Walking in Your Anointing*. Bloomington, IN: Author House, 2007.

## FOR REFLECTION AND DISCUSSION

1. Read Luke 3:16-17; Acts 1:5-8; Acts 2; Acts 4:27-31. What does it mean to be baptized or filled with the Spirit?
2. How is being baptized in the Spirit different from being born again?
3. Why is the baptism in the Spirit important?
4. Read Acts 1:5, 8. How is power the evidence of the baptism in the Spirit? It what ways can that power be manifested?
5. Have you been baptized—overwhelmed with the Holy Spirit? How do you know? What are the evidences in your life?
6. What term do you prefer to give to this experience and why?

CHAPTER 4

# The Baptism in the Spirit and Sanctification

## WHAT DO YOU MEAN BY A "SANCTIFYING" BAPTISM IN THE SPIRIT?

*He shall baptize you with the Holy Spirit **and fire**. His winnowing fork is in His hand, And He will thoroughly clear His threshing floor; and He will gather His wheat into the barn, but He will burn up the chaff with unquenchable fire* (Matt. 3:11-12).

While some people interpret this fire to be God's judgment at the Second Coming, Alliance leaders recognized that in John the Baptist's words about Jesus, the fire is a part of being baptized with the Spirit and is the sanctifying work of cleansing and burning of chaff (or alloy, dross from precious metals) from the believer filled with the Spirit.

*A Baptism of Fire—The Secret of Spiritual Power.* "The secret of spiritual power is the baptism of fire."—A.B. Simpson[112]

*Fire of Intensified Sanctification.* "This does not mean that the Holy Spirit and fire are different, or that the baptism of fire is something distinct from that of the Spirit, but simply that the figure of fire expresses more fully the intensity and power of this divine baptism. It means that the person who is baptized with God is a soul on fire. . . . penetrating, . . . purifying, . . . consuming, . . . refining, . . . melting, . . ."—A.B. Simpson[113]

*Fire That Consumes Dross and Alloy.* "Christ's baptism was by fire, and went to the roots of conduct. The purity He required included motives, aims, and 'the

— *43* —

thoughts and intents of the heart,' and He not only requires but He gives the purity that springs from the depths of our being. Like a flame that consumes the dross and leaves the molten metal pure and unalloyed, so the Holy Spirit separates us from our old sinful and self-life, and burns into us the nature and the life of Christ."—A.B. Simpson[114]

*Burning Up the Self Life.* "The baptism of fire . . . seems to be first a burning up of sin and the self life, then the abiding presence of God in the heart like a consuming fire, accompanied by great joy and an intense love for God and souls."—William Franklin, C&MA missionary and district superintendent[115]

*A Life on Fire.* "A passion for souls is *love on fire.* A spirit of prayer is *prayer on fire.* The baptism of the Holy Spirit is *service on fire.* Sitting at the feet of Jesus is *knowledge on fire.* A God-given utterance is *speech on fire.*" —Edward Armstrong, C&MA evangelist[116]

*A Fire That Burns Through Every Difficulty.* "What is the baptism of fire? . . . I know no fire like the fire of God, the fire of everlasting love that consumed the sacrifice on Calvary. . . . Brother, sister, ask God to baptize you with the Spirit of love. . . . Love is a fire that will burn through every difficulty."—Andrew Murray[117]

*Consuming All That Is Not of God.* "What is the meaning of the 'Holy Spirit?' And what of the term 'Fire?' They have but one meaning. They are the living God. What is 'Baptism with the Holy Spirit and fire?'. . . . What is the character of this baptism with the Holy Spirit and fire? Fire love that consumes all that is not in accord with our Lord Jesus. Faber writes:

> 'Burn! Burn, oh love within my heart.
> Burn fiercely night and day.
> Till all the dross of earthly love
> Is burned and burned away!'

What is its object? To change our character into the likeness of our Lord"—Edgar E. Sellow, Alliance pastor[118]

*Being Filled with the Holiness of Christ.* "Sanctification means filling. The literal translation of the old Hebrew word to consecrate is 'to fill the hand.'. . . Christ Himself must be the supply and substance of our new spiritual life and fills us with His own Spirit and holiness."—A.B. Simpson[119]

THE BAPTISM IN THE SPIRIT AND SANCTIFICATION

*Making Christ Our Sanctification.* "The message [of the C&MA] is the fulness of Jesus through the indwelling Holy Spirit to meet and satisfy every need of spirit, soul and Body. . . . It is not an ecstasy, not merely an experience, not a cold doctrine, but the living, victorious Christ. It is 'Christ our Sanctifier.' This simple phrase expresses at once the mightiest fact and the profoundest philosophy of holiness. It includes . . . the definite baptism with the Holy Spirit, making Christ 'unto us sanctification.'"—F.N. Senft, C&MA President, 1924 Annual Report

*The Experience of Transformation and Appropriation.* "Sanctification, or holiness, is the gift of the Holy Spirit, the grace of the Lord Jesus Christ, the prepared inheritance of all who will enter in, the great attainment of faith, not the attainment of works. . . . The identification of the believer with Christ in death and resurrection is the historical side of holiness; the transformation of the believer in character and conduct through the baptism of the Holy Spirit is the experimental side of holiness. The one is apprehension, the other is appropriation. After the vision of victory comes the realization of victory. Now it is through the presence and power of the Holy Spirit that the vision of victory is transformed into its realization. It is through the incoming of the Holy Spirit that the revelation of the indwelling Christ breaks with comforting cheer upon our despairing hearts, and it is through the Holy Spirit that we are enabled to die unto sin and live unto God."—W.M. Turnbull and C.H. Chrisman, C&MA Board of Managers[120]

## WHAT DOES THE ALLIANCE MEAN BY A "CRISIS" EXPERIENCE?

*The Crisis of the Deeper Life.* "Our holiness flows from contact with God. . . . The result of such contact with Christ is a new Christian experience, a second definite work of grace—a crisis as radical and revolutionary as the crisis of conversion."—George P. Pardington[121]

*A Definite Line of Demarcation.* "We also believe, and this is the emphatic point in our testimony, that this experience of Christ our Sanctifier marks a definite and distinct crisis in the history of a soul. We do not grow into it, but we cross a definite line of demarcation as clear as when the hosts of Joshua crossed the Jordan and were over in the promised land and set up a great heap of stones so that they never could forget that crisis hour."—A.B. Simpson[122]

"One may experience a great crisis in his spiritual life, in which there is such a total surrender to God and such an infilling of the Spirit, that he is freed from the bondage of sinful appetites and habits, and enabled to have constant victory over self instead of suffering constant defeat."—A.J. Gordon[123]

***Both Instantaneous and Gradual—Crisis and Progressive.*** "There is an instantaneous and there is a gradual work of the Holy Spirit. There is an act by which He baptizes us into Himself forever. And there is a process in which He sits down beside the crucible and watches the molten silver until it perfectly reflects His image."—A.B. Simpson[124]

***Romans 12:1 Describes the Crisis.*** "There was a marked difference of opinion among those who taught sanctification. One party taught that the work of sanctification I the life of the believer was completed in one *crisis*; the other contending for a lifelong *process*. Mr. Simpson wisely met this issue by accepting both positions as Scriptural, and combining them in one experience— a *crisis* followed by a *process*. St. Paul in Romans 12:1 describes the *crisis*: 'I beseech you therefore, brethren by the mercies of God, that ye present your bodies a living sacrifice, holy acceptable unto God which is your reasonable service.' And in 1 Thessalonians 5:16-24 he describes the *process*."—William T. MacArthur[125]

***Crisis and Process—Wicket Gate and Narrow Path.*** "Such experience usually takes the two-fold form of a crisis leading to a continuous process. . . . in terms of John Bunyan's 'wicket gate' through which Christian entered upon a 'narrow path': (a) A wicket gate (Crisis). (b) A narrow path (Process). . . . There may be a crisis that, once reached and passed, can transform our whole life an service for God. It is a wicket gate by which we may enter upon an entirely new pathway. Such a crisis occurred in the life of Jacob at Peniel."—Watchman Nee, C&MA pastor's son-in-law[126]

## WHAT DOES IT MEAN TO BE "WHOLLY SANCTIFIED?"

*Now may the God of peace sanctify you completely; and may your whole*
*spirit, soul, and body be preserved blameless at the coming of our Lord*
*Jesus Christ* (1 Thess. 5:23 NKJV)

***The Holy Glory Penetrating Our Whole Being.*** "Beautiful type of the work of sanctifying grace—the holy Shekinah of the divine Spirit and the indwelling Christ in the innermost chamber of the spirit, and spreading their heavenly life and influence abroad through every part until they penetrate every faculty of the soul and every organ of the physical being with their transforming and consecrating power."—A.B. Simpson[127]

"Let your whole being receive the baptism of His presence."—A.B. Simpson[128]

*Sanctification of the Whole Person—Spirit, Soul, and Body.* "There is a distinct baptism of the Holy Spirit for the mind as well as for the spirit. . . . The former gives soundness of judgment, clearness of expression, pungency of thought, power of utterance, attractiveness of style. . . . A sanctified body is a body filled with the Holy Spirit. . . . The whole spirit, soul and body must be trained to abide in Christ." —A. B. Simpson[129]

*If You Want The Vessel Full, the Vessel Must Be Whole.* "If a vessel that ought to be one whole is cracked into many pieces, it cannot be filled. You can take one part of the vessel and dip out a little water into that, but if you want the vessel full, the vessel must be whole."—Andrew Murray[130]

*A Transfusion of the Life of God Within.* "When the tabernacle was finished the Holy Spirit came down and possessed it, and dwelt in a burning fire upon the ark of the covenant between the cherubim. God lived there after it was dedicated to Him. So when we are dedicated to God He comes to live in us and transfuses His life through all our being, . . . so that every movement, every thought, every intention, every desire of our whole being will be prompted by the springing life of God within."—A.B. Simpson[131]

*Not Eradication or Suppression, But Transformation by Christ in You.* "A.B. Simpson . . . found two opposing schools, known as Eradications and Suppressionists—the former contending that in the crisis of sanctification, sin is eradicated, root and branch, leaving the subject freee to love and serve God unhindered; the latter contending that sin with all its possibilities is always present, demanding constant suppression. Mr. Simpson's reply to these was characteristic. He would say, 'It is neither suppression nor eradication; it is Christ in you, the hope of glory.' It was this persistent exaltation of Christ above human experiences that distinguished the Alliance from other bodies of holiness people."—William T. MacArthur[132]

"The Christian and Missionary Alliance has no set doctrine on either of these phrases of the deeper life [eradication or suppression]. We prefer to rise above them, because each is incomplete and extreme, and to emphasize the Christ-life as the secret of holiness. We are not so greatly concerned whether the old man is 'suppressed' or 'eradicated'—our concern is that the Christ Himself be in control of the complete heart and life—then there will be constant victory and the greatest possible holiness."—J. Hudson Ballard[133]

*Christ Living Within.* "Far more sublime and glorious than either eradication or suppression is the truth of the indwelling Christ. Eradication would take out of the heart the principle of sin, while suppression would keep the principle of sin bound down and in subjection in the heart.

But sanctification through the indwelling Christ means that not only the principle of sin, but the heart itself in which the principle of sin resides; yea more—the very person himself in his entire being is nailed to the cross and is raised again in vital and inseparable union with the Lord. So that we may now say with Paul, 'I am crucified with Christ: nevertheless I live; yet not I, but Christ liveth in me: and the life which I now live in the flesh I live by the faith in the Son of God Who loved me and gave Himself for me.' (Galatians 2:20.)"—George D. Pardington[134]

> Once there lived another man within me,
> Child of earth and slave of Satan he;
> But I nailed him to the cross of Jesus,
> And that man is nothing now to me.
> Now Another Man is living in me,
> And I count His blessed life as mine;
> I have died with Him to all my own life;
> I have ris'n to all His life divine.
>                          —A.B. Simpson[135]

## WHAT ARE OTHER SANCTIFYING EFFECTS OF THE BAPTISM IN THE SPIRIT?

*A Love That Annihilates the Power of Self.* "It is power to receive the life of Christ. . . . The baptism of the Holy Spirit will always bring a spirit of love. . . . It brought a love to God that annihilated the power of self."–A.B. Simpson[136]

*Overwhelmed with the Spirit Himself.* "It is not that Christ baptizes us with some special feeling, gift, or blessing, but rather that Christ baptizes us with the Spirit Himself."—A.B. Simpson[137]

*The Spontaneous Life of Intercession.* "To me the greatest phase of the Baptism in the Spirit is the spontaneous life of intercession."—F.F. Bosworth[138]

*No Room for Self.* "If you get filled with God, there will be no room for you." —A.B. Simpson

*A Change in Our Speech.* "The baptism of the Holy Spirit is a baptism for our tongues, and if it does not bring us a new tongue it should bring us a new message, a new unction, a new mighty power, to be silent from the voices of earthly folly, clamor and sin, and charged with heavenly might to witness for Jesus Christ to the uttermost part of the earth."—A.B. Simpson[139]

"A proper baptism of the Holy Spirit will fix our tongues so that we shall stop saying the wrong things and begin to say the right."—Dr. Ira David[140]

"It matters little what gifts and manifestations we possess if we have not the spirit of gentleness and love that will at least let your brother alone and if you cannot agree with him will love him and pray for him in silence. We believe that in almost every instance the test of spiritual health will be found by applying the simple rule which the physician usually first applies to his patient, 'Put out your tongue.'"—A.B. Simpson[141]

*A Disdain for the Things of the World.* "You will be so filled with Him that you will not want the world. It will be the expulsive power of a new affection. The new will expel the old. You will find your greatest delight and joy in God's service, and you will discover that you are miserable and unhappy in the world."—Oswald J. Smith, Pastor of Alliance Tabernacle, Toronto[142]

*Increased Spiritual Benefits.* "There has been a great increase of holy joy. . . . an increased holy stillness, as all the powers of my being have been brought into subjection to the law of the Spirit of life in Christ Jesus. . . . a great increase of love. . . . increased power to witness, . . . increased teachableness, a willingness to learn from the humblest believer in Christ, . . . . increased love for the Word of God, and a glad yielding to its authority. . . . an increased spirit of praise."—Carrie Judd Montgomery[143]

## ADDITIONAL RESOURCES ON THE C&MA DOCTRINE OF SANCTIFICATION

McGraw, Gerald E. and George McPeek. *Empowered! Discovering the Dynamics of Holy Living*. Camp Hill, PA: Christian Publications, 2000.

McGraw, Gerald E. *Launch Out: A Theology of Dynamic Sanctification*. Camp Hill, PA: Christian Publications, 2000.

Pardington, George D. *The Crisis of the Deeper Life*. Camp Hill, PA: Christian Publications, 1991.

Simpson, A.B. *Wholly Sanctified*. Harrisburg, PA: Christian Publications, 1925.

Simpson, A.B. *The Four-fold Gospel*. Harrisburg, PA: Christian Publications, n.d.

Stoesz, Samuel J. *Sanctification: An Alliance Distinctive*. Camp Hill, PA: Christian Publications, 1992.

### ADDITIONAL RELATED SOURCES

Bright, Bill. *Have You Made the Wonderful Discovery of the Spirit-filled Life?* Tract produced by Campus Crusade for Christ.

Murray, Andrew. *Absolute Surrender*. New Kensington, PA: Whitaker House, 1981.

Nee, Watchman. *The Normal Christian Life*. Ft. Washington, PA: Christian Literature Crusade, 1957, 1963.

### FOR REFLECTION AND DISCUSSION

1. Read Luke 3:16-17. What is the baptism of fire? How is the baptism in the Spirit a sanctifying experience?

2. Read Romans 6:-13; 7:23-8:16; 12:1. What is meant by a "crisis experience?" How do these Scriptures describe the crisis experience of the Spirit in sanctification?

3. Read Romans 6:13 and Ephesians 1:13-14. How is the baptism in the Spirit both a crisis and a progressive experience?

4. Read 1 Thessalonians 5:23. What does it mean to be wholly sanctified? Does this mean sinless perfection? Why or why not?

5. Read Colossian 1:27; Romans 8:2, 9-11; Gal. 2:20. What are the differences between sanctification as eradication, suppression, and transformation by the indwelling Christ?

6. Why does the Alliance believe in the third view of sanctification?

# CHAPTER 5

Gifts and Manifestations of the
Spirit-Empowered Life

## DO WE NEED AN ANOINTING FROM GOD?

*Manifestation of His Nearness and Touch.* "Dear friends, I never feel so near to the Lord . . . as when I stand with the Living Christ, to manifest His personal touch and resurrection power in the anointing of the sick."—A.B. Simpson[144]

*Even Jesus Depended upon the Anointing.* "Even our Lord Jesus Christ ministering in the time of His humanity among us depended upon the anointing of the Spirit. . . . When leaders and members of a church do not have the genuine gifts of the Spirit—the true anointing of the Spirit—they are thrown back upon human and natural capabilities."—A.W. Tozer[145]

*Changed into a New Person.* "Samuel to Saul: 'The Spirit of the Lord shall come upon you, and you shall be changed into another man. . . .' What a difference the anointing makes. The Spirit's oncoming makes new men and new women for every calling."—A.B. Simpson[146]

*Impartation of Spiritual Gifts.* "I was ordained to the public ministry at our district conference held in Pittsburgh, Pennsylvania. . . . The speaker said, 'Now, when the hands of the elders are laid upon you, expect the Holy Spirit today to give to you a special gift of God for your ministry.' One of the founders of our society, the Reverend William MacArthur, prayed when the brethren laid their hands on me, 'Oh God, give this young man the gift of evangelism and whatever he needs to accompany this gift.' I returned home. . . . On Sunday my entire congregation was aware that I was different. Something happened to my sermons and for the first time people responded to the invitation to seek the Lord. Men and women began to come forward to the altar in my meetings."—Richard Harvey, C&MA pastor and evangelist[147]

## Should We Seek After Gifts and Manifestations?

*Seek God Himself More Than All Gifts.* "Let us *seek Him, Himself,* in all His satisfying fulness, and let Him give us 'gifts' as best pleases His heart of love." —May Mabette Anderson[148]

"Let us not despise the least of God's gifts. But let us *seek God Himself, not manifestations or gifts,* and He will divide severally to every man as He will. Not the gift but the Giver should occupy our attention."—*The India Alliance* editor[149]

"Seek Him, not gifts or even graces, but Him, Him alone."—Mary Mullen, C&MA missionary[150]

"The safest teaching that we have been able to find is that which is embodied in our Alliance message—'The Blesser more than the blessing.'"—William T. MacArthur[151]

*Expect Without Agenda.* "While we are not to seek outward manifestations, yet it is evident from God's Word that we have a right to expect them (Mark 16:20)."—C.J. Moon, C&MA pastor[152]

"With hearts wide open in the fullest expectancy. . . we are seeking the fullness of God in a way that is acceptable to Him."—William T. MacArthur[153]

## Should We Expect All of the Gifts in Every Church?

*An Ideal Church Will Have All of the Gifts.* "An ideal New Testament church would have all of the spiritual gifts of 1 Corinthians 12 effective among the believers." —Dr. Ira David[154]

*A Crying Need for All the Gifts in Every Assembly.* "We have been burdened for some time over the low ebb of life in the church. Is there not a crying need for the full manifestation of the Spirit in the Church? . . . The nine gifts [of 1 Corinthians 12] are given for the perfection of the body. Should they not be manifest in every assembly if the body is to perform her function fully?" —R.S. Roseberry, Chairman, French West Africa C&MA Mission[155]

*Speaking in Tongues Should Have a Place in Every Spirit-Controlled Church.* "Alliance leaders are quite agreed in believing that speaking with tongues . . . should have a place in every Spirit-controlled church."—J. Hudson Ballard[156]

*Why Not All Gifts Without Controversy?* "Why may we not have all the gifts and all the graces of the Apostolic Church blended in one harmonious whole. . . .

Why may we not have all the supernatural ministries of the early Church? . . .
Why may we not have the ministry of teaching, the gifts of wisdom, knowledge,
the faith of primitive Christianity, and even the tongues of Pentecost, without
making them subjects of controversy, without judging one another harshly,
because each may have all the gifts, and all in such beautiful and blended
harmony?"—A.B. Simpson[157]

*Love's Divine Overflow Manifests Full Exercise of Gifts in the Assembly.* "Love's
divine overflow . . . is God's ideal for all saints. . . . Into their hearts is to be shed
abroad by the Holy Spirit, the very love of God Himself, so that they shall love
their brethren and the men of the world around with an affection that is supernatural. . . . How such a display on earth of the spirit of heaven would revolutionize
the Church! False ambition would find no place. . . . The Holy Spirit, ungrieved
by carnality, would be manifest in such power that His gifts would once again be
in full exercise in the assembly, to the glory of God."—John MacMillan[158]

## WHAT DOES THE ALLIANCE BELIEVE ABOUT APOSTLES AND PROPHETS TODAY?

*The Church Needs the Fivefold Ministry Gifts of Ephesians 4:11-13 for Full
Maturity.* "Does not the apostle tell us that these gifts and ministries were be-
stowed 'till we all come into the unity of the faith and the knowledge of the
Son of God unto a perfect man, unto the measure of the stature of the fulness of
Christ'? Certainly the church has not yet reached that maturity and if these gifts
were need then they are needed still."—A.B. Simpson[159]

"Until the Body, the Church, is complete, these gifts [Ephesians 4:11] will
continue."—A.E. Thompson[160]

*God Has Appointed Them in the Church Permanently.* "In 1 Corinthians 12:18
we read, 'But now God has set the members, each one of them, in the body just
as He pleased.' In verse 28 we read, 'And God has appointed [set] these in the
church: first apostles, second prophets, third teachers, after that miracles, then
gifts of healings helps, administrations, varieties of tongues.' The word *set* [ap-
pointed] is in both cases the same in Greek (*etheto*), and signifies to place, establish, ordain, with the idea of permanency."—William C. Stevens[161]

*God Has Ordained the Five-Fold Ministry, But They Are Not Superior or
Privileged.* "It is true that God has ordained that some in the church should
be apostles, some prophets, some evangelists, some pastors and some teachers, and He has, furthermore, invested these with certain limited authority in
the congregation of the saints; but the notion that they constitute a superior or

privileged class is wholly wrong. They do not, but the exercise of their proper offices within the church easily leads to the idea that they do and this makes for division."—A.W. Tozer[162]

**A.B. Simpson—A Modern Apostle.** "The results of the work of Dr. A.B. Simpson, as viewed one hundred years after his birth, give him an honored place among modern apostles, and earn for him an imperishable name among the great religious leaders of the Church."—Dr. H.M. Shuman, C&MA president[163]

*We Need the Gift of Prophetic Insight.* "This frightening hour cries aloud for men with the gift of prophetic insight. Instead we have men who conduct surveys, polls, and panel discussions."—A.W. Tozer[164]

**A.B. Simpson—A Modern Prophet to the Prophets.** "The prophet . . . has come out of the inner chamber of God's presence with a specific message for a special occasion. . . . It was this mystical element in Dr. Simpson's later ministry, this prophetic office to which he was called that made him more than a great pulpiteer, evangelist, and pastor—he was all these in his early ministry. Now he was lifted into the circle of those to whom are committed to the oracles of God. . . . Dr. Simpson was a prophet to the prophets."—A.E. Thompson, Simpson's biographer[165]

*Real Anointed Prophets of God Like C&MA President Paul Rader Are Needed Today.* "What this world needs now more than anything under heaven is true preaching, real prophets of God, not animated question marks, if you please, to stand in the pulpit, but real prophets of God, anointed by the Holy Spirit and filled with His power. I rejoice that we have had in New York visits from our dear Brother Rader and have had the opportunity of sitting under his message and of seeing that he is one of the Lord's anointed preachers He is not a man made preacher, but he is a prophet of God made such by the Holy Spirit."—John Roach Straton, pastor, Calvary Baptist Church, C&MA-affiliated[166]

**A.W. Tozer—A Twentieth-Century Prophet.**—David J. Fant, Tozer's biographer[167]

*Apostles and Prophets Illumine, Not Proclaim New Authoritative Revelation or Truth.* "The Spirit today is not adding new revelations, or enlarging the Bible, but is illuminating and applying the Word which He has already given. Therefore, no man, whether he claims to be apostle, prophet, or saint, has any right to proclaim any message to his fellowmen whether in known or unknown tongues with the claim that it possesses authority over their consciences."—A.B. Simpson[168]

"I shall not prove to be the apostle of any new revelation or become the exponent of any new truth."—A.B. Simpson[169]

***Real Prophets Are Not Self-Appointed.*** "We have the greatest collection of self-appointed prophets to be found in the Western Hemisphere and they all have their following. Almost every shade of religious belief known is represented here and with few exceptions they boast of being the special custodians of some phase of the full Gospel."—C.H. Chrisman, Pacific District Superintendent[170]

***Real Apostles and Prophets Are Modest, Not Self-Promoting.*** "The air is full of the lofty claims of modern apostles, Elijahs and high stewards, to whom the children of God should, of course, hand over all their surplus funds for apostolic administration. The saddest thing about many of these cases is the apparent sincerity of some of the people who make these claims. Let no one be deceived. The Lord has given us a simple test: 'He that bears record of himself, his record is not true.' When God has a prophet to introduce He will not make it necessary for the prophet to announce his own supernatural claims, but will Himself introduce him, in keeping with the modesty which always becomes the men that are nearest to the Lord, and by such tokens that no man can question, that it is the messenger of God. . . . It is much better to be an epistle than an apostle."—A.B. Simpson[171]

"The holiest apostle can claim no more than that he is an unprofitable servant."—A.W. Tozer[172]

***A Prophet Is Not a Promoter or Religious Manager.*** "Anoint me with the oil of a New Testament prophet. Forbid that I should become a religious scribe and thus lose my prophetic calling. Save me from the curse that lies dark across the face of the modern clergy, the curse of compromise, of imitation, of professionalism. Save me from the error of judging a church by its size, its popularity or its amount of yearly offerings. Help me to remember that I am a prophet—not a promoter, not a religious manager, but a prophet. Let me never become a slave to crowds. Heal my soul of carnal ambitions and deliver me from the itch for publicity."—A.W. Tozer's Ordination Prayer[173]

***True Fiery Apostles Were Distained, Not Exalted.*** "Every superior soul that has done exploits for God was considered extreme and in many cases even deranged. We talk about the saintly John Wesley, a learned Oxford man and founder of the Methodists, but we forget that he was such a fiery apostle that they used to throw eggs and rocks at him."—A.W. Tozer[174]

## HOW CAN WE AVOID DANGERS OF IMBALANCE REGARDING SPIRITUAL GIFTS?

*Avoid Both Pentecostal Excesses and Cold Unbelief.* "There are dangers of excess and fanaticism we admit, and by these the enemy will try to destroy that which is true and prejudice that which is genuine. But there is the middle ground of supernatural reality and power, where we may safely stand, as far on one side from the excesses of Irvingism [a 19th century Pentecostal movement] as it is on the other from the coldness of unbelief."—A.B. Simpson[175]

*Maintain Wholesome and Proper Proportions.* "It has been well said, that the element of proportion is indispensable, both in natural and spiritual things. The atmosphere we breathe depends for its wholesomeness upon the exact proportions in which the different constituents are mingled in the air. A little more carbon, a little more hydrogen, or a little more oxygen, would bring death in a single instant to the whole human race. It is because these elements are so perfectly mingled that the air we breathe brings life and wholeness. It is precisely so with the gifts of the Spirit."—A.B. Simpson[176]

*Don't Magnify One Gift.* "I have known and studied these dear brethren [Pentecostals], and I have preached to them for a long, long time. I have studied them, and I know them very well, and I am very sympathetic with them. There are some churches that are very sane and very beautiful and godly. . . . The movement itself has magnified one single gift above all others and that one gift is the one Paul said was the least. An unscriptural exhibition of that gift results, and there is a tendency to place personal feeling above the Scriptures, and we must never, never do that!"—A.W. Tozer[177]

"Entire openness to all that God has to show and give in the Holy Spirit's promised enduement. But at the same time a firm adherence to the wise and inspired warnings . . . against the undue magnifying of any one gift or the seeking of any kind of power apart from Christ Himself."—A.B. Simpson[178]

*Avoid Confusion and Follow 1 Corinthians 14 Carefully.* "I watched the so-called Pentecostal work carefully and prayerfully. There was much that did not appeal to me. People who claimed to have received the baptism seemed to get in the way of the Spirit. Beginning in the Spirit, they often seemed to fail to walk in the Spirit. They became lifted up, or let self get the ascendancy. Many of the manifestations did not seem at all like the work of the calm, majestic Spirit of God. In many meetings there was much confusion, and God tells us He is not the author of confusion, but of peace. (1 Cor. 14:33, 40). The people often failed to walk in Scriptural lines in regard to unknown tongues, using them in the general assembly, "the whole church," where there was no interpreter, contrary to the Word of God. See 1 Corinthians 14 for careful direction about this matter. . . . I asked Him for quiet, sweet manifestations, which would reveal His majesty and dignity, and not such as would seem like excitement of the flesh."—Carrie Judd Montgomery[179]

*Keep Humble and Loving.* "Let all who have this experience [speaking in tongues] see that they keep low at the feet of Jesus, being filled with His own humility and love."—Carrie Judd Montgomery[180]

"When we find a spirit of censoriousness, division, criticism and spiritual pride on the part of those who claim the highest spiritual attainments, it neutralizes much of their power and influence."—A.B. Simpson[181]

*Don't Force Your Experience on Others.* "If God has honored you with some spiritual gift, be sure to use it as He desires and only as He directs. Don't force your private opinion upon one who is not ready to receive it. Don't even force the Word of God on them. Be gentle and prayerful. 'Let your yieldedness be known to all men.'"—Mary Mullen, C&MA missionary[182]

## WHAT SHOULD BE OUR ATTITUDE TOWARD DESIRING AND RECEIVING MANIFESTATIONS OF THE SPIRIT?

*Ask to Become a Better Person Before Asking for Gifts.* "Many people are looking for some extraordinary gift, or strained experience of the Holy Spirit, when He really wants to come to you in your simple everyday life and help you to be a better wife and mother, a more kind and helpful friend, a more upright and successful business man, a more efficient employee, and a more genial, loving and unselfish member of your household and social circle. . . . Beloved, perhaps it is here that the Holy Spirit wants to come to you first before you have a right to ask Him for the gifts of prophecy, miracles or tongues. He knows better than you your place in life, the needs of those around you and the sort of grace and help best fitted to make you efficient for His glory."—A.B. Simpson[183]

*Seek God Himself.* "God wants to give Himself. He wants to impart Himself with His gifts. Any gift that He would give us would be incomplete if it were separate from the knowledge of God Himself. Seek God Himself. If I should pray for all of the spiritual gifts listed in Paul's epistles and the Spirit of God should see fit to give me all 17, it would be extremely dangerous for me if, in the giving, God did not give Himself, as well. . . . We must repudiate this great, modern wave of seeking God for His benefits. The sovereign God wants to be loved for Himself and honored for Himself, but that is only part of what He wants. The other part is that He wants us to know that when we have Him, we have everything—we have all the rest."—A.W. Tozer[184]

*Be Willing to Receive Any Gift.* "Let us all be sure we are willing to receive any gift, including the gift of tongues; yet let us leave the matter to the will of the Spirit Himself and be deeply thankful and satisfied with what He chooses to bestow. . . . Let no one dare oppose God's true gift. Let each one make sure he is ready for any gift the Spirit 'wills' to send him."—J. Hudson Ballard[185]

*Let Your Spirit Be Open.* "At all times my spirit has been open to God for anything He might be pleased to reveal or bestow."—A.B. Simpson's Diary, Oct. 6, 1912.

*Desire Is Necessary.* "Desire is a necessary element in all spiritual forces. It is one of the secrets of effectual prayer. . . . There is no factor in prayer more effectual than love. If we are intensely interested in an object or an individual, our petitions become like living forces."—A.B. Simpson[186]

"God would keep me still knocking. It is the third degree of prayer."—A.B. Simpson Diary

*Covet Earnestly the Best Gifts, While Pursuing Love.* "The apostle said, 'But covet earnestly the best gifts.' Certainly the nine enumerated gifts in the chapter are the best gifts. We are told to go after them, to desire them, to develop them, 'to covet them.' Surely this does not mean to ignore them. . . . Pursue love, but covet spiritual gifts. If we pursue one without the other, is it strange if we fail of both. . . . Neither zeal for gift without love (as was the case then at Corinth) nor zeal for love without gift (as is the case now) is Scriptural."—Ira E. David, Ph.D.[187]

*Don't Quench the Spirit with Your Mind.* "Every time I would get alone in prayer . . . the showers would come down and all my being was filled with God, excepting that the top of my brain didn't get under. What was the matter? I thought I had to superintend the job. I could not fully trust Him, and so I was keeping this brain of my busy and was delighted with all He was doing, but I was looking after it to see He would do it all right. . . . Although God has blessed me all these years, I have been deprived for many years of the fullness of blessing through that very thing. . . . I am sure I would have spoken in tongues if I had let my brain go under. Because I didn't know how to yield fully, gradually the blessing faded. I didn't know how to depend wholly on Him."—Carrie Judd Montgomery[188]

*Desire What Paul Desired.* "Paul says not to forbid them (1 Cor. 14:39). He also tells us that he who speaks in an unknown tongue, speaks not unto men, but unto God and that 'in the spirit he speaks mysteries (1 Cor. 14:3); also that he "edifies himself.' We are told, however, most plainly, that 'he who prophesies is greater than he that speaks with tongues, unless he interprets, that the church may receive edification.' And yet, in spite of all this, Paul says, 'I wish you all spoke with tongues,' and he thanks God that he speaks with tongues more than they all. Why did he thank God for this gift if it was not truly to be desired?"— Carrie Judd Montgomery[189]

*Plead the Power of the Name of Jesus.* "God revealed to me the NAME of JESUS in special power and enabled me to plead it within the veil for an hour or more until it seemed to break down every barrier and to *command all that I could ask.* . . ."—A.B. Simpson, Diary 1907

*Ask for a Double Portion.* "Lord, show me what the 'Double' means, all Your estimate of it, the Double portion of the Spirit. Double all You have ever done for me. Give me Elisha's blessing, the first born's portion—*all Your gifts and all Your graces.*"—A.B. Simpson, Diary 1907

*Take All That God Promises.* "I had been timid at times about dictating to the Holy Spirit who is sovereign in the bestowal of His gifts, but *now I fully take all that is promised* in HIS NAME."—A.B. Simpson, Diary 1907

*Yield and Obey the Spirit.* "I am determined never to try to get any seeker to speak in tongues until after I see God tries to get them to do so, but then if they are not yielding or cooperating properly, I will instruct them to yield and obey the Spirit."—F.F. Bosworth[190]

*Hunger for God and Trust Him to Keep You from Fanaticism.* "Follow the hunger of your heart until God satisfies you. Listen, if you really want God instead of some gifts, if you really are hungry for holiness and the joy life, the clean life, wholly kept from sin, and then get into fanaticism, I know a Holy Spirit that will bring you back where you belong."—Paul Rader[191]

*Seek God Himself Above All Else.*

> Once it was the blessing, now it is the Lord;
> Once it was the feeling, now it is His Word;
> Once His gifts I wanted, now the Giver own;
> Once I sought for healing, now HIMSELF alone.
> —A.B. Simpson

## ADDITIONAL RESOURCES

King, Paul L. *Genuine Gold: The Cautiously Charismatic Story of the Early Christian and Missionary Alliance.* Tulsa, OK: Word and Spirit Press, 2006.

Schroeder, David E. *Walking in Your Anointing.* Bloomington, IN: Author House, 2007.

"Spiritual Gifts: Expectation without Agenda," C&MA position paper, C&MA website, www.cmalliance.org

## FOR REFLECTION AND DISCUSSION

1. Read 1 Corinthians 12, Romans 12:6-8; Ephesians 4:11. What gifts of the Spirit are operating in your life now? How can you grow in the exercise of those gifts?

2. What new gifts might God want you to consider exercising?

3. Read Ephesians 4:11-16. How can the five-fold ministry of Ephesians 4 be implemented in the Alliance today?

4. Read 1 Corinthians 14:1. Do you desire spiritual gifts? As you seek God, what desires is He placing in your heart? What gifts that you do not have now does God desire you to desire?

5. Read Psalm 37:3-4. Do you desire what God desires or what you desire? How do you go about desiring what He desires rather than what you desire?

6. Read the Alliance position paper "Spiritual Gifts: Expectation without Agenda" (see C&MA website). What does it mean to expect gifts and manifestations of the Spirit without agenda? Are you seeking gifts and manifestations or are you seeking God Himself? How can you seek God more than gifts?

7. Read 2 Timothy 1:7. Are you fearful of gifts because of excesses you have seen or heard about? What is the source of that fear? Read 1 Corinthians 13:1-8 and 14:1, and 1 John 4:18. How do you conquer that fear?

CHAPTER 6

# Understanding the Gift of Prophecy

## WHAT IS PROPHECY?

*Direct Messages of the Holy Spirit.* "It is a divine inspiration enabling the possessor to speak direct messages of the Holy Spirit for the spiritual profit of the hearer. . . . The prophetic message has more immediate reference to the particular condition of he hearer and the need of immediate spiritual help."—A.B. Simpson[192]

*Words Unmistakably Dictated by God.* "The Holy Spirit, has, no doubt, in thousands of instances wrought upon the understanding of the speaker so that he found himself uttering words that were unmistakably dictated by Him."—William T. MacArthur[193]

*A Word in Season.* "Prophecy is the power to receive and give forth special messages of the Holy Spirit for edification, exhortation and comfort of His people. It is not so much the ministry of teaching as the special testimony from time to time along the line which the prophet describes as the 'word in season to him that is weary.'"—A.B. Simpson[194]

*A Quickening Touch, Not Authoritative Words in Addition to Scripture.* "True prophecy is a perpetual ministry in the New Testament church. It is nothing less than receiving the Spirit of God and giving forth the messages of God to men under His inspiration and power. This does not mean new messages of authority in addition to the Holy Scriptures, but it does mean the Holy Scriptures themselves interpreted and applied under the quickening touch of the Spirit of God."—A.B. Simpson[195]

*A Promised Assurance of Faith.* "Faith turns the promise into a prophecy. . . . When faith claims it, it becomes a prophecy, and we go forth feeling that it is something that must be done because God cannot lie. . . . Faith is the echo of God's voice. . . . God has spoken 'It is done.' Faith has answered, 'It is done.'"—A.B. Simpson[196]

*A Spirit-Inspired Testimony.* "Testimony is a prophecy that the Spirit accompanies [Rev. 19:10]."—George D. Watson, C&MA convention speaker[197]

*A Burning Message.* "Come out with your simple testimony of some truth, that has helped you, and that you have been told to pass on for the help of others. Fear not to speak the message which the Holy Spirit has burned into your soul for the quickening and the rousing of your brethren. It will be a word in season for some weary soul."—A.B. Simpson[198]

*Spirit-Inspired Preaching.* "Speaking for God under the inspiration of the Spirit, preaching in the Holy Spirit."—*Signs of the Times*, C&MA publication[199]

*A Message from the Inner Chamber of God's Presence.* "The prophet . . . has come out of the inner chamber of God's presence with a specific message for a special occasion . . . the circle of those to whom are committed to the oracles of God."—A.E. Thompson, C&MA missionary and Simpson biographer[200]

## What Are Some Examples of Prophecy in the Alliance?

*Prophetic Words to A.B. Simpson.* While preaching at the Alliance Convention in Chicago, Simpson shared with the congregation prophetic words he had received from the Lord many years earlier. He recalled a time more than thirty years earlier in which he was traveling around the country "trying to get hold of other people's blessing." The conviction of the Holy Spirit was so heavy upon him, that he felt like the pounding in his heart would crush him. Rushing out into the woods, he heard the Lord saying to him, "Child, haven't you got Me? What more do you want? I am all these things."

On another occasion he traveled five hundred miles to get a blessing at one of Moody's meetings. After being there just a few hours, God said to him, "Go back home." So he obeyed. When he got home, he threw himself face down before the Lord, then God said, "You have Me and I am the whole Convention, now use Me."[201]

*Prophetic Word to John Woodberry.* In 1892 after a series of financial reverses, 37 year-old businessman John Woodberry surrendered to the call to ministry God had place on his life in his early twenties. He and his wife were soon introduced to the C&MA through a prophetic word from a stranger to go to a certain address. His daughter recounts the story:

> At the door one morning appeared a stranger, who began with the words, "I've a message from God for you," and ended with "I have faith that you will go." When the door closed, queries and ridicule

interchanged over such strange guidance as that. What! Go to Grand Rapids—85 Baxter Street—and there learn the Way more perfectly? But some one's faith had laid hold on God. By nightfall they were both so uncomfortable that in the morning they were on their way. The greeting they received was alike surprising: "Are you Mr. and Mrs. Woodberry? Captain _____ said you were coming!" And he was right. In that Alliance Home truths were unfolded, such as they had never dreamed of, as Mrs. Dora Dudley, open Bible upon her knee, led them on from salvation to the deeper knowledge of sanctification, divine healing, and the glorious return of Christ.[202]

*Prophetic Word to Missionary Mary Davies.* Mary G. Davies, a missionary to Africa, spoke on "The Ninety-first Psalm," sharing a prophetic word God had given her in a time of danger and fear: "My child, it is about time you practice what you preach. Don't you remember what you told the people in the meeting this morning, how I spoke to you in the night, and showed you how very secure God's children are when abiding in the secret place of the Most High? . . . Don't you remember I showed you how I had given My angels charge over you, to keep you in all your ways? . . . Don't you remember how I said, you shall not be afraid of the 'terrors' by night?"[203]

## ARE PROPHECIES 100% ACCURATE?

*Don't Elevate Impressions to Infallibility.* "The basic principle underlying all such cases of mistaken judgment . . . is always and forever to be when closely scanned, an undue exaltation given to personal 'impressions' and 'assurances' believed to be from God.

So infallible are these 'impressions' and 'revelations' supposed to be, that the one believing them truly believes he will be unfaithful to God should he question them. And when, in the course of events, these 'revelations' do not round out into actualities, there are but two courses open: either to admit that he was mistaken in his impressions, or find some 'scapegoat' on whom to place the failure. These dear ones are wholly sincere in their course, and, what is still sadder, they are usually very spiritual and lovely souls. So earnest are they, and so assured that their 'revelations' have been from above, that they are ready to denounce all who do not accept their view—even though such may be the most Christ-like and spiritually intelligent souls with whom they are bringing in contact—as 'under Satanic power.'"—May Mabette Anderson[204]

*We Are Fallible Transmitters of an Infallible God.* "Beloved, let us understand and admit one for all, that we are exceedingly *fallible* creatures. So very *fallible*, in fact, that, though our Father may be very desirous of imparting to us some truth and though He may breathe into the soul in all His Divine purity, yet when we undertake to give it voice and pour it out in verbal phrase to others, we are more than apt—unless we lie low at His feet in deepest humility—to so tarnish and becloud it by our clumsy touch and exaggerated language, as will place it beyond the Divine recognition.

A revelation may be truly from God. Yet, being such imperfect transmitters and interpreters of the Divine thought as is true of each one of us, one may easily be mistaken in the interpretation given to such revelation. Those who confidently aver that marvelous experiences have been given them, accompanied by visions and repeated assurance that a certain one who is ill has been already healed or is to be healed in the future, and then following such assurance the sick one dies without healing having been experienced—such persons either misinterpreted God's revelation, or have mistaken the voice of the Adversary for that of the Holy Spirit."—May Mabette Anderson[205]

**Even the Most Inspired Words Are Not Equal to Scripture.** "When Jonathan Edwards preached his memorable sermon from the text, 'Their feet shall slide in due time,' and the people held onto the pillars of the buildings to keep themselves from slipping into hell, his words must have been prompted by the Holy Spirit, as truly as though they had been uttered in an unknown tongue, but they were not of equal value with the words of the Bible, even as chaff is not of equal value with wheat.

The Holy Spirit, has, no doubt, in thousands of instances wrought upon the understanding of the speaker so that he found himself uttering words that were unmistakably dictated by Him, and yet they had a human coloring and *inherent fallibility*. Likewise the unknown speech, even when uttered by the most devout and consecrated, has nevertheless an element of the human in it, which forbids its being placed on a parity with the Word of God, but that which is purely human frailty must not be confounded with that which is demoniacal. We are persuaded that there is much that is neither of God nor the devil, but is simply human: wisdom or folly as the case may be."—William T. MacArthur[206]

**We See Truth Imperfectly in a Mirror.** "We see truth not directly and clearly, but as it were 'in a mirror,' and with consequent distortion. Thus we can prophesy only imperfectly, and our utterances never convey the fulness of the truth which we desire to state."—John A. MacMillan[207]

**Can Be a Mixture with the Natural.** "All of the gifts must be exercised in faith and in a humble spirit. Some of them are so blended together that is it difficult to know where one starts and another ends. The inspirational gifts of tongues, interpretation and prophecy are the most likely to be mixed with the natural, and for this reason Paul has given teaching in order that they may be understood and controlled."—A.E. Adams, C&MA pastor[208]

***Revelation Is Partial.*** "Knowledge and prophecy in this present life are imperfect owing to our own imperfection. . . . We prophecy in part. All here is imperfect, and our knowledge as yet merely covers the imperfect, and that imperfectly . . . partial revelations."—John A. MacMillan[209]

***Blow Away the Chaff; Retain the Wheat.*** "The leaders of the early church recognized the need of giving full liberty for the ministry of the Spirit through its members, but they also reserved the right to pass judgment upon prophetic utterances, as the apostle instructed them: 'Quench not the Spirit. Despise not prophesyings. Prove all things; hold fast that which is good' (1 Thess. 5:19-21). The widespread prevalence of error, of the spurious, the worthless, and the unprofitable in religious life, points to the high importance of this injunction to discriminate and to exclude that which falls shorts of the scriptural standard. Some one has expressed it thus: 'Blow away the chaff, but retain the wheat.'"—John A. MacMillan[210]

## WHAT CAUTIONS SHOULD WE HAVE ABOUT PROPHECY?

***Beware of Seeking Prophecy Like Seeking a Fortuneteller.*** "One of the most alarming tendencies of this movement has recently developed in several places in the form of a prophetic authority which certain persons are claiming over the consciences of others and men and women are seeking counsel and guidance from them in the practical matters of private duty, instead of looking directly to the Anointing which they have received of him and obeying God rather than men. It is said that in some instances Christian men and women go to these new prophets almost as the world goes to the clairvoyant and fortuneteller, and follow their advice with a slavish superstition that may easily run into all the dangers of the confessional or the delusions of spiritualism."—A.B. Simpson[211]

***Beware of Self-Will.*** "There is a subtle danger of attaching too much importance to supernatural utterances and interpretations of tongues, considering that they are the very infallible Word of the Spirit of God. It is easy to say, 'The Spirit says,' etc., 'The Lord told me so and so,' when it is quite possible that it is a matter of our own self-willfulness. The Apostle Paul did not accept such leadings as the infallible will of the Lord for him (see Acts 21). Some would make the prophets of the Lord mere fortune-tellers."—Robert Jaffray[212]

***Beware of Uncontrolled or Uncontrollable Impulses.*** "The prophetic inspiration was by no means an overwhelming impulse, which rendered a man no longer able to control himself (1 Cor. 14:32). Such was the case when the inspiration was from Satan (1 Cor. 12:1, 2). But the Holy Spirit does not break down the nature of man, but acts in harmony with his constitution."—Frank S. Weston, C&MA pastor[213]

## WHAT IS A BALANCED VIEW OF THE GIFT OF PROPHECY?

*Be More Ambitious to Prophesy Than to Speak in Tongues.* "The teaching on tongues as the evidence makes them more ambitious to speak in tongues than to prophesy. Prophecy, which Joel said would be the most prominent result of the Baptism in the Spirit (Joel 2:28), and which Paul taught was the most valuable 'manifestation of the Spirit,' is not sought in many Pentecostal meetings nor even recognized as an evidence of the Baptism where it is already manifested."—F.F. Bosworth[214]

*Test All Impressions and Revelations by the Word of God.* "We must not depend on impressions that do not harmonize with the word of God. . . . Always stand firmly upon God's Word, and not upon the impressions of those around you."—Carrie Judd Montgomery[215]

"All so-called revelations since [the closing of the New Testament Canon] must be submitted to the test of the written Word."—John A. MacMillan[216]

"No word from any human lips, no matter how strongly it may seem to be authenticated by blessing on the speaker, should have the slightest weight as affecting the infallible word of God."—A.B. Simpson[217]

*Distinguish Between Impressions and Convictions.* Simpson, commenting on the partially mistaken prophecies Paul had received warning him about going to Jerusalem (Acts 21:4, 10-14), remarked, "We must learn to distinguish between mere impressions and the deeper convictions of the entire judgment under the light of the Spirit, and between the voice of the Shepherd and the spirit of error. This He will teach us, and teach us more and more perfectly through experience."–A.B. Simpson[218]

*Get the Full Mind of the Lord.* "We are not to ignore the Shepherd's personal voice, but like Paul and his companions at Troas we are to listen to all the voices that speak and gather from all the circumstances, as they did, the full mind of the Lord."—A.B. Simpson[219]

*Wait for Confirmation.* "God does give us impressions but not that we should act on them as impressions. If the impression be from God, He will Himself give sufficient evidence to establish it beyond the possibility of a doubt. We read of the impression that came to Jeremiah concerning the purchase of the field of Ana-thoth. Jeremiah, however, did not act upon this impression until after the following day when his uncle's son came to him and brought him external evidence by making a proposal for the purchase. Then Jeremiah said, 'I knew that this was the word of the Lord' (Jer. 32:8). He waited until God seconded the impression by a providence."—A.B. Simpson[220]

*Don't Go By Someone Else's Impression.* "Do not rise from your bed or walk on your lame foot because somebody tells you to do so. That is not faith, but impression."—A.B. Simpson[221]

*Don't Always Be Seeking a Word from God.* "In the life of the Spirit we need not be in bondage and always expecting some strained or supernatural word from the Lord."—A.B. Simpson[222]

*Listen for a Still, Small Voice.* "God was not in the earthquake, the whirlwind, or the fire, but in the still small voice. The natural heart is prone to look for signs, wonders, and startling manifestations of the divine presence and power. But we miss the voice of God when we look for these things and often invite the counterfeit of the enemy's demonstrations and delusions."—A.B. Simpson[223]

*Go Deeper with God Rather Than Trusting Surface Impressions.* "The shallow nature lives in its impulses, its impressions, its intuitions, its instincts and very largely in its surroundings. The profound character looks beyond all these and moves steadily on. . . . When God has deepened us, then He can give us His deeper truths, His profoundest secrets, and His mightier trusts."—A.B. Simpson[224]

## WHO CAN PROPHESY?

*Anyone with a Burning Message from the Holy Spirit.* "Fear not to speak the message which the Holy Spirit has burned into your soul for the quickening and the rousing of your brethren. It will be a word in season for some weary soul."—A.B. Simpson[225]

*Every Believer Can Have a Prophetic Message.* "Every Christian worker and minister should have in a very real way a prophetic message, a message not obtained from books and scribes, but warm from the mouth of God, and fresh from the Holy Spirit."—A.B. Simpson[226]

*According to Your Faith.* "Let us be willing to speak as the oracles of God and prophesy according to the proportion of our faith."—A.B. Simpson[227]

## ADDITIONAL RESOURCES WITH A SIMILAR VIEW OF PROPHECY AS THE EARLY C&MA

Deere, Jack. *Surprised by the Voice of God: How God Speaks Today Through Prophecies, Dreams and Visions.* Grand Rapids: Zondervan, 1996.

Grudem, Wayne. *The Gift of Prophecy in the New Testament and Today.* Wheaton, IL: Crossway Books, 1988.

## FOR REFLECTION AND DISCUSSION

1.  Define and describe the gift of prophecy? What are the purposes of prophecy?

2.  Have you heard the gift of prophecy exercised? What did you think about it?

3.  Read Exodus and 1 Cor. 14:5. Moses and Paul said that they desired for all to prophesy. Why?

4.  Do you desire to prophesy? Do you believe God desires that you prophesy?

5.  How does a person know he or she has a prophetic word from the Lord?

6.  Have you ever had a word of prophecy? How did you know it was a word from the Lord?

7.  Why are prophecies not infallible?

8.  How do you discern whether a prophecy is true, false, or mixed?

9.  Who should judge prophecies?

10. Read Psalm 46:10. Get still before the Lord and listen. What is the Holy Spirit saying to you?

CHAPTER 7

# Understanding Speaking in Tongues

## IS SPEAKING IN TONGUES A HUMAN LANGUAGE OR A HEAVENLY LANGUAGE?

*May Be Human or Heavenly.* "It may be a human tongue, or it may be a heavenly tongue. For the apostle distinctly speaks of both the tongues of men and of angels."—A.B. Simpson[228]

*Can Be a Divine Ecstasy.* "It appears to be a divine ecstasy which lifts the soul above the ordinary modes and expressions of reason and utterance.... The spirit is the higher element and in the gift of tongues appears to overlap the mind altogether, and find its expression in speech quite unintelligible to the person himself and yet truly expressing the higher thought and feeling of the exalted spiritual state of the subject."—A.B. Simpson[229]

"... the express of divine emotion."—A.B. Simpson[230]

"At other times, in my private devotions, or with some friend of the same mind, I have been given sweet, ecstatic utterances which seemed indeed like the tongues of angels."—Carrie Judd Montgomery[231]

*An Ecstatic Overflow—The Artless Freedom of the Spirit's Voice.* "I remember a dear old black saint, now in heaven, who used to accentuate the most important periods and passages in the sermon, or the meeting, by sometimes springing to her feet with a burst of ecstatic overflow that no language could express. It was a sort of inarticulate cry, while her face literally blazed in ebony blackness with the light of glory. She was simply beating time to one of God's great strains, and while the ear of exquisite taste was sometimes offended, I believe the Holy Spirit was pleased, and the true heart of His Church ought always to make room for the artless freedom of the Spirit's voice. There are no monopolies in the Church of Jesus Christ, and reverent faith will always say, 'Let the Lord speak by whom He will.'"—A.B. Simpson[232]

*A Vibrant Rapturous Response from Our Inner Springs.* "There came over me a sense of God's overshadowing presence, and I felt there was nothing to do but to bend lower and lower under the weight of His overshadowing. . . . By the blessed constraint of the Spirit, I was prostrated at His feet. . . . From the very inner springs of my being there began to well up a wordless melody of praise and thanksgiving to God. After a little while, without any conscious effort of my mind or will, there flowed sweetly and calmly utterances in another tongue, in perfect cadence and rhythm. My whole being was vibrant with rapturous response. . . I was satisfied, satisfied, satisfied, not with the new song in a new tongue, not with the ecstasy, but with God, with Himself."—Henry Kenning, A.B. Simpson's song leader and Missionary Training Institute instructor[233]

*May Be Expressed in the Languages of the World in Intercession.* "For a few minutes I talked to Him in a tongue unknown, and then He seemed to say, 'You have wanted to pray, now begin.' I began to pray at Jerusalem, and for the first time in my life I felt my prayer was fully satisfying His heart, because it seemed like the travail of His own soul. I seemed to be in Jerusalem, suffering and praying as in His very stead. When it seemed my heart was poured out for Jerusalem, I began the usual round of prayer at Japan, China, Tibet, India, and so on, and as I prayed the language changed as I prayed for the different places. . . . Then I supposed He had been giving me the language of all the people for whom I had been praying."—Mary B. Mullen[234]

*May Occasionally Be Expressed as Preaching in Other Languages Unknown to the Speaker*

- *Eastern Indian Tongue.* Akola, India orphanage—Boy with a message in tongues, preached repentance for two hours in a language he did not know to an Islamic boy, June 1908[235]
- *Chinese Tongue.* Man in China converted through preaching in tongues who understood him perfectly, May 1909[236]
- *Native American Tongue.* A.G. Ward was preaching with an interpreter to the Indians of the Fisher River reservation about two hundred miles north of Winnipeg. As he was preaching under the anointing of the Spirit, he began to speak in tongues. His interpreter exclaimed, "Why, you are now speaking to us in your own language!"—reported of A.G. Ward, C&MA field evangelist, Western Canada and Director of C&MA Mission in Winnipeg[237]

*Other Examples of Praying and Praising in Tongues Identified as Actual Languages*

- *Hebrew and German.* At Indianapolis C&MA Easter Sunday, 1907, a 17-year-old girl fell under power and spoke in tongues in 3-4 languages, including Hebrew and German[238]
- *German.* Baptist pastor's wife healed at Alliance convention, fell under the power of the Spirit and spoke in tongues in German, October 1907, New Jersey[239]
- *Indian and Chinese dialects.* Several times the Holy Spirit spoke through Carrie Judd Montgomery in tongues understood by missionaries as Indian and Chinese dialects. Harriette Shimer, a Quaker missionary to China, heard her praying and singing in Chinese throughout the week. She did not know much about the Pentecostal movement and was really somewhat opposed to it. Her experience with Carrie changed her mind. On one occasion, a couple from China and their two sons, heard her speak in Chinese, and understood exactly what she said.[240]
- *Indian Dialect of Tamil.* Henry Kenning, A.B. Simpson's songleader, spoke in tongues, confirmed by an Alliance missionary to India that he was speaking in pure Tamil.[241]
- *Chinese.* "I was taken up with my God, but I found I was speaking Chinese and other tongues. Oh such days! Such weeks! Such months I never had before in all my days!"—Mrs. Etta Wurmser, C&MA pastor, church planter, and Bible school director[242]
- *Arabic.* A.G. Argue was praying in the home of George and Annie Murray, Scottish C&MA missionaries to Palestine. Suddenly, he burst out speaking in tongues. The Murrays understood him and revealed that he was speaking in Arabic, which Argue had never learned.[243]
- *African Kefonti Dialect.* Sally Botham, who was planning to go to the mission field in Congo, "sat on the floor before a large map of the world and began praying in tongues. It seemed that as she prayed for each country the Lord gave her a different language." When she prayed in tongues for the Congo, two Alliance missionaries, Lucy Villars and Mary Mullen, recognized the language as "Kefonti," one of the dialects of the Congo. One of them spoke up, saying, "Why, she is speaking in the Congo language! She is telling people to get ready, for Jesus is coming soon!" They translated further utterances as, "the fountain of blood is flowing from Calvary, sufficient for all our sins, and sufficient for a world of sinners."—C&MA General Council, Nyack 1907, certified by A.B. Simpson[244]

- *Thai.* One student who was an MK (Missionary Kid) from Vietnam spoke in perfect Thai, though she had never learned the language.[245]

## WHAT ARE THE BENEFITS OF TONGUES?

*Expressing What the Mind Cannot Fathom or Express.* "It appears to be a divine ecstasy which lifts the soul above the ordinary modes and expressions of reason and utterance. . . . The spirit is the higher element and in the gift of tongues appears to overlap the mind altogether, and find its expression in speech quite unintelligible to the person himself and yet truly expressing the higher thought and feeling of the exalted spiritual state of the subject."—A.B. Simpson[246]

". . . a burst of ecstatic overflow that no language could express. . . . a sort of inarticulate cry, . . . . the artless freedom of the Spirit's voice."—A.B. Simpson[247]

*Filling the Hunger of Your Heart.* "My desire was for a relationship. In fact, the thought that I might speak in tongues was a very real deterrent to me. I was not seeking an emotional experience or signs of any kind. . . . Gently, beautifully, wonderfully, God met the need of my hungry heart, and I knew that He had filled me with His own blessed Self. Quietly, while seated, I began of my own volition, but enabled by God's imparted ability, to speak in a language which I had not learned but given to me by the Holy Spirit."—Paris Reidhead, Sudan Interior Mission missionary, friend of A.W. Tozer and later C&MA pastor[248]

*A Channel of Fellowship with the Heavenly World.* "[The Apostle Paul] does not ignore the gift of tongues by any means, but recognizes it as the distinct mark of divine power and presence, and a very glorious and blessed channel or direct fellowship with the heavenly world, and in some sense a real opening of the doors between the earthly and the heavenly."—A.B. Simpson[249]

*Entering on Holy Ground.* "As we come to [this] class of tongues, let us take the shoes off our feet, for the ground whereon we stand is holy. . . . This is where the supernatural predominates to such a degree that God is more in evidence than man, or simply the operation of the Spirit upon man. It is a speaking manifestation of Deity—a supernatural Spirit-given utterance to men clothed with power and authority from on high."—W. T. Dixon, C&MA pastor[250]

*Deepening of Spiritual Life and Zeal.* "Many of these experiences appear not only to be genuine but accompanied by a spirit of deep humility, earnestness, and soberness, and free from extravagance and error. And it is admitted that in many of the branches and states where this movement has been strongly developed and wisely directed, there has been a marked deepening of the spiritual life of our members and an encouraging increase in their missionary zeal and liberality."—C&MA Annual Report, 1907-1908.

*A Fresh Spring and Deeper Dimension.* "There welled up deep within me a fresh spring of spiritual water—bubbling and bubbling. . . . Everything seemed to have come into a deeper dimension."— Joy Boese, C&MA missionary nurse[251]

*The Acme of Revival.* "The acme of the revival seemed reached when Miss Wink spoke in an unknown tongue for fully thirty minutes. . . . 'It was not a meaningless jargon. . . . She uttered distinct words and in such tones of sweetness as I have never heard. . . . it was clearly the story of the crucifixion she was relating.'"—Dr. F.E. Marsh, Simpson associate, relating a report of an Alliance meeting[252]

*Strengthening the Inner Man.* "It is their being strengthened with might by His Spirit in the inner man. . . ."—William T. MacArthur[253]

*Intensive Worship.* "When the Holy Spirit came on the day of Pentecost, why did the believers break out into ecstatic language? Simply, it was because they were rightly worshiping God for the first time. Intensive worship unexpectedly leaped out of their hearts."—A.W. Tozer[254]

*Five Benefits to Robert Jaffray.* "Personally I have never received such a spiritual uplift as when I received this blessed Baptism and spoke in tongues. The anointing then received 'abides' unto this day. These are a few of the many benefits that I would mention:

- *Deeper Love and Understanding of the Word of God.* "A deeper love for, and understanding of, the Word of God than ever before."
- *A Sense of Our Powerlessness and the Power of Prayer.* "A knowledge of my utter strengthlessness and of the power of the Name and the Blood of Jesus in prayer as never before."
- *A Greater Anointing in Witnessing and Preaching.* "An unction in witnessing and preaching greater than ever before."
- *Greater Control of Our Human Tongue.* "A control of the 'unruly member' in daily life since the Lord took peculiar charge of my tongue."
- *Greater Awareness of Spiritual Warfare.* "A clearer understanding of the mighty works of the Holy Spirit and of evil spirits, in these last days of the Present Age."—Robert Jaffray[255]

*A Stepping Stone to Greater Gifts.* "May it not be that the Spirit usually gives the 'tongues' first to test us and see whether or not we may be trusted with greater gifts of the Spirit which may be indeed of more value in the Christian ministry."—Robert Jaffray[256]

*Taming Our Tongue.* "There may be this reason also, that if the Spirit can get hold of a man's tongue He has what corresponds, according to James, to the bit in the horse's mouth and the rudder of the ship, and so in turn the whole body may be bridled by the Spirit of God."—Robert Jaffray[257]

*Sweeter Prayer and Worship.* "God graciously gave me this gift fourteen years ago [1906], and nearly every day in prayer and worship I still speak in tongues, and it is one of the sweetest things in my Christian experience."—F.F. Bosworth[258]

*Overflowing Praise.* ". . . an overflowing spirit of praise."—A.E. Thompson[259]

*Supernatural Intercession.* ". . . the blessedness of this experience—the heavenly intoxication of the supernatural song, or the blissful agony of supernatural intercession; yet these are among the blessings indicated in our Apostle's description of the Spirit-filled life—to quote him further, he says: 'Praying with all prayer and supplication in the spirit.'"—William T. MacArthur[260]

*Double Equipment of Mind and Spirit.* "We do not say that these things cannot be enjoyed in the understanding as well; but Paul had the double equipment, which he so much desired that the others also should enjoy, and declared he would pray and sing with both his spirit and his understanding."—William T. MacArthur[261]

*Reaches the Highest and Best of Our Heavenly Inheritance.* "Tongues are valuable . . . in proportion as the speaker communes with God. . . . It seems to us that is not possible to reach the highest and best of our heavenly inheritance apart from them."—William T. MacArthur[262]

*Greater Consciousness of God's Presence—Beyond All Dreams.* "Out from my innermost being rolled a volume of language unknown to me, while my soul was filled with 'joy unspeakable and full of glory,' which found vent in this new operation of the Spirit. I was literally drunk with 'new wine.' This 'weight of glory' remained for days, while the consciousness of the divine presence within was greater than I had ever dreamed possible in this life."—Bertha Pinkham Dixon, Alliance pastor's wife[263]

*Greater Liberty and Divine Unction.* "I have far greater liberty and Divine unction on me in dealing with souls, and there has come into my life an overflow of love and joy with a deep settled peace planted in the depths of my soul, a something that is inexpressible and indescribable."—H.L. Blake, C&MA pastor[264]

*Expressing the Holy Spirit's Burden.* "It would seem as if in these last days God had sometimes to give a new tongue to adequately express the burdens of the Holy Spirit's prayer. Therefore, we cannot always expect to fully understand our own prayers, but must often pour out our hearts before Him in wordless agony and unutterable desire, knowing 'that He who searches the hearts knows the mind of the Spirit, because He makes intercession for the saints according to the will of God.'"—A.B. Simpson[265]

*Deeper Death in Surrender to God.* "I had longer for a deeper death, and an experience where the power of God would be manifested in my life. . . . This desire deepened, and the death deepened. . . . About this time we had a special season of waiting upon the Lord for a deeper revelation of Himself, and one night . . . the joy of the Lord flooded my entire being, until it seemed I could not stay in this world. Then the Spirit seemed to say, 'Now I am ready for the tongue,' and I said, 'Lord I covet the best gifts, please answer my prayer for love, wisdom and power to intercede for others.' This seemed to check the outpouring of the Spirit, and I said, 'Lord, if you want my tongue to speak an unknown language, take it, take it,' and the third 'take it' was spoken in another language, and for a few minutes I talked to Him in a tongue unknown."—Mary B. Mullen[266]

*Increased Depths of Power, Prayer, Love, and Sweetness.* "One lady I had known for years as a sanctified and anointed teacher of God's Word. She was not satisfied and pressed on by faith into the fullness of the Holy Spirit. Her experience was most satisfactory, such appreciation for the blood, such power to witness, increased intercessory prayer, such a baptism of divine love. She spoke in tongues, but kept the gift in its proper place. One of the dear Beulah workers also received the fullness, and we all could realize the increased depths of sweetness, humility, and power which took possession of her life."—Carrie Judd Montgomery[267]

*Rejuvenation of Body and Mind.* "The old, tired feeling went like the dropping of an old garment. My memory was quickened and my nerves steadied instantly."—Mattie Perry, C&MA evangelist and director of Elhanan Bible Institute and Children's Home[268]

*It Is the Residue—Like Icing on the Cake.* "This [Pentecostal baptism] was like the 'residue of the oil' (Leviticus 14:18, 25) that flowed down upon the hem of Aaron's robe, and that God was doing this thing for all who would receive."—Mrs. William T. MacArthur, wife of Simpson's close friend and associate[269]

## CAN A PERSON SPEAK IN TONGUES IN ONE'S OWN LANGUAGE?

*The Holy Spirit Can Take Control of Your Language.* "One timid young woman, whom we know well, had been praying earnestly for her baptism. One night the Spirit came down upon, and for an hour or more the Holy Spirit took her tongue, and made her praise God, as never before in all her life. She was conscious that the Holy Spirit was controlling her tongue, but she was praising the Lord in her own language."—Dr. T.J. McCrossan[270]

*Another Tongue All in English.* "One night the blessed Holy Spirit came down upon me. I saw a light, far brighter than the noon-day sun—a perfect blaze of glory. Hundreds of tongues of fire seemed to dart forth upon and about me. For an hour or more great billows of glory, indescribably beautiful from light and colors, began to roll through my soul like mighty breakers over a sandy beach. No outsider needed to tell me that the Holy Spirit had entered my life in a new way. Then the blessed Spirit took possession of my tongue, and for an hour or more made me praise the Lord Jesus in a way I had never praised Him before. I was literally speaking with another tongue as the Spirit gave to me to utter forth, but it was all in English."—Dr. T.J. McCrossan[271]

*Tongues of Glory in Your Own Language.* "My whole being was filled with the glory of God. Wave after wave passed over my soul until every thing seemed like a bright shining light. I could see nothing of this world and still I realized what was going on. . . . All is could say was, Glory! Glory! Some were expecting that I would speak in an unknown tongue. For nine days there was such a halo of glory over me that I could wake up in the night and for hours I could fell the glory of the Lord surging through my mortal frame. God said, 'Are you no satisfied with your tongue of glory?' And I said, 'Yes, Lord.' It just seemed that I could not stand any more of this demonstration of the power of God. Now when the power of the Spirit comes on me, I have to say, glory, three times before I get my own tongue back again as it was before. No matter what the people may think or say I know that I have experienced the tongues of glory, what God wanted me to have."—C&MA Pastor Mary Gainforth[272]

## WHAT IS SINGING IN THE SPIRIT?

*A Melody from Within the Veil—From Another World.* "A young girl came under the power and her spirit was caught up to the throne. She sang a melody, without words, that seemed to come from within the veil, it was so heavenly. It seemed to come from another world."—October 1907 at the C&MA convention in Simpson's Gospel Tabernacle[273]

*Intoxication of Supernatural Song.* ". . . the blessedness of this experience—the heavenly intoxication of the supernatural song, or the blissful agony of super-natural intercession; . . . these are among the blessings indicated in our Apostle's description of the Spirit-filled. . . . Paul had the double equipment, which he so much desired that the others also should enjoy, and declared he would pray and sing with both his spirit and his understanding."—William T. MacArthur[274]

*Drawn into the Presence of God.* "We have frequently heard young people sing in other tongues, as the Spirit gave them utterance; singing with a voice so vast-ly superior to their own natural voice, that there was no comparison. No inter-preter was present on these occasions, and yet I felt certain these were genuine languages (having studied five different languages), and I know from the tone, facial expression and marvelous joy that it was the work of the Holy Spirit. There was something about it so sweet, so attractive, so helpful, something that actually drew one into the very presence of God."—Dr. T.J. McCrossan[275]

*Celestial Harmony from My Innermost Being.* "A heavenly choir . . . a low humming that gradually rose in harmonious crescendo as six individuals in different parts of the audience rose spontaneously to their feet and a full tide of glorious melody poured forth in ecstatic worship and praise. . . . from my inner-most being heavenly music poured forth like strains through the pipes of some great organ. . . . the flowing forth of celestial harmony like a foretaste of divine rapture."—Alice Reynolds, teenage girl from Indianapolis Alliance Church[276]

*A Perfect Song—Transcendently Beyond This World.* "Something in the tone of voice gripped my soul. . . . I listened to the song [in tongues], and I seemed entranced. . . . I was dumbfounded. Such purity of tone, such perfect poise of resonance, such evenness of the registers ascending and descending, and most remarkable of all, such astounding breath-control as I have never heard. . . . too beautiful for words . . . indeed eloquent with a message from another world. . . . with all the beauty and rapture that the voice seemed to speak, there was an indefinable and indescribable *something* that seemed to breathe the holiest and profoundest worship. . . . merged in something transcendently beyond—the worship and adoration of God."—Pastor Henry Kenning, music instructor at Nyack Missionary Training Institute[277]

*Singing with a Heavenly Choir.* "Presently as they seemed to come to a pause in the singing, at the end of a strain. He turned around so gracefully to me, and looked at me and said, 'Well, My child, what would you like to have?' And I said, 'Oh, Lord, I would like to join Your choir,' and then I seemed to tremble at what I had said, 'join that choir!' He turned and looked toward the choir, and then at me and said, 'My child, you may,' and then all the strength left me, and I said, 'Well, I can't now, I wouldn't dare.' But He made a motion to me with His baton, and it seemed I was lifted right up and was set down in the choir. I began to sing with them a little and what do you suppose? I was singing the 'latter rain' song in tongues, which I afterwards interpreted and wrote into English. They all seemed to join in with me and after it was all over they sang another great chorus. I listened, and the great Leader, my glorified Christ, motioned to me and I sat down, and I thought, Oh, what singing! The old Ohio Quartette never could sing like that and I found myself singing also. . . .

Oh, what glory I was in for an hour. I took out my watch and saw that for just an hour I was lost to this world. Oh, what a vision of Jesus and of heaven! Indescribable! I have just sketched the outline. Oh, what glory there was in my soul."—David Wesley Myland, Alliance Pastor, Columbus, Ohio, and District Evangelist[278]

## WHAT ARE SOME EXAMPLES OF INTERPRETATION OF TONGUES?

*Pastor Myland's Latter Rain Song in Tongues and Interpretation.* "The glory died away and I came to myself singing in tongues. It passed away and immediately I began to reach for my Bible. I took out a piece of blank paper and began to write with my left hand, tried to write with my pencil between the first and second finger. I could not get along very fast and involuntarily took it over into my right hand, the hand that had been so badly swollen, and I found I was healed; the sores were there but I was healed. There wasn't a particle of pain or stiffness, and I wrote the words of the Latter Rain Song, word for word, as fast as I could write; never changed a word, wrote the melody, tried it on the piano, and found it a beautiful melody."—David Wesley Myland, Alliance Pastor, Columbus, Ohio, and District Evangelist[279]

This is the song that he wrote as an interpretation of singing in tongues, called "The Latter Rain Song" and also "Pentecost Has Come":

> There's a Pentecost for all the sanctified.
> Heaven's Witness true, which cannot be denied,
> And the Spirit's gifts are being multiplied
> In God's holy church today.
>
> CHORUS:
> Oh, I'm glad the promised Pentecost has come,
> And the "Latter Rain" is falling now on some;

Pour it out in floods, Lord, on the parched ground,
Till it reaches all the earth around.

There's a Pentecost for every trusting soul,
Of your life the Spirit now will take control.
Filling, sealing, quickening, healing, making whole,
By God's holy pow'r today.

There's a Pentecost for every yielded heart,
And the "holy fire" God's Spirit will impart;
To obey His will you gladly then will star
In God's holy work today.

There's a Pentecost for those who wait and pray
With surrendered will, O seek it then today;
Christ will baptize all His saints who will obey
With the Spirit's tongues of fire.[280]

*Intepretation of Tongues for Healing from Breast Cancer.* "I was awakened with the power of the Lord upon me and as I began praising Him in the unknown tongue, He gave me the interpretation, 'This thing I will cast off from thy being.'. . . I got up that morning and ate my breakfast, but soon realized that God was working in that cancer, and it seemed to be literally pushing out of my breast." Five days later she saw a vision of Christ and His presence filled the room. She was lifted up off her bed on her feet with no effort of her own. The pain was gone and a week later the cancer dropped off her chest "like a hard, heavy stone."[281]

*Interpretation Through Sign Language, Not Verbally.* "The acme of the revival seemed reached when Miss Wink spoke in an unknown tongue for fully thirty minutes. . . . 'Usually after such a speech there is a [verbal] interpretation of the meaning. Miss Wink gave none . . . But those who heard her say it was clearly the story of the crucifixion she was relating. She pointed to her head as where Christ had worn the crown of thorns; indicated the pierced side, and nail prints in the hands by gestures which all could understand.'"—Dr. F.E. Marsh, Simpson associate relating a report of an Alliance meeting[282]

## WHAT SHOULD BE OUR ATTITUDE TOWARD SPEAKING IN TONGUES?

*It Is Dangerous to Oppose or Despise Tongues.* "The church of Christ today may receive the Gift of Tongues. Every local church of Christ should have, in some of its members, the manifestation of this gift. . . . It is a dangerous thing to oppose or despise this, one of the immediate manifestations of the Blessed Spirit of God."—J. Hudson Ballard[283]

**Don't Be Afraid of It.** "Get alone in your room and wait on the Lord until you are filled. You say, 'I might speak in tongues.' Well, if you do, Hallelujah. I am afraid of you if you are afraid of something the Holy Spirit gives from above. . . . Why not be willing, if the Lord sends it, to speak in tongues? . . . Paul tells us how to regulate the gifts, not to eliminate them."—Paul Rader, C&MA President[284]

**Be Willing to Receive It.** "Every Christian should be willing to receive this gift (tongues) if it please the Spirit to bestow it upon him."—J. Hudson Ballard[285]

"The gift of tongues may be received by any regenerate person. Children readily receive the gift."—German pastor Jonathan Paul, friend of A.B. Simpson and speaker at Simpson's Gospel Tabernacle[286]

**Be Willing to Receive the Least of Gifts before Being Entrusted with Greater Gifts.** "May it not be that the Spirit usually gives the 'tongues' first to test us and see whether or not we may be trusted with greater gifts of the Spirit which may be indeed of more value in the Christian ministry."—Robert Jaffray[287]

**Desire What Paul Desired.** "Paul says not to forbid them (1 Cor. 14:39). He also tells us that he who speaks in an unknown tongue, speaks not unto men, but unto God and that 'in the spirit he speaks mysteries (1 Cor.14:3); also that he 'edifies himself.' We are told, however, most plainly, that 'he who prophesies is greater than he who speaks with tongues, unless he interprets, that the church may receive edification.' And yet, in spite of all this, Paul says, 'I want you all to speak with tongues,' and he thanks God that he speaks with tongues more than they all. Why did he thank God for this gift if it was not truly to be desired?"—Carrie Judd Montgomery[288]

"Paul had the double equipment, which he so much desired that the others also should enjoy, and declared he would pray and sing with both his spirit and his understanding."—William T. MacArthur[289]

**Desire Tongues, But Prefer Prophecy.** "Tongues are desirable, yet prophecy is preferable."—A.E. Thompson, C&MA missionary[290]

**Speak Out the Inexpressible That Is in Your Heart.** "If you have, in some simple form, the old gift of tongues welling up in your heart, some Hallelujah which you could not put into articulate speech, some unutterable cry of love or joy, out with it!"—A.B. Simpson[291]

## ADDITIONAL RESOURCES ON SPEAKING IN TONGUES SIMILAR TO HISTORIC C&MA UNDERSTANDING

Christianson, Larry. *Answering Your Questions about Speaking in Tongues.* Bloomington, MN: Bethany House, 1968, 2005.

Hayford, Jack. *The Beauty of Spiritual Language.* Dallas: Word Publishing, 1992. (Note: Dr. Hayford attended an Alliance church as a teenager and learned of speaking in tongues from his Alliance pastor whom he heard praying in tongues. He was a featured speaker at the C&MA General Council at Anaheim, California in the 1990s, where this book was sold.)

## FOR REFLECTION AND DISCUSSION

1.  Read 1 Corinthians 12:10. What are speaking in tongues and interpretation of tongues?

2.  Why is speaking in tongues so controversial?

3.  Read 1 Corinthians 14:5. Why is speaking in tongues desirable? Discuss the benefits of speaking in tongues.

4.  Why does Paul say that prophecy is preferable unless tongues are interpreted?

5.  How can excesses and extremes regarding speaking in tongues be avoided without quenching the genuine gift of tongues?

6.  Have you or a friend had an experience of speaking in tongues? What was it like?

7.  Are you willing to speak in tongues if God desires it for you?

# Understanding Other Spiritual Gifts and Manifestations

## WHAT IS THE GIFT OF FAITH?

*Special Mountain-Moving Faith.* "It is not saving faith, . . . but it is the special faith that fits us for effective service; the faith that removes mountains of difficulty, the faith that uproots sycamore trees of evil, the faith that knocks until doors are opened, the faith that equips the evangelist for the winning of souls and the work for the accomplished of great and mighty things in the pulling down of strongholds and the building up of the kingdom of God."—A.B. Simpson[292]

*The Secret of Jesus' Power—The Faith of God Himself.* "No gift of the Spirit is of more unspeakable value than the gift of faith. It was of this the Master said to His disciples, when they asked Him the secret of His own power, 'Have the faith of God.'"—A.B. Simpson[293]

*Spirit-Imparted Faith.* "This 'faith of God' is the faith the Holy Spirit imparts to God's saints, just in proportion as we allow Him to control our lives. 1 Corinthians 12:9 tells us that 'faith' is one of the gifts of the Spirit, and this 'Spirit-imparted faith' is the faith of God."[294]

## WHAT ARE SUPERNATURAL WORDS OF WISDOM OR KNOWLEDGE?

*A Word in Season or Revelation.* "The word of knowledge . . . is also spoken of as the Word of Wisdom. It is not a general stock of crystallized knowledge laid up by mere human study, but it is a particular revelation as we need to use the Word for each occasion and service. . . . 'a word in season to him who is weary.'"—A.B. Simpson[295]

*A.B. Simpson's Supernatural Knowledge of Someone Resisting the Holy Spirit.* "Brother Simpson asked all that were willing to consecrate everything to God and to accept Him in the future as their Physician to stand on their feet. When the invitation was given to go forward for anointing, I still held back, riveted to my seat by a power I could not resist. All the seats were filled but one that the dear Lord had placed there for me. Brother Simpson said, 'I feel some one is resisting the Spirit, and I beg of you don't do it.' Then came the words very clearly to me, what was I that I could resist God, and I was carried to the front seat not knowing how. Once there all fear fled and I felt I was in the presence of God.

When Brother Simpson placed the oil upon my brow I felt that I just reached out and touched Jesus, and the power of the Holy Spirit overcame me. For half an hour I knew no more and then I began praising God. The witness was within that the work was done. I soon found the symptoms all gone and a new life and health flowing through my body that I had never known before. I could sing and talk for Jesus all the time without weariness or pain, a thing I had never been free from for twenty-three years."[296]

*John Salmon's "Telegram from God."* Although the aged John Salmon had gone into retirement after his worldwide trip to China, his supernatural ministry in the Spirit had not abated in his final years. In December 1917, about six months before his death, Salmon dreamed of vast group of foreigners surrounding a woman pleading for something to eat. She was alone without any help. When he awoke he asked God the meaning of the dream, and the Lord responded, "I want you to help her." He replied, "Well, Lord who is it?" And the Lord said, "It is Mrs. Cole in North China." Then he said, "Well, Lord, how much shall I send her?" "Send her $50." He sent the money the next morning, not knowing that at about the same time Jean Cole had been praying for funds to come in to feed starving people in North China displaced by flooding. Cole called the incident a "telegram from God."[297]

*William Christie's Supernatural Knowledge and Prophetic Word.* In one incident of supernatural knowledge, a former Tibetan lamaistic priest named Dkon-Mchog-Bastan-Adzin, had become severely ill, and had tried to find relief for seven years through sorcery and witchcraft. He was lying on a bed when Christie was summoned by the man's wife to pray for him. Christie "was swept by a strong impression that if this man would forsake heathenish ways, and put his trust in Jesus Christ, the power of God would be manifested, and he would be healed." As a result the man confessed Jesus as his Savior and the family burned all of the lamaistic paraphernalia. Then Christie "rebuked the disease in the name of Jesus" and "suddenly the former priest felt a touch of life, and he arose," and was totally healed.[298]

*Glenn Tingley's Supernatual Knowledge over the Radio.* "A woman who continually prayed for her cruel and drunken husband told us that he had cursed 'that religious program' to which she listened daily. Finally, one day he was so enraged at her devotion that he picked up the radio and crashed it on the floor. Miraculously, the little shattered box kept right on talking! He had just raised his foot to smash it into silence when my voice challenged him:

> 'You may not want to hear what I have to say! You may throw this radio on the floor! You may stomp it to pieces, but friend, God loves you and Christ died for your sins!'

"Amazed and gasping, the man turned to his wife and screamed, 'He sees me! He actually sees what I'm going to do!'"—Glenn Tingley, C&MA pastor and evangelist[299]

As a result, the man came to Tingley's Gospel Tabernacle and turned his life to Christ.

*Evangelist's Supernatural Impression as Woman Walks into Meeting.* "An evangelist sat on the platform one evening, waiting for the hour to open the service. He was suddenly impressed to repeat, "Whosoever hates his brother is a murderer, and you know that no murderer has eternal life abiding in him." A young lady had just entered her pew when this Scripture was quoted. She was under deep conviction for salvation, but held a grudge against one whom she would not forgive. The passage quoted cut her to the heart, and such guilt pressed her spirit that she immediately yielded to Christ and was saved.—cited by W.W. Newberry[300]

## WHAT ARE THE GIFTS OF HEALING AND MIRACLES?

*A Distinct Enduement of Faith and Power.* "A distinct enduement of the workers who are called to it with the faith and power of God."—A.B. Simpson[301]

*Necessary in the Church and Should Be Prominent.* "We find as a matter of course and of necessity 'gifts of healing' taking just such rank and prominence as they did in our Lord's personal ministry on earth."—William C. Stevens[302]

*Not a Magic Power.* "This does not mean some kind of magic or magnetic power possessed by some individuals enabling them to remove diseases by a touch."—A.B. Simpson[303]

*Not the Power of a Person, But the Power of the Holy Spirit.* "They are spiritual gifts, but never apart from the Giver. They are not powers possessed by the individual, but the power of the Holy Spirit personally, working through him."—A.B. Simpson[304]

*A Real Power to Lead People to Receive Healing From the Divine Healer.* "At the same time a very real power to help God's sick and suffering children to know and receive Him as their healer and life. Just a God gives to some the special ministry of leading souls to Christ, so He gives to others as distinct a ministry in leading sufferers to receive the healing power of the Great Physician."—A.B. Simpson[305]

*The Difference Between Gifts of Healing and Gifts of Miracles.* "The working of miracles are distinguished from the gifts of healing, inasmuch as healing is not always or even usually miraculous . . . . The miracle rather is intended by its sudden and startling character to attract attention and to bear witness in some extraordinary way to the power and majesty of God. . . . . The miraculous is an element of the Spirit's enduement."—A.B. Simpson[306]

## SHOULD ONLY ELDERS OR THOSE WITH GIFTS OF HEALING PRAY FOR THE SICK?

*All Preachers, Teachers, and Writers.* "All preachers, teachers, writers, and all others who hand out the Word of Life to the people should keep this direction (James 5:14) as continuously before the people as sickness itself constantly confronts them."—William C. Stevens[307]

*Laymen.* "Even laymen may pray for the sick."—F.F. Bosworth[308]

*Women.* "The right of women to act as elders. . . . It is right for women to anoint and pray for the sick, until God raised up men elders, and then to stand at their side and help."—A.B. Simpson[309]

*The Humblest Believer.* "This power is not associated with the apostles in any distinctive way. It is through the Holy Spirit by faith in the name of Jesus. These are general conditions, met by the apostles in a preeminent degree, but open to the humblest believer."—William C. Stevens[310]

## HOW SHOULD WE REGARD HEALERS?

*Trust the Divine Healer, Not the Human Instrument.* "I have never allowed anyone to look to me as a healer, and have had no liberty to pray for others while they placed the least trust in either me or my prayers, or aught but the merits, promises and intercessions of Christ alone. My most important work has usually been to get myself and my shadow out of people's way, and set Jesus fully in their view."—A.B. Simpson[311]

***Don't Claim to Be A Healer, But a Witness of Jesus' Power.*** "We do not claim to be healers and wonderworkers, but simply witnesses for the power of Jesus to do all He has promised."—A.B. Simpson[312]

"No man can claim that he is a healer or a power or anything but a helpless instrument whom God may be pleased to use in a given case. . . . In the ministry of healing, the part of the instrument is to lead the sufferer to know the will and the Word of God, to trust Him for himself, and then when he truly and trustingly comes, to claim with and for him the blessing promised and the seal and earnest of the Holy Spirit."—A.B. Simpson[313]

***Get Out of the Way and Put the Focus on Jesus.*** "I have never allowed anyone to look to me as a healer, and have had no liberty to pray for others while they placed the least trust in either me or my prayers, or aught but the merits, promises and intercessions of Christ alone. My most important work has usually been to get myself and my shadow out of people's way, and set Jesus fully in their view."—A.B. Simpson[314]

***Trust Jesus, Not Someone Else's Word.*** "Do not rise from your bed or walk on your lame foot because somebody tells you to do so. That is not faith, but impression."—A.B. Simpson[315]

***True Healing Ministry Is Not Superior Salesmanship.*** "Another field where tearless men have done us untold harm is in prayer for the sick. There have always been reverent, serious men who felt it their sacred duty to pray for the sick that they might be healed in the will of God. It was said of Spurgeon that his prayers raised up more sick persons than the ministrations of any doctor in London. When tearless promoters took up the doctrine it was turned into a lucrative racket. Smooth, persuasive men used superior salesmanship methods to make impressive fortunes out of their campaigns. Their big ranches and heavy financial investments prove how successful they have been in separating the sick and suffering from their money. And this in the name of the Man of Sorrows who had not where to lay His head!"—A.W. Tozer[316]

***Shun Public Parades and a Wondering-Seeking Spirit.*** "It is very solemn ground and can never be made a professional business or a public parade. Its mightiest victims will always be silent and out of sight, and its power will keep pace with our humility and holiness. . . . We greatly deprecate the indiscriminate anointing of all who come forward. . . . We hope the wonder-seeking spirit will not be allowed to take the place of practical godliness and humble work for the salvation of men."—A.B. Simpson[317]

*Alliance Healing Meetings Avoid Sensationalism.* "In striking contrast with many evangelists who have visited Toronto, the preaching of evangelist Bosworth is characterized by an entire absence of sensationalism or any endeavor to excite emotional outburst on the part of the hearers. He is a plain man and preaches the plain old-fashioned Gospel."—Newspaper report of F.F. Bosworth's C&MA-sponsored healing evangelism meetings[318]

*Be Careful Not to Criticize.* "Let us then be more careful how we criticize these noble men of God who are winning thousands to Jesus Christ. Remember, they all emphasize 'the healing of the soul' as the all important matter, and will not pray for any sick person, if they can help it, who has not first given himself or herself to the Lord Jesus Christ."—Dr. T.J. McCrossan[319]

## CAN "HOLY LAUGHTER" BE BIBLICAL AND FROM GOD?

### Scriptural Examples of Holy Laughter
1. "You greatly rejoice with joy inexpressible and full of glory" (1 Pet. 1:8).
2. "The disciples were filled with joy and with the Holy Spirit" (Acts 13:52).
3. "Jesus rejoiced in Spirit" (lit., "leaped or danced with much joy") (Luke 10:21).
4. Sarah said, "God has made me laugh" (Gen. 21:6).
5. "God will fill your mouth with laughter" (Job 8:21).
6. "Our mouth was filled with laughter" when the Lord set the Israelites free (Ps. 126:2, 5, 6).

This is not a common ordinary joy, but a joy that comes out of the overflow of the Spirit—a spontaneous overflowing joy from the awesome presence and power of God.

*Holy Laughter as an Effect of Being Filled with the Spirit.* "Some of the effects of being filled with the Spirit are . . . fullness of joy so that the heart is constantly radiant. This does not depend on circumstances, but fills the spirit with holy laughter in the midst of the most trying surroundings."—A.B. Simpson[320]

*Simpson's Experience of Holy Laughter.* "The Spirit came with a baptism of holy laughter for an hour or more and I am waiting for all He has yet to give and manifest."—Simpson's Diary, Sept. 12, 1907.

*Ziemer's Experience of Holy Laughter.* "Oh, glorious rapture of the soul! I arose, shouted, and sang, and laughed in the Spirit until I cried for very joy as the flood-tide of God's grace rolled in over my soul again and again with purifying and cleansing power. I felt the holy fire of God burning in my soul. . . . The Lord Jesus Christ was baptizing me with the Holy Spirit according to His Word and power."—Rev. L.H. Ziemer[321]

*Holy Laughter as Intense and Sublime Worship—Tozer.* "I once saw a man kneel at an altar, taking Communion. Suddenly he broke into holy laughter. This man laughed until he wrapped his arms around himself as if he was afraid he would burst just out of sheer delight in the presence of Almighty God. . . . So worship is capable of running from the very simple to the most intense and sublime."—A.W. Tozer[322]

*Holy Laughter as a Manifestation of the Presence of God.* Writing on "The Presence of God," Ira David testified, "There is a Holy Spirit laugh, the laugh, from your feet to the roof of your head, contagious."[323]

*Unspeakable Joy.* "It seemed as if a strong hand passed like a fluttering dove from my head down, and was felt in every part of my being. This was followed by an unspeakable joy and holy laughter." . . . The joy of the Lord flooded my entire being, until it seemed I could not stay in this world."—Mary B. Mullen[324]

*Overflow of Soul in Tozer's Meeting.* "What prayers! What faith! What expectancy! What conviction! What groaning in the Spirit! What claiming of promises! What heart-searching! What victory! God in His faithfulness and love could not help but fulfill His own precious promise : 'Call unto me, and I will . . . show you great and mighty things, which you know not.'. . . One young man, after the Spirit had filled and overflowed his soul, cried out with holy laughter, 'It's too much! It's too much! I can't stand any more!'"—Nyack President Dr. Thomas Moseley, reporting in the *Alliance Weekly* of Tozer's revival meeting at Nyack[325]

## ARE SENSATIONS OF HEAT, ELECTRICAL CURRENT, OR SHAKING FROM GOD?

Trembling or shaking seems to be a response to the overwhelming presence of the Lord and the moving of the Holy Spirit, sometimes in fear, sometimes in joy, sometimes connected with a sense of humbling, sometimes just with a sense of the awesomeness of God.

*A Healing Effect of Prayer and Anointing.* "The effect of prayer and anointing is sometimes like an electrical shock in a mild form. . . . Many members of my congregation have experienced this aid in some form, often by a direct cure of some ailment, physical as well as spiritual."—A.B. Simpson[326]

*A Penetrating Fire.* "A distinct sense of warmth—at times a penetrating fire—filled my whole body. . . . God showed me plainly that it was the Holy Spirit. . . . It continued for more than 6 hours. . . I got alone with God and on my face opened all my being to Him to fill. . . . At the same time there was a deep sense of much more to come and that my heart could not be satisfied without all the fullness of His power."—A.B. Simpson's Diary, Sept. 13, 1907.

*A Fire Burning Within.* "The third one was filled, and for days there seemed to be a veritable fire burning within her."—Dr. T.J. McCrossan, writing of a woman baptized in the Spirit[327]

*Whiteside—Thrilled Like an Electrical Flash.* "Like a flash of electricity, I was instantly thrilled. Every point of my body and nerves was controlled by a strange sensation that increased in volume, until I bowed lower and lower to the floor. I was filled with the ecstatic thrill. My physical frame was unable to stand the strain."—E.D. Whiteside[328]

### Scriptural Examples of Such Manifestations

- *The Philippian jailer trembled* and fell at Paul's feet (Acts 16:29).
- *A hand touched Daniel and he was set trembling* on his hands and knees (Dan. 10:8-11).
- *"Fear and trembling" when Titus arrived* (2 Cor. 7:15).
- *"Rejoice with trembling"* (Ps. 2:11).
- *"Tremble, O earth, before the Lord"* (Ps. 114:7).
- *"Humble and contrite spirit who trembles at My word"* (Isa. 66:2).
- *Woman trembled when the healing power of Jesus was imparted to her* (Luke 8:46-47).
- *"All men . . . will shake at My presence"* (Ezek. 38:20).
- *"The place was shaken"* at the filling of the Spirit (Acts 4:31).

## WHAT IS FALLING DOWN UNDER THE POWER OF THE SPIRIT"?
## IS IT BIBLICAL AND FROM GOD?

Note: In early writings it was often called *"prostrated* under the power of God."

*Being Overpowered by the Holy Spirit.* "A very mighty and continued resting of the Spirit down upon my body until it was almost overpowering and continued during much of the night."—Simpson Diary, August 28, 1907.

*An Overshadowing Weighty Presence.* "There came over me a sense of God's overshadowing presence, and I felt there was nothing to do but to bend lower and lower under the weight of His overshadowing. . . . by the blessed constraint of the Spirit, I was prostrated at His feet. . . . My whole being was vibrant with rapturous response. . ."—Henry Kenning[329]

*Weakened by a Delightful Weight of Glory.* "A 'weight of glory' rested upon my head, which I could distinctly feel, and even see in the Spirit. I was filled with joy and praise to God with an inward depth of satisfaction in Him which cannot be described. To be thus controlled by the Spirit of God and to feel that He was speaking 'heavenly mysteries' through me was most delightful. The rivers of living water flowed through me and divine ecstasy filled my soul. I felt that I drank and used up the life and power as fast as it was poured in. I became weak physically under the greatness of the heavenly vision."—Carrie Judd Montgomery[330]

*An Extra Spiritual Blessing.* "It is the prayer of faith that heals. Going under this power seems, however, to bring an extra spiritual blessing."—T.J. McCrossan[331]

*Physically Weakened by the Power of God.* "Like a flash of electricity, I was in-stantly thrilled. Every point of my body and nerves was controlled by a strange sensation that increased in volume, until I bowed lower and lower to the floor. I was filled with the ecstatic thrill. My physical frame was unable to stand the strain."—E.D. Whiteside[332]

*"People Fell as Dead."* "At service after service . . . I saw people fall as dead under the power of God."—C&MA Field Supt. Dean A.C. Peck_

"We read of revivals on the Pittsfield and Litchfield circuits: 'The work of God in convicting, converting and sanctifying souls was very evident . . ., sometimes the people fell as if shot down in battle, and would lay without strength from one-half hour to two hours, when they would arise happy in God.'"—Dr. T.J. McCrossan, citing the *History of U.S.A. Methodism* [333]

"We read regarding one of Peter Cartwright's meetings: 'In about 30 minutes the power of God fell on the congregation in such a manner as is seldom seen. The people fell in every direction, right and left, front and rear. It is supposed that not less than 360 fell like dead men in battle.' On page 115 he tells of one meeting where, out of an audience of 20,000, three thousand fell prostrate under this same strange power, and arose saved, and praising God.—Dr. T.J. McCrossan, citing the *History of U.S.A. Methodism*[334]

*Those Praying for the Sick Fall Under the Power in Alliance Meetings.* "At the time of prayer for the sick, wave after wave of holy emotion rolled over us, and shouts of victory arose as the sick were healed. Some who were assisting were prostrated by the power of God."—Wilbur F. Meminger, C&MA Field Evangelist[335]

*A Willingness to Surrender to God.* "This was the beginning of a school in which I soon learned that the Holy Spirit wanted to have control of my body in a new way, as well as my soul and spirit. After I understood it was Him, I said, 'Lord, I am willing to fall over, or do anything ridiculous, if Thou cast be gloried in that. Soon after this I realized He had really subdued me and the baptism came."—Mary B. Mullen[336]

*Losing One's Balance from the Wind of the Spirit.* "The very air seems charged with supernaturalism and the atmosphere is spiritual, and wonderful and blessed things are taking place all about one so that the tendency is that the 'rushing mighty wind' would cause one to lose one's balance as it were. . . . It is very easy for one who has had no such experience to coldly criticize one's actions who is under the power, but he knows nothing of what it means till he has himself realized the power of God."—Robert Jaffray[337]

*Wave After Wave of the Spirit.* "Since I have been consecrated to the work of the Lord and received the baptism of the Holy Spirit I have been prostrated under the power of God. At one time it seemed that my whole being was filled with the glory of God. Wave after wave passed over my soul until every thing seemed like a bright shining light. I could see nothing of this world and still I realized what was going on."—Pastor Mary Gainforth[338]

*A Power Encounter Leading to Salvation.* "In one meeting we saw 48 persons, while sitting in the audience, go down under this same strange power. A dozen or so of these were very sick, and were healed while under this power. The rest were sinners, but while under this same power, they were converted, and came out of it praising God."—Dr. T.J. McCrossan[339]

*Healing Through Falling Under the Power.* In Victoria, McCrossan accompanied Charles Price and assisted him in praying for people for healing. In one particular instance, Price asked McCrossan to join him in laying on hands praying for a Chinese pastor's wife who was dying from tuberculosis. He described what happened: "The result was that God sent a mighty power (somewhat like bolts of electricity) down our arms into her body. Personally, we could hardly endure it, but we knew well it was God answering prayer, for we saw that she had fallen into a peaceful sleep." For about half an hour she lay still on the platform, though "her dress was constantly twitching and moving just over her lungs. Suddenly she leaped to her feet perfectly well."[340]

*Biblical Examples of Falling Under the Power of the Spirit.*

- *Balaam Fell Down with Vision and Prophecy.* Balaam, in his poetic prophecy, says he was falling down as he received a vision: "The oracle of him who hears the words of God, and knows the knowledge of the Most High, who sees the vision of the Almighty, *falling down,* yet having his eyes uncovered" (Num. 24:16).
- *Queen of Sheba Fainted with Awe* (1 Kings 10:5; 2 Chron. 9:4)—"There was no spirit left in her." Some commentators like Jonathan Edwards view Queen of Sheba's fainting as an expression of this phenomenon.
- *Priests Unable to Stand to Minister Because of the Glory of the Lord* (2 Chron. 5:13-14).
- *Ezekiel Fell on Face from Awe of God* (Ezek. 1:28; 3:23; 44:4)—three occasions of falling on his face at the manifestation of the glory of God. Many commentaries indicate this was not a voluntary falling, but a supernatural result of the awesomeness of God's presence.
- *Daniel Fell on Face from Fear* (Dan. 8:17).
- *Daniel Fell from Vision and Voice from God* (Dan. 10:8-10). Daniel had three manifestations of this phenomenon when he saw a vision and heard a voice. First, his strength was sapped. Then he fell forward into a deep sleep or unconsciousness. Then, a hand touched him and he was set trembling on his hands and knees.
- *Peter, James and John Fell on Their Faces in Fear* (Matt. 17:16-18).
- *Soldiers Fell When Jesus Says, "I Am!"* In the Garden of Gethsemane, when the soldiers approached Jesus, and He said, "I am [He] [the "he" is not found in the Greek], they all fell backward at the awesomeness of the statement of Jesus that He is the "I am" (John 18:5-6).
- *Paul Fell from Flash of Light from Heaven.* Paul at his conversion on the Damascus road fell when he saw the light from heaven flashing about him (Acts 9:3-4).

- *Peter Fell into a Trance* (Acts 10:9-11).
- *Philippian Jailer Trembled and Fell at Paul's Feet* (Act 16:29). Jonathan Edwards cites this as an example of the phenomenon.
- *John Fell at a Vision of Jesus.* John writes, "And when I saw Him, I fell at His feet as a dead man" (Rev. 1:17).

These all appear to be a response to the overwhelming power and glory of God in fear, conviction, revelation, or blessing.

## BUT ISN'T SUCH FALLING DEMONIC OR HYPNOTISM?

*Not Hypnotism or the Power of Suggestion* "This power is not hypnotism. . . . The Evangelist urges the people to come to the platform in the spirit of prayer with their eyes and thoughts centered on the Lord Jesus. Most of them, when prayed for, have their eyes closed, and the Evangelist closes his eyes, when he prays, and asks the Lord to manifest His power and cure them. . . . No Hypnotist can possible hypnotize you if he closes his own eyes, has you close your eyes, and tells you to look to God alone. This is an utter impossibility, so we know this power is not hypnotism."—T.J. McCrossan[341]

*Not Devil Power.* "Again we have discovered that this is not devil power. . . . All who are genuinely under this power praise the Lord Jesus in a marvelous manner. Many of them have visions of their Lord in Heaven. Some see Him on the cross, and, praise God, many are baptized with the Holy Spirit before the Holy Spirit is through with them. Does Satan so act?"—Dr. T.J. McCrossan[342]

*But Some Falling Is Done in the Flesh.* "Mrs. Jones, a worldly-minded Christian, comes to be prayed for. She has not spent hours in prayer like her spiritually minded friend, Mrs. Smith. Mrs. Smith is prayed for first. When the Evangelist anoints her and puts his hands upon her head, seemingly bolts of electric power flash down his arms into her, and she falls prostrate, and is wonderfully healed. Mrs. Jones is then anointed and prayed for, and falls down because Mrs. Smith fell, although no power whatever was felt by the Evangelist. Mrs. Jones, of course, is not healed, and, her pride being wounded, she is glad to testify against the Evangelist."—T.J. McCrossan.[343]

## DOES GOD SPEAK THROUGH DREAMS AND VISIONS?

*Yes, God Still Speaks Through These and Other Means.* "The Creator has never left the creature to walk solely in the light of his own reason, but has spoken to him by voice, vision, dream, angel, prophet, His Son, His Holy Spirit, and His inspired written Word."—W.W. Newberry[344]

*Hours of Vision and Revelation Elevated Above the Clouds.* "The Lord Jesus still gives His people hours of vision and revelation when they are elevated above the clouds and shadows of the present and permitted to come into closer touch with eternal things."—A.B. Simpson[345]

*Simpson's Dream That Launched the Alliance.* "I was awakened from sleep trembling with a strange and solemn sense of God's overshadowing power, and on my soul was burning the remembrance of a strange dream through which I had at that moment come. It seemed to me that I was sitting in a vast auditorium and millions of people were sitting around me. All the Christians in the world seemed to be there, and on the platform was a great multitude of faces and forms. They seemed to be mostly Chinese. They were not speaking, but in mute anguish were wringing their hands, and their faces wore an expression I can never forget. As I woke with that vision on my mind, I trembled with the Holy Spirit, and I threw myself on my knees, and every fiber in my being answered, 'Yes, Lord, I will go.'"—A.B. Simpson[346]

*Simpson's Dream of Trials and Testings.* "In the beginning of this life of faith God gave me a vision which to me was a symbol of the kind of life to which He had called me. In the dream a little sailboat was passing down a rapid stream, tossed by the winds and driven by the rapids. Every moment it seemed as if it must be dashed upon the rocks and crushed, yet it was preserved in some mysterious way and carried through all perils. Upon the sails of the little ship was plainly painted the name of the vessel in one Latin word, *Augustiae*, meaning 'Hard Places.' Through this simple dream the Lord seemed to fortify me for the trials and testings that were ahead, and to prepare me for a life's journey which would be far from a smooth one, but through which God's grace would always carry me in triumph."—A.B. Simpson[347]

*Simpson's Vision of Christ and Heaven.* "I ventured to ask Him for a special token and soon after He did give it—a very mighty and continued resting of the Spirit down upon my body until it was almost overpowering. . . .

"One afternoon it seemed as if heaven was opened and I was permitted to see myself seated with Christ in the heavenlies within the veil . . . ."—A.B. Simpson, Diary, August 1907

## How Should We Regard Dreams and Visions?

*Impressions of a Personal Message from the Voice of God—But Rare.* "I had one of those rare dreams which leave behind them an impression of the voice of God. . . . I awakened with the quiet sense that God had spoken to my heart with a personal message . . ."—A.B. Simpson[348]

*Don't Expect Them Frequently.* "Not always should we look for these celestial uplifts; it would not be wholesome. Two or three times in his life, the Apostle Paul had such special visitations from His Master."—A.B. Simpson[349]

*Don't Place Too High Importance to Them.* "God sometimes reveals His will by means of dreams and visions, but their value, when compared with other evidences—guidance through common sense, providences, the Holy Spirit, and the Bible—is held to be of minor importance."—W.W. Newberry[350]

*Get Confirmation from Other Sources.* "We may be deceived unless we have confirmatory evidence from collateral sources."—W.W. Newberry[351]

*Look for a Three-fold Leading—The Vision, the Spirit and the Providence.* "While Peter thought on the vision, the Spirit said unto him, Behold three men seek thee (Acts 10:19). We have a three-fold leading. Three lines of evidence converge to convince. . . The vision, the Spirit, and the providence unite to assure Peter that he is to go to the Gentiles and preach the gospel to them."—W.W. Newberry[352]

*God's Safety Brakes—The Checks of the Spirit.* "Paul in Acts 16:6, 7, was 'forbidden of the Holy Spirit—the Spirit suffered them not.'. . . As abruptly as the engineer puts on the safety brake, Paul found himself stopped, forbidden to go further. . . The checks of the Spirit are God's safety brakes."—W.W. Newberry[353]

*Avoid Extreme Asceticism.* "Good people who shut themselves up in cells and closets in weeks of fasting and prayer without proper exercise, nourishment or sleep, or without any change of mental or spiritual attention, are very apt to see visions and dream dreams that do not always come from above."—A.B. Simpson[354]

*Recognize Many Sources of Dreams.* "A diseased condition of the mind or body accounts for many of them; aroused mental activity at the time of retiring gives rise to dreams about the things just studied; trouble will pray upon the mind in sleep and cause dreams; overeating and drunkenness will produce them; the personalities of the underworld have access to the mind while in sleep (and some dreams are certainly from this source), while others come from the power of God resting upon the mind."—W.W. Newberry[355]

## HOW DO WE KNOW A VISION OR DREAM IS FROM GOD?

"Usually true of the dreams which are from the Lord: They will remain fresh and vivid in the memory for many days. The mind will be continually reverting to them. Like thoughts, which are produced by the Spirit, they will stay in the mind until recognized or fulfilled. . . . Other dreams . . . vanish like the mists, and often no trace of them is left but the vague memory that we have dreamed."— W.W. Newberry[356]

## ADDITIONAL RESOURCES

Deere, Jack. *Surprised by the Power of the Spirit.* Grand Rapids: Zondervan, 1993.

Deere, Jack. *Surprised by the Voice of God.* Grand Rapids: Zondervan, 1996.

King, Paul L. *Genuine Gold: The Cautiously Charismatic Story of the Early Christian and Missionary Alliance.* Tulsa, OK: Word and Spirit Press, 2006.

King, Paul L. "Holy Laughter and Other Phenomena in Evangelical and Holiness Revival Movements," *Alliance Academic Review 1996*, Elio Cuccaro, ed. (Camp Hill, PA: Christian Publications, 1998), 107-122. Accessible at www.allianceacademicreview.com.

Schroeder, David E. *Walking in Your Anointing.* Bloomington, IN: Author House, 2007.

## FOR REFLECTION AND DISCUSSION

1. Read 1 Corinthians 12:1-9. Describe some of the gifts and manifestations of the Holy Spirit. Have you observed or experienced those manifestations?

2. Why are manifestations such as trembling, holy laughter, and falling under the power of the Spirit so controversial?

3. Read the Scriptures cited above regarding expressions of holy joy and laughter. What is the source of those manifestations? Have you ever experienced something like that in your life or known someone who has? What was it like? Did it draw you closer to God?

4. Read the Scriptures cited above regarding expressions of falling under the power of the Spirit. Have you ever experienced something like that in your life or known someone who has? What was it like? Did it draw you or someone else closer to God?

5. Read the Scriptures above cited regarding expressions of trembling or other sensations. Have you ever experienced something like that in your own life or known of someone who has? What was it like? Did it draw you or someone else closer to God?

6. Have you ever received a dream or vision you believe was from God? How did you know it was from God?

7. Have you ever experienced a dream or vision you believe was from an evil source? How did you know?

CHAPTER 9

# Healing in the Spirit-Empowered Life

## How Does the Alliance View Sickness and Healing?

*Focus on the Christ the Healer, Not on the Healing.*

> "Once it was the blessing, now it is the Lord;
> Once it was the feeling, now it is His Word;
> Once His gifts I wanted, now the Giver own;
> Once I sought for healing, now HIMSELF alone."
> —A.B. Simpson

*Healing Involves the Wholeness for the Whole Person.* "God has made us a trinity and there is an interdependence between spirit and soul and body which we cannot ignore. The presence of disease is a hindrance not only to our spiritual usefulness but to our higher experiences, . . . divine healing . . . has a reflex influence on every other part of our nature."—A.B. Simpson[357]

*Holiness Is Wholeness.* "Healing is intimately connected with the spiritual life. . . . Holiness brings healthiness and helpfulness. Holiness is wholeness. A pure heart, a peaceful conscience, and a spirit of rest in God combine the elements that go to make up soundness. Joy is a stimulant, peace a sedative, righteousness a tonic better than all the drugs."—A.B. Simpson[358]

"Holiness is the best preservative of youthfulness, freshness, sweetness, and joy."—A.B. Simpson[359]

"The more we give ourselves to experience personally sanctification by faith, the more we shall also experience healing by faith."—Andrew Murray[360]

*Salvation Is Wholeness and Soundness.* "The beautiful expression, 'your salvation' (Psalm 67:2), includes the idea, not only of salvation, but of healing, too, or, more correctly, of that fullness of blessing which the old word *health* so perfectly expressed. The Saxon *hale* gives us the perfect meaning, and it just describes the wholeness and soundness and wholesomeness which the gospel brings into all our life . . . enabling us to say, 'All is well.'"—A.B. Simpson[361]

**Total Healing May Involve Deeper Root Causes.** Commenting on Mark 2:5 where Jesus addresses the adult paralytic as "child," Simpson recognized in this story the need for a deeper spiritual healing, writing, "In dealing with the sick, we must realize the deeper causes of their physical conditions."—A.B. Simpson[362]

"If one is sick and desires healing, it is of prime importance that the true cause of the sickness be discovered. This is always the first step toward recovery. If the particular cause is not recognized, and attention is directed toward subordinate causes, or to supposed but not real causes, healing is out of the question."—Andrew Murray[363]

**More Than Healing—Quickened in the Higher Life.** "There is a still higher phase of this precious truth [Divine Healing] . . . 'Your youth is renewed like the eagle's' (Psalm 103:5). This is the quickening life of Christ in our mortal flesh, giving vitality and spring to the body. . . . This is more than being headlined of disease and redeemed from death. It is being quickened in the higher life and filled with the vigor and energy of our Lord."—A.B. Simpson[364]

"We can touch each moment that conquering Hand that never lost a battle, that never relinquished a trust, that never grows weak or weary; and strong in the strength of Christ, we can do all things hand in hand with Him."—A.B. Simpson[365]

## IS IT GOD'S WILL TO HEAL?

**It Is God's Nature to Heal and Restore.** "The Indians have a tradition that wherever the rattlesnake is found there always grows in the neighboring forests a little plant which is a certain antidote to the fatal sting. And so redemption springs in all its healing power amid the very earliest seeds of sin and misery, and God prepares His balm of healing even before the serpent has time to strike his fatal blow. How marvelous His resources! How wonderful His love!"—A.B. Simpson[366]

**Sickness Is Contrary to God's Kingdom.** "Sickness is contrary to the kingdom of heaven. . . . Disease is interference with His original and established laws. It is the sign of an invader somewhere in His kingdom. . . . God's answer is the restoration of His law from this daring infringement. . . . He treated sickness as a disorder in His kingdom, a menace to His honor and authority."—William C. Stevens[367]

***God Is More Glorified by Sanctified Health.*** "It is a prevalent idea that piety is easier in sickness than in health, and that silent suffering inclines the soul to seek the Lord more than the distractions of life. For these reasons, sick people hesitate to ask for healing from the Lord. They believe that sickness may be more of a blessing to them than health. To think thus is to ignore that healing and its fruits are divine. . . . Although many sick people may have glorified God by their patience in suffering, He can be still more glorified by a health which He has sanctified."—Andrew Murray[368]

***Healing Is God's Normal Provision for the Believer.*** "Divine healing . . . is His normal provision for the believer. It is something that is included in our redemption rights, something that is part of the gospel of His grace, something that is already recognized as within His will and not requiring a special revelation to justify us claiming it."—A.B. Simpson[369]

## Is Healing Provided for in the Atonement?

***The Cross Is the Remedy for Both Sin and Sickness—A Redemption Right.*** "If sickness has come into the world through sin, which is conceded, it must be got out of the world through God's great remedy for sin, the cross of Jesus Christ. . . . If healing is provided for by Jesus Christ, then it is a redemption right which we may humbly yet boldly claim while walking obediently with the Lord."—A.B. Simpson[370]

***Forgiveness and Healing Go Hand-in-Hand—Psalm 103:1-5.*** "'Bless the Lord, O my soul, and forget not all His benefits: who forgives all your iniquities, who heals all your diseases, who redeems your life from destruction, who crowns you with loving kindness and tender mercies, who satisfies your mouth with good things, so that your youth is renewed like the eagle's.' Why does he use the word 'redeem?' Simply because he is thinking . . . the healing of his diseases is through the redemption."—A.B. Simpson[371]

***By His Stripes We Are Healed—Isaiah 53:4-5.*** "As He has borne our sins, so Jesus Christ has borne away our sicknesses, yes, and even our pains, so that abiding in Him, we may be fully delivered from both sickness and pain. Thus 'For by His stripes we were healed!'"—A.B. Simpson[372]

"The clear meaning is, that Jesus did take upon Himself our diseases and mental trouble in precisely the same way that 'He bore our sins in His own body upon the tree.'"—Russell Kelso Carter, Simpson associate, author of the hymn "Standing on the Promises"[373]

*The Magna Charta of Divine Healing—Matthew 8:1-17.* "Matthew 8:1-17 is the Magna Charta of divine healing."—William C. Stevens[374]

"Matthew's translation [of Isaiah 53:4] bears out in every part the application of this verse to the healing of the body."—A.B. Simpson[375]

*Christ Is the Sickness Bearer as Well as the Sin Bearer—Matthew 8:16-17.* "In the atonement of Christ there seems to be a foundation laid for bodily healing. . . . We have Christ set before us as the sickness bearer as well as the sin bearer of His people. . . . Something more than sympathetic fellowship with our suffering is evidently referred to here. The yoke of His cross by which He lifted our iniquities took hold also of our diseases. . . . The passage seems to teach that Christ endured vicariously our diseases as well as our iniquities."—A.J. Gordon, Simpson associate[376]

*Jesus Suffered, Bled, and Died for Our Sickness as Well as Our Sins—1 Peter 2:24.* "Here note two facts: (1) That the word for 'healed' here, both in the Septuagint and in the Greek New Testament is *iaomai*, a verb that always speaks of physical healing in the New Testament. . . . Yes, Peter here (1 Peter 2:24) clearly teaches that Christ not only suffered, bled, and died for our sins, but also for our physical healing."—Dr.T.J. McCrossan, C&MA pastor, professor and Greek scholar[377]

*Redeemed from the Curse of the Law—Galatians 3:13.* "In Gal. 3:13 we read: 'Christ has redeemed us from the curse of the law, being made a curse for us.'. . . What was the curse of the law? In Deut. 28 God names the blessings promised to the obedient, and then enumerates the curses that will fall upon those who will not hearken unto His voice and do all His commandments. He names the diseases which are known as 'the curse of the law.'. . . When Jesus redeemed us from the curse of the law, He redeemed us from . . . the whole list of diseases named in that curse. . . . Tell me the name of your disease and I will tell you one from which you have been redeemed and can be healed."—F.F. Bosworth[378]

"Of course we know that it was a far-reaching and eternal curse, but it was also a temporal curse, a physical curse, a curse involving sickness, suffering, infirmity, disease, pain. . . . Read Deut. 28:15-22. Therefore, it is perfectly scriptural to say Christ has redeemed us from consumption, fever, inflammation, having been made curse for us."—A.B. Simpson[379]

## WHAT IS THE ROLE OF FAITH IN HEALING?

***Not Faith Healing, But Divine Healing.*** "We are not advocates of 'faith healing' and never used that term. We do believe God heals His sick and suffering children when they can fully trust Him."—A.B. Simpson[380]

***God Is the Source of Healing; Faith Is the Channel.*** "It is not the faith that heals. God heals, but faith receives it."—A.B. Simpson[381]

***Faith Is Live Contact with a Living Savior.*** "There is no power in prayer unless it is the prayer of God Himself. Unless you are in contact with Christ the living Healer, there is no healing. . . . Faith is more than believing; it is a living contact with a living Savior."—A.B. Simpson[382]

***Don't Try to Work Up Your Faith.*** "If I need faith for anything, I don't try to work up faith, I don't agonize in prayer until I get a certain degree of faith; I just say, 'It is Your faith, not mine; You have it for me, just as You have the blood, and the power, and the cleansing, It is all Yours, and I just borrow it for the time. Lend me Your faith for this hours,' and I take His faith, and depend upon it to be mine, I go forward and act as if I had it, and I find that He meets me and gives me the blessing of confidence in His healing and His power."—A.B. Simpson[383]

***Don't Have Faith in Your Own Faith.*** "Faith is hindered most of all by what we call 'our faith.'"—A.B. Simpson[384]

> The Shepherd does not ask of thee
> Faith in thy faith, but only faith in Him.
> And in this He meant in saying, "Come to Me"
> In light or darkness seek to do His will
> And leave the work of faith to Jesus still.
> —Cited by Carrie Judd Montgomery[385]

"Faith in faith is faith astray."—A.W. Tozer[386]

***Our Confidence Must Be in Christ and God's Character.*** "I cannot recommend that anyone have faith in faith. . . . Our confidence must not be in the power of faith but in the Person and work of the Savior Jesus Christ. . . . I have been memorizing the Scripture ever since I was converted, but my faith does not rest on God's promises. My faith rests upon God's character. Faith must rest in confidence upon the One who made the promises."—A.W. Tozer[387]

***Claim the Faith of God.*** "Jesus does not say to us, 'Have great faith yourselves.' But He does say, 'have the faith of God.'"—A.B. Simpson[388]

"We must claim the faith of God, letting the Spirit of Jesus sustain our faith with His strong faith."—A.B. Simpson[389]

*Pray for Special Faith.* "If you have any question about your faith for this, make it a special matter of preparation and prayer. Ask God to give you special faith for this act. All our graces must come from Him, and faith among the rest. We have nothing of our own, and even our very faith is but the grace of Christ Himself within us. We can exercise it, and thus far our responsibility extends; but He must impart it, and we simply put it on and wear it as from Him."[390]

"This faith [Mark 11:22-24 and James 1:6-7] is a special work of the Holy Spirit."—A.B. Simpson[391]

*Let Jesus Work His Faith into Us.* "Jesus is the author and finisher of our faith, and He will work *His own faith* in our hearts. Let us give up our own poor attempts at faith and take the faith of the Son of God. The Lord Jesus has faith in His own power to make good all His promises."—Carrie Judd Montgomery[392]

*Then Act in Faith.* "We believe that God is healing before any evidence is given. It is to be believed as a present reality and then ventured on. We are to act as if it were already true."—A.B. Simpson[393]

*But Act Only with Clear Assurance from God—Not on Human Faith or Word.* "Act your faith . . . not to show your faith, or display your courage, but *because* of your faith, begin to act as one that is healed. . . . But it is most important that you should be careful that you do not do this on any other human faith or word. Do not rise from your bed or walk on your lame foot because somebody tells you to do so. That is not faith, but impression." [394]

*Faith Is a Point of Contact.* "Faith in connection with our healing. . . .[is] this point of contact, this organ of receptiveness, this open mouth of the soul—confidence in God, appropriating faith."—A.B. Simpson[395]

*Faith Is Activated by Connecting with God.* "We must trust as if all depended upon God and we must work as if all depended on us. . . . The blessings which God has to impart to us through the Lord Jesus Christ do not wait upon some sovereign act of His will, but are already granted, completed and prepared and simply awaiting the contact of a believing hand to open all the channels of communication."—A.B. Simpson[396]

## ARE POINTS OF CONTACT (LAYING ON HANDS, ANOINTING, PRAYER CLOTHS, ETC.) VALID METHODS OF HEALING?

The concept of a point of contact as an expression of faith is rooted in two Biblical passages, especially in relationship to healing: 1) James 5—anointing with oil and laying on hands, and 2) Mark 5:27-28—the woman touching the hem of Jesus' garment. In these Scriptures, touch or physical contact appears to be an aid or accompaniment to faith.

*Points of Contacts Are Stepping Stones to Our Faith.* "Jesus still uses a few outward signs as steppingstones to our faith. Anointing with oil in the name of the Lord is not a means in a medical sense; it is simply an outward sign to suggest through the senses more vividly the spiritual reality which it signifies. . . . The Lord addresses us through every vehicle which can convey to us His thought and His touch."—A.B. Simpson[397]

*Laying on of Hands and Anointing with Oil Are Points of Contact.* "Sometimes a man needs a visible sign, appealing to his senses, which may come to the aid to sustain his faith and enable him to grasp the spiritual meaning. The anointing, therefore, should symbolize to the sick one the action of the Holy Spirit who gives the healing. . . . We also should regard it, not as a remedy, but as a pledge of the mighty virtue of the Holy Spirit, as a means of strengthening faith, a *point of contact* and of communion between the sick one and members of the Church who are called to anoint him with oil."—Andrew Murray[398]

*A Point of Contact Is Touching Jesus Himself.* "It involves not only our hand but His personality. Faith must recognize the Lord Jesus Himself and come into immediate contact with Him before it can draw His healing virtue or His comforting love."—A.B. Simpson[399]

"Let each contact with the blood be contact with the Lamb, more particularly with His gentleness and meekness. Let your faith touch just the hem of His garment and power will go out from Him."—Andrew Murray[400]

*A Point of Contact Is a Touch of Faith.* "There is a touch of faith as well as a touch of God. . . . The blessings which God has to impart to us through the Lord Jesus Christ . . . are already granted, completed and prepared and simply awaiting the contact of a believing hand to open all the channels of communication."—A.B. Simpson[401]

*Clothing Charged with Power of Spirit Through Contact with Jesus Himself.* "The charging of clothing with the power of the Holy Spirit was by no means unknown, for when Jesus went about doing good, there were times when His clothing was so filled with power that it was only necessary to touch the fringe of His garment, and as many as touched were made perfectly whole. More than that, when on the Mount of Transfiguration, His raiment was so surcharged with the Spirit from within His holy body that it was ablaze with heavenly light. But on no occasion was power manifested in a fabric which was not in contact with His sacred person."—William T. MacArthur [402]

**Activate Your Faith by Laying Hands on Yourself.** Jesus sometimes touched a particular part of a person's body for healing—putting his fingers in the ears of a deaf mute and touching his tongue with His own saliva (Mark 7:33-34). On other occasions he put saliva or mud on the eyes of the blind (Mark 8:23-25; John 9:6-7). You may not have someone near by to lay hands on you, but you can lay hands on yourself in faith—touching and praying over a particular part of your body that is diseased or in pain. Missionary John MacMillan, acted out his faith, combining his belief in the believer's authority and exercising this principle of point of contact by making it his practice to lay hands on various parts of his body:

"Just after leaving a building after having anointed another missionary, Mac-Millan slipped on an incline by a spring and painfully twisted his ankle on a stone. Placing his hands on the injured spot, as was his custom in prayer, he prayed for healing. He records that he received an instant answer to prayer—no sprain or swelling, just a bruise, and he gave God the glory!"[403]

"As a professor in the Missionary Training Institute at Nyack, New York, [John MacMillan] shared with his students one of his secrets of receiving healing and maintaining health. He made it his practice daily to lay hands on various parts of his body, praying for divine healing and health in each part. In this way he experienced the divine energizing he talked so much about throughout his writings."[404]

**Other Points of Contact in Scripture.** Throughout biblical times and church history, God has used numerous unusual means as points of contact of faith for the purpose of cleansing or healing or for consecration and impartation of power. Some of the points of contact in Scripture include:

- Priests anointed with blood for protection, cleansing, or consecration (Exod.12:7:24:8; Lev. 4:16-18; 8:23-24).
- Isaiah laid a fig cake on Hezekiah's boil and he was healed (2 Kings 20:7).

- Elijah and Elisha stretched out their bodies on boys who had died (1 Kings 17:17-24; 2 Kings 4:32-35)
- Blessed salt—Elisha healed bad water by putting salt in it (2 Kings 2:19-22)
- Blessed water—Naaman dipped in water seven times at Elisha's command (2 Kings 5:1-14)
- Elisha put a stick in water and a lost ax head floated to the top (2 Kings 6:4-7).
- Moses put a branch in water and healed the poisonous waters (Exod. 15:23-25).
- Elisha put flour in poisonous stew (2 Kings 4:38-41).
- A dead man was raised to life when his body touched Elisha's bones in his grave (2 Kings 13:20-21).
- Peter's shadow passing over the sick (Acts 5:15-16)
- Prayer cloths/handkerchiefs (Acts 19:11)

Power can be transmitted through a physical touch when done in faith and when we make real contact with Christ. A touch in faith may at times result in physical manifestations from the Holy Spirit such as heat, electrical impulse, falling or swooning, etc., but they are not always to be expected or sought.

***Prayer Cloths Occasionally Used in Alliance Meetings.*** In April 1921, A. E. Funk reported on the Pittsburgh C&MA Convention, saying it was like the 5th and 19th chapters of Acts with extraordinary meetings and special miracles.[405] Acts 5 is uniquely significant for supernatural revelatory knowledge, signs and wonders, healings, and exorcisms. Acts 19 records speaking in tongues, prophesying, healing and exorcism through the use of cloths as a point of contact of faith. By pointing out these particular chapters of Acts, Funk seems to be indicating that phenomena unique to these chapters had occurred in these meetings.

## WHAT CAUTIONS DO YOU HAVE ABOUT SUCH POINTS OF CONTACT?

***Don't Depend Upon the Touch or Feeling—Depend on Jesus.*** "Just identify yourself with Jesus, and say, 'Jesus is within; not I, but Christ; He is my righteousness and my faith, and He is my bodily life too.'. . . Be sure that you do not depend upon the anointing, be sure that you do not depend upon the touch—these are like Gehazi's staff. Be sure that you do not depend on any feeling. Be sure that you are not looking for any thrill or any physical sensation. Keep your mind off all these."—A.B. Simpson[406]

*Don't Regard It as a Magic Power.* "This does not mean some kind of magic or magnetic power possessed by some individuals enabling them to remove diseases by a touch."—A.B. Simpson[407]

*Not a Mysterious Current.* "It is not a mysterious current which flows into one body from another. . . . Such an influence is repudiated by all who act as true ministers of divine healing."—A.B. Simpson[408]

*Don't Go into the Handkerchief Business.* "Some have quite gone into the handkerchief business. . . . While I was in the West large packages of letters addressed to the sick were brought for my blessed, also bundles of handkerchiefs to be prayed over and some asked that the handkerchiefs might be anointed. From all this we humbly asked to be excused. We cannot reconcile this wholesale handkerchief business with the unostentatious behavior of the apostles. It savors of an unwholesome love for the spectacular."—William T. MacArthur [409]

*Some Semblance of Truth, But Not Common—Special Miracles for a Purpose.* "Not that there is no semblance of truth in the thing. . . . Would God that we were so filled with the Holy Spirit that our very clothing might possess the healing virtue! But God deliver us from these shallow pretenses. . . . It must be remembered moreover that this was not a normal experience even with Peter and Peter. . . . And no instructions are to be found among the inspired writings to govern its exercise. We must therefore conclude that it was just as the Scripture states, 'special miracles' no doubt for a special purpose."—William T. MacArthur[410]

*Points of Contact Are Signs and Aids to Faith, Not Inherent Healing Power.* "Hezekiah's sickness was a fatal one. It is foolish to talk about his being healed through a mere poultice of figs of a disease that was declared by God Himself to be unto death. . . . The figs (used by Isaiah on Hezekiah's disease) were merely a sign to help his faith to rise from the natural to the supernatural, just as the oil of anointing is a sign of the touch of the Holy Spirit, but has not in itself any inherent healing power."—A.B. Simpson[411]

It would thus appear from Scripture and Alliance history that such points of contact as prayer cloths may be appropriate on some occasions as aids to faith, but cannot be used indiscriminately or magically. Nor should they be used as fundraising gimmicks. A touch in faith may at times result in physical manifestations from the Holy Spirit such as heat, electrical impulse, falling or swooning, etc., but they are not always to be expected or sought. Such phenomena can also be of the flesh or even a demonic counterfeit.[412]

# HOW DOES MENTAL ATTITUDE AFFECT HEALTH AND HEALING?

*Focus on Self and Symptoms May Hinder Healing.* "A man went to Bethshan Healing Home in England to receive prayer for healing. He talked continually about himself and his symptoms, and this prevented him from getting hold on the Lord for healing. At last those who had charge of the Home told him that he would have to leave the Home unless he stopped talking about himself, and his bad feelings. They said, "You can talk about the Lord Jesus, but you must not say anything more about yourself." So when he would forget, and begin to say something about himself, they would lift a warning finger, and he would manage to change the sentence, before it was finished, into some word of praise or exaltation of the Lord Jesus. Not long after this the man was healed."—Carrie Judd Montgomery[413]

*Fear Encourages the Devil's Power in Your Life.* "We must not give place to the devil. Nothing encourages him so much as fear, and nothing dwarfs him and drives him away so quickly as audacity. If you for a moment acknowledge his power, you give him that power. If you for a moment recognized that he is in you, you will find that he is in you. If you let the thought or consciousness of evil into your spirit, you have lost your purity."—A.B. Simpson[414]

*Negative Attitudes Will Affect Your Health.* "If you want to keep the health of Christ, keep from all spiritual sores, from all heart-wounds and irritations. One hour of fretting will wear out more vitality than a week of work, and one minute of malignity, or rangling jealousy or envy will hurt more than a drink of poison. Sweetness of spirit and joyousness of heart are essential to full health. . . . We do not wonder that some people have poor health when we hear them talk for half an hour. They have enough dislikes, prejudices, doubts and fears to exhaust the strongest constitution. Beloved, if you would keep God's life and strength, keep out of the things that kill it."—A.B. Simpson[415]

"A flash of ill temper, a cloud of despondency, an impure thought or desire can poison your blood, inflame your tissues, disturb your nerves and interrupt the whole process of God's life in your body!"—A.B. Simpson[416]

# IN WHAT OTHER WAYS DOES GOD HEAL?

*Through Confessing Our Healing.* "It is not enough to think it, to feel it, to resolve it; we must say it. . . . We must confess Him in order to be saved; so we must receive and keep our sanctification, our healing, and the answers to our prayers by acknowledging God, even before we see His working."—A.B. Simpson[417]

"Faith will die without confession."—A.B. Simpson[418]

Speaking of the woman who touched Jesus' garment (Luke 8:48): "She did not feel first and then believe, but she believed and then she felt. But her blessing must be confessed. Christ will not allow us to hold His gifts without acknowledgement."—A.B. Simpson[419]

"We should claim this gracious relationship to the fullest degree for our own flesh and bones, and refuse the sicknesses that seek to fasten upon our physical frames."—John A. MacMillan[420]

*Through Exercising the Authority of the Believer.* "It is ours to take hold jointly with the Spirit—for as He takes hold with us we must also cooperate with Him—against the things and the forces which assail our individual lives with a faithful and firm refusal of their right to control our bodies or our circumstances. Too often the Christian passively accepts whatever comes to him as being the will of the Lord, yielding without resistance at times to the wiles of the enemy himself. True faith in conflict is a steadfast and earnest will for victory. . . . That 'God hath spoken' is the ground upon which every forward step in the spiritual life must be taken."—John A. MacMillan[421]

*Through Expecting Strength, Not Weakness.* "Don't expect to have a spell of weariness and reaction, . . just go calmly forward, . . . expecting Him to give you the necessary strength to carry you through."—A.B. Simpson[422]

*Through Looking to Jesus, Not at Your Symptoms.* "God told Moses to lift up the brazen serpent, which was a type of Christ. Those who were dying were carried to where they could look at the type of Christ, and all who looked received the double cure and were healed (Numbers 21). . . . If the children of Israel could look at the type of Christ and received healing, why can not we look at the antitype, Christ Himself, and be healed? . . . Everyone who looked at the brazen serpent was healed. They didn't get healed looking at their swollen bodies that had been bitten by the serpents, but by looking at the type of Christ. You can never get faith by looking at symptoms or at yourselves, but you can look to Jesus, and meditate on God's faithfulness, until faith will come into existence with out and effort, and then your diseases will evaporate like a mist before the sun."—F.F. Bosworth[423]

*Through Drawing Life from Jesus.* "I find that healing, like salvation, is retained by constantly looking to Jesus, drawing our life from Him moment by moment. Oh, it is a blessed experience to be leaning on His breast, breathing our very life from Him."—Mary Gainforth, pastor, Alliance Faith Mission, Trenton, Ontario

*Through Abiding in Christ.* "It is from close and trustful confidence alone that we can claim His healing.... We must get under His very wings and in the bosom of His love before faith can claim its highest victories in our inmost being.... This is the secret of divine healing. It is union with the One who is our physical Head as well as the source of our spiritual life."—A.B. Simpson[424]

*Through the Lord's Supper.* "The Lord's Supper is very intimately connected with our physical life, and it brings us to the actually bodily strength of the Lord Jesus Christ, if we rightly partake.... [It] is deeper than mere healing; it is the actual participation in the physical strength, vitality and energy of our risen Lord."—A.B. Simpson[425]

"Many a flagging spirit, fainting under a host of temptations, has had a fresh touch of God and a restoration of soul at our Lord's table. Eating worthily and discerning with contrition anew the Lord's body has brought healing to the physical life."—R.D. Kilgour, C&MA pastor, speaking at an Ordination service[426]

"The wine is an emblem of the blood of Jesus for the remission of sins, and the bread is an emblem of His body broken for the healing of every man's body.... Discerning His broken body will bring deliverance from our diseases, and appropriating His shed blood will cleanse us from our sins." —F.F. Bosworth[427]

"Brother Birdsall ... was all run down in health, having jaundice and weeping eczema.... When we had the Lord's Supper, he put the bread in his mouth, really appropriating the Lord's body for the first time in his life. What was the result? God's lightning struck his body and made him whole, and he gained twenty pounds the next thirty days. The weeping eczema left his body and he has been well ever since... Mrs. Rosa McEvoy had paralysis of the optic nerve for fifteen years.... She ate the Lord's Supper, discerned the Lord's body with faith, and was healed. She does not even have to wear glasses."—F.F. Bosworth[428]

*Through Soaking Prayer.* In July 1899 Mrs. N. S. Dean, who had been bedfast or wheelchair bound for 17 years due to a spinal condition, was dramatically healed. One of the workers spent time with her and hours in prayer for her, what today would be called "soaking prayer." When the worker laid her hand on Mrs. Dean's right leg, Mrs. Dean immediately had a "prickling, tingling sensation." Later she felt a twitch in her back that enabled her to sit upright. Though the worker did not know of the curvature of the spine, she received a prophetic impression from the Lord of Isaiah 55:2, "I will make the crooked places straight." The "impression deepened into a certainty" when she laid her hands on Mrs. Dean again and Mrs. Dean felt the prickling sensation again.

She continued to command the spine to be straightened. The process took about six hours. "I stood upon my feet twice, which I had not done for 17 years." The worker was "wonderfully baptized with a spirit of praise." A light appeared upon the face of Mrs. Dean and her face was transfigured. The worker continued to pray five hours a day for three weeks, resulting in stiff and atrophied muscles being strengthened. One day her ribs creaked "like an old saddle" as they were adjusted into proper place through prayer. Her short leg was lengthened an inch with a grating sound.—*Alliance Weekly*, 1901[429]

*Through Yielding to God.* "Some suffering Christians have been so anxious to get well and have spent so much time in trying to claim healing, that they have lost their spiritual blessing. God sometimes has to teach such persons that there must be a willingness to be sick before they are yielded enough to receive His fullest blessing."—A.B. Simpson[430]

*Through Harmony with God's Will.* "We shall often find that God is dealing with men and women through their very sickness and we want to be careful first to get them into harmony with His will and spiritually prepared for the blessing of healing."—A.B. Simpson[431]

*Through Maintaining the Joy of the Lord.* "The spirit of joy, freedom from anxious care and worry, a generous and loving heart, the sedative of peace, the uplifting influence of hope and confidence—these are better than pills, stimulants and sedatives, . . . making it true in a literal as well as a spiritual sense, that 'the joy of the Lord is your strength.'"—A.B. Simpson[432]

## Is It OK to Use Medicine and Doctors?

*Medical Science Has a Place.* "Medical Science has a place in the Natural Economy."—A.B. Simpson[433]

"There is no faith in merely refusing a physician. There must be the direct touching of the heavenly physician."—A.B. Simpson[434]

*Use Medicine and Doctors Thankfully.* "Let us avail ourselves of all that science has revealed as contributory to our best estate. Let us use these things thankfully. But never forget that they only help the natural."—Kenneth MacKenzie[435]

*Don't Abandon Medicine Unless God Clearly Indicates.* "We do believe God heals His sick and suffering children when they can fully trust Him. At the same time we believe that no one should act precipitously or presumptuously in this matter, or abandon natural remedies unless they have an intelligent, Scriptural and unquestioning trust in Him alone and really know Him well enough to touch Him in living contact as their Healer."—A.B. Simpson[436]

He encouraged the development and perfecting of "every possible human remedy against all forms of disease so long as they do not exclude or antagonize His higher way. . . . It would be most un-Christlike for us to denounce it or oppose it wherever it has its true place."—A.B. Simpson[437]

"Unless they have been led to trust Christ entirely for something higher and stronger than their natural life, they had better stick to natural remedies."—A.B. Simpson[438]

*In Many Cases God Does Not Give Faith to Abandon Medicine.* "We do not mean to imply . . . that the medical profession is sinful, or the use of means always wrong. There may be, there always will be, innumerable cases in which faith cannot be exercised," and there is "ample room for employment" of such "natural means."—A.B. Simpson[439]

*Simpson's Mentor in Divine Healing Used Medicine upon Occasion.* "Dr. Cullis believed in setting broken bones and in taking medicine except where faith was perfectly free and spontaneous, notably in incurable cases. . . .Taking a little bottle from his pocket, [Cullis] said, 'Now I know that this will stop my headache in a few minutes. Knowing that, I think it would be wrong to trouble the Lord about it, or expect Him to effect the cure in any unusual way.'"—R. Kelso Carter, associate of A.B. Simpson, writing of Dr. Charles Cullis, through whose teaching Simpson was healed[440]

*Most Missionaries Use Medicine and Health Principles.* "Most of the [C&MA] missionaries have used quinine and other remedies freely and are instructed to observe most carefully the rules of the climate for rest and food and clothing."—R. Kelso Carter[441]

*God Uses a Variety of Methods for Healing.* "Christ heals human bodies today by his own direct supernatural touch, sometimes through the physician and medicine, sometimes without medicine, sometimes when medicine is confessedly powerless, and sometimes overcoming the unwise use of medicine.

The Holy Spirit's leading is the touchstone."—S.D. Gordon, C&MA Convention speaker[442]

*Ask the Divine Physician for His Prescription.* "What about the use of means? . . . The answer is this: Ask Christ. Get in touch, if you are not already. Then when the need comes, ask him. He will tell you. . . . He is a true physician, for he advises."—S.D. Gordon[443]

*Divine Healing Is Receiving Christ Our Strength, Not Giving Up Medical Care.* "Divine Healing is not giving up medicines, or fighting with physicians, or against remedies. It is not even believing in prayer, or the prayer of faith, or in the men and women who teach Divine Healing. . . . But it is really receiving the personal life of Christ to be in us as the supernatural strength of our body, and the supply of our life."—A.B. Simpson[444]

## WHAT ABOUT THOSE WHO ARE NOT HEALED?

*Consider the Sovereignty of God.* "Divine healing fully recognizes the sovereignty of God and the state and spiritual attitude of the individual."—A.B. Simpson[445]

"Sometimes the Master is taking home His child and will He not, in such cases, lift the veil and show the trusting heart that its service is done? How often He does! . . . A dear young girl in Michigan who for some time claimed healing, awoke one day from sleep, her face covered with the reflection of heaven, and told her loved ones that the Master had led her to trust for life thus far, but now was taking her to Himself. It is well, and let no one dare to reproach such a heart with unfaithfulness."—A.B. Simpson[446]

*Healing in the Atonement Does Not Mean Universal Healing.* "The doctrine of healing in the atonement says not that universal healing is therefore available, but rather that physical healing is available to believers on the ground of the blood atonement."—Dr. Keith Bailey[447]

*Some Provisions of the Atonement Are For the Future Life.* "Absolute sinless-ness . . . is ours through the atonement, but it is to be ours in fullness only in the future life. Again, a condition of the body not subject to weariness is pur-chased by the atonement, but will not be enjoyed in this life."—Dr. J. Hudson Ballard[448]

*We Get the First Fruits in This Life, But Not the Full Benefits.* "But while we do not get the full benefits for the body secured for us by the atoning death of Jesus Christ in the life that now is but when Jesus comes again, nevertheless, just as one gets the first fruits of his spiritual salvation in the life that now is, so we get the first fruits of our physical salvation in the life that now is. We do get in many, many, many cases of physical healing through the atoning death of Jesus Christ even in the life that now is."—R.A. Torrey, friend of A.B. Simpson and C&MA convention speaker[449]

***Sometimes God Gives Divine Strength Rather Than Healing.*** "Whatever the explanation, it is a fact that of those who take Christ as their Healer some are not healed of their diseases or delivered from their infirmities in the sense that the diseases wholly disappear or the infirmities are entirely removed. They could not get a doctor's certificate of good health nor, because of physical unsoundness, could they take out a life insurance policy. Yet such persons daily experience a supernatural quickening of their bodies which gives them freshness and strength and in some instances extraordinary physical endurance. Indeed, they seem to have something more than Divine Healing; they have Divine Life. Theirs indeed is a paradoxical experience. Instead of being bedridden or helpless invalids they keep going in the strength of Jesus, not only carrying their own burdens but stretching out a helping hand to others. Surely it is one thing to sink down under the power of disease or the weight of infirmity; but it is quite another thing to rise above the power of disease and the weight of infirmity and in the strength of the ascended and glorified Christ not only have a victorious spirit but bear fruit, yea, the 'much fruit' that shall abide the day of His coming."—George P. Pardington[450]

***God's Finer Touches.*** Simpson describes how some believers receive healing in their earlier Christian experiences, "but when we meet them a little later in their life, we often find them struggling with sickness, unhealed and unable to understand the reason of their failure. It is because God is leading them into a deeper spiritual experience. He is teaching them to understand His guidance, and some people cannot be guided any other way than by a touch of pain. . . . God is teaching them His finer touches."—A.B. Simpson[451]

***Pray Until You Get a Clear Answer.*** Citing Paul's thorn in the flesh, Simpson taught: "Paul certainly prayed until he got an answer from heaven, and so we should claim deliverance at the very least until we get a refusal as clear and divine as he did."—A.B. Simpson[452]

"We have Paul's example for steadfastly praying in faith for its removal, until we get an answer from the Lord about which there can be no mistake."—Russell Kelso Carter[453]

"Healing is to be expected. Paul himself expected healing in his own case [his thorn in the flesh] until God definitely revealed to him that it was not His will in that particular instance."—R.A. Torrey[454]

*Expect as Much Healing as the Spirit Guides.* "How far may Christ's healing be expected? . . . We may have all we can take, as His Spirit guides our taking."—S.D. Gordon[455]

*Health and Strength Until Our Work Is Done.* "The Word places a limit to human life, and all that Scriptural faith can claim is sufficiency of health and strength for our life-work and within its fair limits."—A.B. Simpson[456]

"The promise of healing is not physical immortality, but health until our life work is done."—A.B. Simpson, paraphrasing Oliver Cromwell and Charles Spurgeon, who said, "A man is immortal until his work is done."[457]

*Don't Let the Devil Condemn You for Lack of Healing.* "No Christian should allow the Adversary to whip him because he is not healed, when he is conscious of a perfect acquiescence in the will of God."—R. Kelso Carter[458]

*There Is Faith and Victory Even in Death.* "It is a beautiful picture of faith that even infirmity and approaching dissolution cannot subdue or even cloud, reminding us that the Christian's last hours may be his brightest and that the sublimest triumphs of his life should be in the face even of his foes. Have we not all seen such victories, in which the withering frame and worn out forces of nature and the very frailty of the outward temple made it more transparent to the glory that was shining out from within."—A.B. Simpson[459]

## Additional Resources on Faith and Healing

Bailey, Keith M. *Divine Healing: The Children's Bread.* Harrisburg, PA: Christian Publications, 1977.

Bosworth, Fred F. *Christ the Healer.* Grand Rapids: Fleming H. Revell, 1973.

King, Paul L. *Moving Mountains: Lessons in Bold Faith from Great Evangelical Leaders.* Grand Rapids: Chosen Books, 2004.

King, Paul L. *Only Believe: Examining the Origin and Development of Classic and Contemporary Word of Faith Theologies.* Tulsa, OK: Word and Spirit Press, 2008.

McCrossan, T.J. *Bodily Healing and the Atonement*. Tulsa, OK: Kenneth Hagin Ministries, 1982, edited edition).

Müller, George *The Autobiography of George Müller*. Springdale, PA: Whitaker House, 1984.

Murray, Andrew; A.J. Gordon; A.B. Simpson. *The Three Classics on Divine Healing*. Compiled and edited by Jonathan Graf. Camp Hill, PA: Christian Publications, 1992.

Simpson, A.B. *The Gospel of Healing*. Harrisburg, PA: Christian Publications, 1915.

Simpson, A.B. *The Lord for the Body*, revised edition. Camp Hill, PA: Christian Publications, 1996.

Simpson, A.B. *Seeing the Invisible*. Camp Hill, PA: Christian Publications, 1994.

## FOR REFLECTION AND DISCUSSION

1. Discuss the principles of healing of A.B. Simpson, F.F. Bosworth, and T.J. McCrossan.

2. Read Isaiah 53:4-5; Matthew 8:16-17; 1 Peter 2:24. How do Alliance leaders understand healing in the atonement from these verses?

3. Read Deuteronomy 28 and Galatians 3:13. Are illness and disease scripturally regarded as curses? How are believers redeemed from the curse of the law?

4. What is the role of faith in healing?

5. When is appropriate to use and not to use medicine?

6. How much health and healing can we expect in this life?

7. How should we respond when healing doesn't come?

8. Which of these Alliance healing principles are the most meaningful to you?

CHAPTER 10

———— ◆ ————

# Worship in the Spirit-Empowered Life

*But the hour is coming, and now is, when the true worshiper will worship*
*the Father in spirit and truth* (John 4:23 NKJV).

## HOW DO WE WORSHIP IN SPIRIT AND TRUTH (JOHN 4:23-24)?

*Restore the Missing Jewel of Worship.* "The purpose of God in sending His Son to die and rise and live and be at the right hand of God the Father was that He might restore to us the missing jewel—the jewel of worship; that we might come back and learn to do again what we were created to do in the first place—worship the Lord in the beauty of holiness, to spend our time in awesome wonder and adoration of God, feeling and expressing it, and letting it get into our labors. . . . Power for service? Yes, but that's only half of it, maybe only one-tenth of it. The other nine-tenths are that the Holy Spirit may restore to us again the spirit of worship."—A.W. Tozer[460]

*Avoid Both Religious Ritual and Worldly Ways.* "The Spirit may be grieved by the method of public worship in a congregation. It may be either so stiff and formal that there is no room for His spontaneous working, or so full of worldly and unscriptural elements as to repel and offend Him from taking any part in a pompous ritual. An operatic choir and a ritualistic service may effectually quench all the fire of God's altar, and send the gentle Dove to seek a simpler nest."—A.B. Simpson[461]

*The Highest Calling—Worship Before Work.* "The highest calling of the saint is not so much to work for a cause, as to worship God and pour out the fulness of the heart in adoration and praise to Him alone. God made us for Himself and our supreme business is to glorify God."—A.B. Simpson[462]

*Put Worship in the Hands of the Spirit, Not Men.* "The Word must clear away all the mists of Obscurity. It takes worship out of the hands of men and puts it in the hands of the Holy Spirit. . . . It is impossible to worship God acceptable apart from the Holy Spirit. The operation of the Spirit of God within us enables us to worship God acceptably."—A.W. Tozer[463]

*Intensive Worship Leaps Spontaneously Out of Our Hearts.* "When the Holy Spirit came on the day of Pentecost, why did the believers break out into ecstatic language? Simply, it was because they were rightly worshiping God for the first time. Intensive worship unexpectedly leaped out of their hearts. It was nothing planned or perpetuated by some 'worship leader.' God was in their midst. Whenever there is a move of the Holy Spirit, it is always a call for God's people to be worshipers of the Most High God above everything else."—A.W. Tozer[464]

*Worship Expresses Delightful Awe, Astonished Wonder, and Overpowering Love.* "Worship is to feel in your heart and express in some appropriate manner a humbling but delightful sense of admiring awe and astonished wonder and overpowering love in the presence of that most ancient Mystery, that majesty which philosophers call the First Cause but which we call Our Father Which Art in Heaven."—A.W. Tozer[465]

*The Presence of God Is More Important Than the Program.* "The Presence is more important than the program. . . . In our times the program has been substituted for the Presence. The program rather than the Lord of glory is the center of attraction. So the most popular gospel church in any city is likely to be the one that offers the most interesting program; that is, the church that can present the most and best features for the enjoyment of the public. These features are programmed so as to keep everything moving and everybody expectant. . . . Even persons who may honestly desire to serve God after the pattern shown us in the mount are deceived by the substitution of the program for the Presence, with the result that they never really become mature Christians. . . . Seek to cultivate the blessed Presence in our services. If we make Christ the supreme and constant object of devotion the program will take its place as a gentle aid to order in the public worship of God. If we fail to do this the program will finally obscure the Light entirely."—A.W. Tozer[466]

## WHAT IF I DON'T LIKE OLD OR MODERN WORSHIP STYLES?

*Embrace Both the Old and the New.* ". . . a most delightful and remarkable collection of the very best hymns, both old and new . . . perfectly adapted to the most sober taste and the most old-fashioned church services, while at the same time full of new, fresh hymns."—A.B. Simpson[467]

*Old Wineskins of Worship Will Burst and Lose God's New Wine.* "New wine put into old wineskins would have no allowance for stretching, and the result would be the rending of the wineskins and the loss of both the wineskins and the wine. . . . The same struggle still goes on when people try to hold on to old forms, habits and methods of worship . . . I remember terrific struggles in my early experience as a minister . . . daring to introduce modern hymns and tunes. . . and many other things that are simply nonessentials. There is no sacredness in antiquity."—A.B. Simpson[468]

*Ask For the Ancient Paths.* "We are to 'stand . . . in the ways, and ask for the old paths, where is the good way, and walk therein.' (Jer. 6:16)."—A.B. Simpson[469]

*Old Truths Become Present Truths—God's Message to the Times.* "There are certain truths which God emphasizes at certain times. . . . From age to age God speaks the special message most needed, so that there is always some portion of divine truth which might properly be called *present* truth [2 Peter 1:12], God's message to the times."—A.B. Simpson[470]

## IS EMOTION APPROPRIATE IN WORSHIP?

*Deepened in God Through Waves of Holy Emotion.* "Wave after wave of holy emotion rolled over us. We were all deepened in God."—Wilbur F. Meminger, Field Evangelist and District Superintendent[471]

*Where Emotion Has Vanished, God's Glory Has Departed.* "The church from which emotionalism has vanished is already moribund. When 'amens' and 'hallelujahs' are no longer heard in Alliance assemblies, we may write 'Ichabod' over our doors, for the glory of the Holy One has departed."—John MacMillan[472]

*Genuine Worship Can Be Ecstatic.* "I once saw a man kneel at an altar, taking Communion. Suddenly he broke into holy laughter. This man laughed until he wrapped his arms around himself as if he was afraid he would burst just out of sheer delight in the presence of Almighty God. . . . So worship is capable of running from the very simple to the most intense and sublime."—A.W. Tozer[473]

*Genuine Worship Is Both Order and Spirit, But Not Routine.* "The theory is that if the meeting is unplanned the Holy Spirit will work freely, and that would be true if all the worshipers were reverent and Spirit-filled. But mostly there is neither order nor Spirit, just a routine prayer that is, except for minor variations, the same week after week, and a few songs that were never much to start with and have long ago lost all significance by meaningless repetition. In the majority of our meetings there is scarcely a trace of reverent thought, no recognition of the unity of the body, little sense of the divine Presence, no moment of stillness, no solemnity, no wonder, no holy fear."—A.W. Tozer[474]

*Danger of Cold Formalism in Guise of Spirituality.* "It is refreshing to the devout heart to meet a saint of God, whose soul has been so blest by the conscious presence of his Lord, that he has been overwhelmed by the flow of the full tides of heavenly love. Some will tell us that such experiences are the result of an emotional nature, but this is not correct. It is true that the outward manifestation may be molded by the individual temperament, but the deep inner experience is the result of the revelation of Christ to the human spirit by the Holy Spirit. And, when the Spirit of God is pleased to visit the yielded heart in power, He takes for the time complete control. Then the lips are tuned as never before to utter the praises of Jehovah in His chosen tabernacle of the threefold being of the believer.

Such experiences used to be much more common than they are today. There is a practicality to much of the religion about us—a combination of unbelief and spiritual coldness that decries emotion. . . . But, while the control of emotionalism may at times be an indication of a growth in spirituality, there is the serious danger that it may be, on the other hand, the result of the incoming of a cold formalism under the guise of a deeper godliness. Unhappy the congregation that has lost all emotionalism from its worship."—John MacMillan[475]

## IS REPETITIVE WORSHIP BIBLICAL OR VAIN REPETITION?

*God Is Glorified in Repeated Worship.* "Shortly after that a power came upon me as I was bended lowly in prayer and praise, and straightened me upright and in this attitude I continued for a length of time repeating over and over again: 'Glory to Jesus, Glory to Jesus,' till by and by I got down on the straw covering the ground of the Tabernacle."—John Salmon C&MA Vice President[476]

*The Spirit Leads Us in Repeated Worship.* "The Spirit alone was leader in the meetings. . . . One chorus that was quietly sung again and again was 'Deeper yet, under the cleansing blood.'. . . Heart sobs, Holy Spirit groans, prostrations of spirit. . . . a marvelous and unprecedented visitation of the Holy Spirit in our midst."—*Alliance Weekly*, of the Nyack Revival of 1906[477]

*Worship in Heaven Is Repeated Again and Again By Angelic Beings.* "One [seraph] cried out to another, saying, 'Holy, holy, holy, is the Lord of hosts; the whole earth is full of His glory" (Isaiah 6:3).

*Same Phrase Repeated 26 Times in Psalm.* ". . . . For His mercy endures forever." (Psalm 136:1-26).

*Heavenly Creatures Worship Day and Night.* "The four living creatures . . . do not rest day or night, saying, 'Holy, holy, holy, Lord God Almighty, who was and is and is to come'" (Rev. 4:8).

*Elders Repetitively Worship in Heaven.* "Whenever the living creatures give glory and honor and thanks to Him who sits on the throne . . . the twenty-four elders fall down before Him . . . saying, 'You are worthy, O Lord, to receive glory and honor and power; for You created all things, and by You all things exist." (Rev. 4:9).

## SHOULD SPIRITUAL GIFTS SUCH AS PROPHECY AND TONGUES BE ALLOWED IN ALLIANCE MEETINGS?

*If You Have a Message or a Tongue—Out with It!* "Fear not to speak the message which the Holy Spirit has burned into your soul for the quickening and the rousing of your brethren. It will be a word in season for some weary soul. And if you have, in some simple form, even the old gift of tongues welling up in your heart, some Hallelujah which you could not put into articulate speech, some unutterable cry of love or joy, out with it!"—A.B. Simpson[478]

*A Place in Every Spirit-Controlled Church.* "Alliance leaders are quite agreed in believing that speaking with tongues is one of the gifts of the Spirit and should have a place in every Spirit-controlled church."—J. Hudson Ballard[479]

*Let All Things Be Done—Decently and in Order.* "One of the most important chapters in the New Testament, and one of special value at this time, is the fourteenth chapter of First Corinthians, and one of the most significant statements in that chapter is in the thirty second and thirty-third verses, 'The Spirits of the prophets are subject to the prophets, for God is not the author of confusion, but of peace, as in all the churches of the saints,' to which we might add the concluding verse of the chapter, 'Let all things be done decently and in order.'"—A.B. Simpson[480]

*Freedom within Biblical Order.* "This [1 Cor. 14:26] allows perfect freedom and fellowship, but at the same time demands perfect order. . . . This clearly means that the Holy Spirit does not overrule our individual judgment and carry us off our feet in wild and reckless incoherency, but He holds His messages subject to our sanctified judgment and will, and permits us to act as rational and responsible beings, speaking or keeping silence as may seem to us most unto edification."—A.B. Simpson[481]

"We insisted upon holding everything strictly to the Pauline regulations. . . . We have not deviated from our first position—that anything that was not Pauline was not of God, there we expect to remain."—William T. MacArthur[482]

*Permissible, But Not Appropriate in Every Service.* "I believe if we are going to be Biblical we would have to say that speaking in tongues in a public service is admissible if it is interpreted. . . . I do not think it is appropriate to have speaking in tongues in every service."—Dr. Keith Bailey, Vice President of Church Ministries, 1978[483]

*Avoid Temptation to Speak Out of Order.* "I was tempted to pray in public in these different languages, but I know this was not of God, as I tried the spirits, because underneath was a secret temptation to let the people know of the gift He had given me."—Mary Mullen, C&MA missionary[484]

*Let Message in Tongues Be Given—Pray for Interpretation.* "If God should give someone a message in tongues in your congregation—and He might—let him deliver it without interpretation, but pray God, to give the interpretation to someone."—T.J. McCrossan[485]

## Is Dance Appropriate in Worship?

*Dance Can Be Sacred and Grand.* "We witnessed a sacred dance by a company of about fifty of the women. . . . They swayed their bodies and moved their feet and arms, keeping time to the music. And the effect was truly grand."—A.B. Simpson, of an African-American Alliance church[486]

*God Approves Whole-Soul Outbursts of Praise.* "So the Ark of the Lord was brought into the City of David amidst shouting and the sound of the trumpet and dancing. . . . It was David's whole-souled, sincere outburst of thanksgiving to his God, of which spirit God approved, and accepted."—*Alliance Weekly*[487]

*God Is Pleased with Dance as an Offering to Him.* "The Psalmist says that his offering in the tabernacle of Jehovah will consist of 'sacrifices of shouting.' He was not afraid to express before the great congregation his love and praise. There was an occasion when he even 'danced before the Lord with all his might,' at the bringing up to Jerusalem of the ark of the covenant. With such offerings God is well pleased."—John MacMillan[488]

*A God-Intoxicated Man Dances to God's Delight.* "What made David run? What makes the child run and shout with glee on a summer morning? What brings the lover to the door where his beloved dwells? David was a God-intoxicated man. He had gazed on God until he was enraptured and that rapture he could not always contain. While still a young man, in the presence of the holy Ark he let himself go in an ecstatic dance that delighted God as much as it outraged the coldhearted Michal."—A.W. Tozer[489]

*Joyous Dancing May Be the Power of the Spirit upon People.* "There is a degree of joy that manifests itself in physical demonstrations [dancing] that cannot be denied or resisted without resisting the Holy Spirit."—W.W. Newberry, C&MA pastor, in *Alliance Weekly*[490]

*But Avoid Fleshly Expression.* "There is, however, great need in that every movement of the flesh be held in the place of crucifixion in all these demonstrations."—W.W. Newberry[491]

*Beware of Judging People for Expressing Their Joy in Dance.* "The dancing and holy joy that David manifested aroused antagonism in the heart of Michal. She despised him in her heart. The power of the Holy Spirit on God's people has often brought down upon them the indignation and opposition of half-hearted Christians. They condemn all religious fervor as fanaticism. Judgment came upon Michal and it has often happened that people who have criticized the power of the Spirit on other people have suffered in their experience."—W.W. Newberry[492]

"David's wife saw David (as she looked through a window) leaping and dancing before the Lord, and she despised him in her heart. . . . Have you ever heard . . . of some people who have been so overcome with joy and thanksgiving toward God that they have done things similar to what David did in his delight, and people of a different point of view have looked on and despised them in their hearts? There is a very deep lesson to be learned from this haughty despising on the part of Michal. . . . We must always remember, in looking at any form, that it is the spirit that actuated the form that is what is to be criticized, and not the mere form itself. . . . One ought to be very careful how they criticize others' actions. Here was a rebuke from the Lord, and a terrible rebuke it was. In this case, it was despising what God honored that brought this result."—*Alliance Weekly*[493]

## What Is the Meaning of Communion?

*The Real Presence of Christ.* "It is a service of communion, not only bringing the remembrance of the Lord, but bringing His own personal presence in living communion with us and loving fellowship with one another." . . . . [It] is the real presence . . . of Christ in the Lord's Supper."—A.B. Simpson[494]

"The communion will not have ultimate meaning for us if we do not believe that our Lord Jesus Christ is literally present in the Body of Christ on earth. There is a distinction here—Christ is literally present with us—but not physically present. . . . When we come to the Lord's table, we do not have to try to bring His presence. He is here! . . . . There is nothing else like this in the world—the Spirit of God standing ready with a baptism of the sense of the presence of the God who made heaven and earth."—A.W. Tozer[495]

*Impartation of the Life and Grace of Jesus.* "It is . . . communication of His life and grace to us. It is thus a means of grace and channel of actual spiritual impartation from Him to those who are in living fellowship with Him."—A.B. Simpson[496]

*Elevation to a Higher Level.* "Knowing the sense of His presence [through Communion] will completely change our everyday life. It will elevate us, purify us, and deliver us from the dominion of carnal flesh to the point where our lives will be a continuing, radiant fascination!"—A.W. Tozer[497]

*Celebration of Jesus.* "The Lord's table, the communion, is not as a picture hung on the wall or a chain around the neck reminding us of Him. It is a celebration of His person—a celebration in which we gladly join, because we remember Him, testifying to the world and to each other of His conquering and sacrificial death—until He comes!"—A.W. Tozer[498]

*Mystic Expectancy, Fresh Touch from God, and Restoration of Soul.* "Oh, I charge you, do not set forth the Sacraments as bare and naked signs. Fill the vessels with spiritual meat and drink. Awaken the conscience and faith of God's people. Let them come to these sacred and solemn moments in a mystic expectancy and with a valid assurance of God's spiritual blessing upon them, and never with the settled conclusion that nothing whatever is to be expected or received in the manner of a fresh revelation of Christ. Many a flagging spirit, fainting under a host of temptations, has had a fresh touch of God and a restoration of soul at our Lord's table. Eating worthily and discerning with contrition anew the Lord's body has brought healing to the physical life."—R.D. Kilgour, C&MA pastor, speaking at an Ordination service[499]

## ADDITIONAL RESOURCES

Tozer, A.W. *The Purpose of Man*. Ventura, CA: Regal, 2009.

Tozer, A.W. *Worship: The Missing Jewel*. Camp Hill, PA: Christian Publications, 1992.

Webber, Robert E., ed. *The Biblical Foundations of Christian Worship*, Vol. I. Peabody, MA: Hendrickson, 1993.

## FOR REFLECTION AND DISCUSSION

1. Read John 4:23-24. How can you worship in spirit and in truth?
2. In your life and your church is the presence of God more important than the program?
3. Read 1 Corinthians 11. What is the meaning of Communion to you?
4. What is the appropriate place of emotion in worship services?
5. Read Psalm 136; Isaiah 6:1-4; Rev. 5:8-9. Is repeating words or phrases in worship meaningful to you? Why or why not?
6. Read 1 Corinthian 12 and 14. When would manifestations of prophecy, word of knowledge, word of wisdom, or tongues and interpretation be appropriate in worship services?
7. Read Psalm 47:1; 63:3-4; 150. What bodily expressions of worship do you find in these Scripture verses?

# CHAPTER 11

## Discernment in the Spirit-Empowered Life

### THE SIGNATURE THEME OF THE ALLIANCE

*Believe not every spirit; but try the spirits to see if they be of God*
(1 John 4:1).

*Alliance spokespersons had an almost uncanny way of discerning potential difficulties that enthusiastic Apostolic Faith adherents seemed prone to overlook. Within several years, some Pentecostals would echo Alliance appeals for prudence and balance. For the moment, however, the cautions seemed to go largely unheeded.*
—Historian of Pentecostalism Edith Blumhofer[500]

*Teach all "seekers after truth" to "try the spirits" and "discern the things that differ."*
*Distinguish between divine fervor and dangerous fanaticism*
—A.B. Simpson[501]

### ARE ALL SUPERNATURAL MANIFESTATIONS FROM GOD?

*Some Manifestations May Not Be from the Holy Spirit.* "Today hundreds of God's saints really speak with other tongues when baptized with the Holy Spirit. . . . We have also heard many good people speak with other tongues when we felt absolutely sure that the Holy Spirit had nothing to do with the speaking. . . . Our own experience leads us to the conclusion that, wherever people really believe they must speak in tongues to be baptized with the Holy Spirit, a large percentage either speak mere 'gibberish' or a real language, which the Holy Spirit has nothing whatever to do with."—T.J. McCrossan[502]

*Some Manifestations May Be Human Self-Willfulness.* "It is easy to say, 'The Spirit says,' etc. 'The Lord told me so and so' when it is quite possible that it is a matter of our self-wilfulness. The Apostle Paul did not accept such leadings given through the utterances of others as the infallible will of the Lord for him (See Acts 21.)"—Robert Jaffray[503]

"There were several cases of the Gift of Tongues [at the 1907 C&MA General Council] and other extraordinary manifestations, some of which were certainly genuine, while other appeared to partake somewhat of the individual peculiarities and eccentricities of the subjects; so that I saw not only the working of the Spirit, but also a very distinct human element, not always edifying or profitable."—Simpson's Diary, May, 1907.

"There are messages in both the known and unknown tongue with which the Lord has nothing to do; and it may not be of the devil either."—W. T. Dixon, C&MA pastor[504]

*Some Manifestations May Be Satanic Counterfeits.* "There have been many instances where [seeking for] the gift of tongues led the subjects and the audiences in to the wildest excesses and were accompanied with voices and actions more closely resembling wild animals than rational beings, impressing the unprejudiced observers that it was the work of the devil."—A.B. Simpson[505]

"The gift of tongues above all others opened the way for scenes of much excitement and the possibility of Satanic counterfeit. There are languages spoken in hell as well as heaven."—A.B. Simpson[506]

## What Is the Gift of Discernment of Spirits?

*The Power to Distinguish the False and the True.* This was the one gift that Simpson encouraged people to seek: "It is quite remarkable that this gift immediately precedes the last two, namely, tongues and interpretation of tongues. It would seem as if at this point there were peculiar need for the power to distinguish the false and the true. The gift of tongues above all others opened the way for scenes of much excitement and the possibility of Satanic counterfeits."—A.B. Simpson[507]

*Diagnosing Whether Evil Spirits Are Afflicting Torments of Body and Mind.* "Very common are vexing conditions of body and of mind, and torments of body and mind; and it is noticeable that just such conditions are attributed in Scripture to demoniacal presence and afflictions. Yet such explicit rules of diagnosis are not given as to dispense with the need of the Spirit's gifts of discernment, by which to detect the evil spirits, their lodging places, and their particular operations."—William C. Stevens[508]

*A God-given Supernatural Instinct.* "We have no business to be afraid of evil spirits, for He has given us 'power over all the power of the enemy,' and He can give supernatural discernment of spirits. . . . The air is full of voices and it is impossible, in the natural wisdom of man, to discern the spirits. Only by a God-given, supernatural instinct, only by 'trying the spirits' in the Scriptural way may we be saved from evil influences that fill the 'air' in these last days. In order to try a spirit it is necessary that one be separated from and not in any sense under the influence of that spirit at the time of the trial (cf. John 4:1-3)."—Robert Jaffray[509]

*A Quickening in the Soul—Distinguishing the Human from the Spirit.* "I noted first a quiet but real quickening in my own soul, . . . so that I saw not only the working of the Spirit, but also a very distinct human element, not always edifying or profitable. And God led me to discern and hold quietly to the divine order for the gifts of the Spirit in 1 Cor. 12-14. At the same time I could not question the reality of the gifts, and I was led to pray much about it, and for God's highest will and glory in connection with it."—A.B. Simpson[510]

*Distinguishing Manifestations of the Spirit from False Manifestations.* "The Lord gave me a spirit of discernment so that I was enabled to know the difference between false manifestations and those which come from God. . . . It is most necessary to have this discernment in spiritual matters. We cannot lean to our own understanding but must trust the leading of the Holy Spirit, for it is still true, as in Job's time, that when the sons of God come together, the devil comes also (Job 1:6)."—Carrie Judd Montgomery[511]

*Your Spiritual Nature Will Revolt in Recognition of the False.* "You will feel at once that is not of God. It will be harsh and repelling; your spiritual nature will revolt."—Dr. T. J. McCrossan [512]

*A Strong Conviction of the Presence of Evil.* "The conviction seized me that there was no disease present, but simply an evil spirit."—William T. MacArthur[513]

"A.B. Simpson once said that he could feel the demon powers attack when on ship board, and nearing a heathen land."—W.T. Norton, Ramabai's Mukti Mission, India[514]

*Discerning a Spirit of Bondage.* "I recall the case of a person who came to me for spiritual counsel and relief. He began by several humbling confessions which were most sincerely and we have no doubt accepted by the Lord in His abundant mercy and grace. But we discerned a spirit of bondage and a severity and harshness in dealing with himself which deprived him of the comfort which the Lord mean for him in His forgiving grace and love."—A.B. Simpson[515]

***Distinguishing Insanity from Demonic.*** "Having met the insane frequently, . . . I can detect the symptoms [of insanity or demons] more quickly that most people, and I do hereby testify that I found no trace of insanity, or lack of mental poise in either of these cases [of demonization]."—William T. MacArthur[516]

***A Clear Inner Knowing from the Spirit.*** "God's people need to pray for discernment. If they will wait on the Lord, He will give them discernment by the power of the Holy Spirit, and they will know at once when the enemy is trying to counterfeit the work of the Holy Spirit."—Carrie Judd Montgomery[517]

## SHOULD WE SHUN OR FORBID THE GIFTS BECAUSE OF FEAR OF COUNTERFEITS?

***The Devil Wants to Frighten You—Don't Let Him.*** "There is indeed ample evidence of the prevalence of fanaticism, but it would seem as if the adversary had particularly intended that this very thing should frighten us off from the special gifts and blessings which God has for His Church at this time."—A.B. Simpson[518]

***Don't Be Scared of Satan's Scarecrows.*** "Many of God's dear children have been hindered in waiting upon Him by fear of certain manifestations and spiritual movements which may not always be wholly scriptural in their methods and results. The enemy loves to use these things as scarecrows to keep away God's children from genuine blessing. Let us . . . simply wait upon God without fear."—A.B. Simpson[519]

***Trust God to Keep You from a Counterfeit.*** "Can we not trust our heavenly Father to keep His promise to us, "if a son shall ask bread of any of you which is a father, will He give him a stone him, a stone? Or if he ask a fish, will he for a fish give him a serpent? Or if he ask an egg will He offer him a scorpion? If ye then, being evil, know how to give good gifts to your children, how much more shall the heavenly Father give the Spirit to them that ask Him."—A.B. Simpson[520]

"God knows how to give without a counterfeit or misleading."—A.B. Simpson[521]

***Be Watchful—Not Fearful—And Boldly Press On.*** "Let us not be less watchful but let us be less fearful, and just because the adversary is trying to impose upon the credulous and sensational his deceptions, let us the more earnestly and boldly press on for the real blessing and the fulness of power which we need to day as never before just because of the activity of the adversary."—A.B. Simpson[522]

*Fear Cheats Us Out of the Spirit's Blessings.* "There is a great danger of fear of the works of the devil to such an extent that we shall lose all courage to seek earnestly for the true and full endowment of the Spirit for which our souls hunger. I have met some who are so prejudiced on account of why that have seen that they say they have no desire to ever speak in tongues, forgetting that tongues is one of the gifts of the Spirit. Let us not allow the enemy so to drive us away from, and cheat us out of, the real blessings of the Spirit because he has counterfeited in some cases the gift of tongues. We have no business to be afraid of evil spirits, for His has given us 'power over all the power of the enemy,' and He can give supernatural discernment of spirits."—Robert Jaffray[523]

"Well, my brother, I will not be frightened out of my rightful heritage. I will not be scared out of my birthright because some others didn't know what to do with the birthright or have found something else that has nothing to do with the birthright. I want all that God has for me!"—A.W. Tozer[524]

*Don't Depreciate the Genuine Gold.* "We must not allow the counterfeit to depreciate the genuine gold."—Simpson's 1907 Annual Report.

*Fight False Fire with True Fire.* "The way to fight false fire is by the true fire."—A.B. Simpson[525]

*It Is the Enemy Who Causes Fear of Counterfeits.* "It is perhaps true that many earnest and sober Christians have become so much afraid of extreme and unscriptural manifestations in meetings for united prayer that they have not been waiting upon God as earnestly as in time past. This is one of the enemy's snares to frighten us away from the mercy seat. Let us trust God to keep us from the devil's counterfeit and to give us a genuine blessing, even 'the spirit of love and power and a sound mind,' and let us wait upon Him with confidence for the outpouring of the Holy Spirit."—A.B. Simpson[526]

*Overcome Fanaticism with Truth, Not Criticism or Opposition.* "The way to meet and overcome fanaticism is not to oppose all unusual spiritual manifestations, but to accept that which is truly of the Lord and then from the standpoint of a friend gently and wisely correct the spirit of extravagance which you can never do if you take your place among the critics and the enemies of 'spiritual gifts.' The only way to meet error is to go all the way with truth."—A.B. Simpson[527]

*Beware of Offending the Holy Spirit.* "If you say this is all of Satan, you will surely offend the Holy Spirit, and He may forsake you, and leave you as powerless as He has left many others. Friend, we had better obey Paul's word and 'Forbid not to speak with tongues.' Let us take 'the middle of the road attitude' on this subject."—Dr. T.J. McCrossan[528]

*Don't Be Afraid of What the Spirit Gives.* "Get alone in your room and wait on the Lord until you are filled. You say, 'I might speak in tongues.' Well, if you do, Hallelujah. I am afraid of you if you are afraid of something the Holy Spirit gives from above. . . . Why not be willing, if the Lord sends it, to speak in tongues? . . . Paul tells us how to regulate the gifts, not to eliminate them."— Paul Rader, C&MA President[529]

*It Is Dangerous to Oppose or Despise Manifestations.* "Every Christian should be willing to receive this gift (tongues) if it please the Spirit to bestow it upon him. It is a dangerous thing to oppose or despise this, one of the immediate manifestations of the Blessed Spirit of God." —J. Hudson Ballard[530]

*Claim the Protection of the Blood of Jesus.* "I had seen a few manifestations which I knew were of God, but I had seen so many things which were not. . . . I said, 'Father, I believe You are doing a mighty work, but I believe also that the Enemy is there and at work to counterfeit and hinder. . . . Father, if You have anything more for me, I want it.' I had to ask Him to take away all fear. One day Jesus said to me, 'My precious blood will keep you away from every evil, from everything that is not of God.'"—Carrie Judd Montgomery[531]

*Put Up with Mixture, and Trust God to Guard.* "To prevent wild-fire we do not think that preventives should be invented. We believe that 'mixture' is inevitable where God moves in power, and think that is safer to let God guard the door to danger, and put up with some mixture, rather than teach that God can and cannot do this and that, as a means of guarding against danger. God is larger than our human theories, and it is both highly unbecoming and dangerous to be too extravagantly positives in asserting what He is or is not able to do."—N.H. Harriman, C&MA pastor[532]

*Avoid Psychic Manifestations.* "Avoid gatherings where psychical manifestations are much in evidence."—Mary McDonough, C&MA author[533]

"Such bodily powers as clairvoyance, clairaudience, hypnotism, etc., are possible of development, but the use of them under present conditions leads invariably to intercourse in some form with evil spirits, and so is forbidden."—John A. MacMillan[534]

## HOW DID THE EARLY ALLIANCE VIEW THE PENTECOSTAL MOVEMENT?

*No Doubt God Started It.* "There is no doubt but that God graciously inaugurated this 'revival.'"—May Mabette Anderson, C&MA author and teacher[535]

"It is the river of God, but not yet as clear as crystal."—associate of A.B. Simpson[536]

*In Sympathy with Balanced Experiences.* "Our State workers and field superintendent, Dr. Henry Wilson, were all in perfect accord with the testimony given by those who received their Pentecost, and expressed themselves in thorough sympathy with the experiences as witnessed in our midst." The meetings continued to be "modest and steady."—C&MA pastor Warren Cramer[537]

*Danger of Extremes for or Against Manifestations.* "Some are deceived into the error that all supernatural manifestation is of God, and are so easily led off into extravagances and fanaticism and thus bring much dishonor on the work and the name of the Lord. Others equally deceived and misled declare that the whole movement is of the devil."—Robert Jaffray[538]

*Both Approval and Disapproval by Henry Wilson.* "This work is of God, and no man should put his hand on it."—Dr. Henry Wilson, Simpson associate, speaking of the Pentecostal movement in Alliance circles.[539]

"I am not able to approve the movement [in the town of Alliance, Ohio, not a part of the C&MA], though I am willing to concede that there is probably something of God in it somewhere."—Dr. Henry Wilson, as cited by Tozer[540]

"In a time of upheaval, the scum floats to the top. . . . mountain climbing is lonely work—the farther you go up the mountain the more people you leave behind you. This shows a recognition of three classes, one of which definitely sought the restoration of the faith of the Apostles to the church that mighty works might be done in the name of Jesus, the son of God. Another class held back, and still another became fanatical."—Dr. Henry Wilson, cited by C&MA pastor's wife Bertha Pinkham Dixon[541]

*Both the Counterfeit and the Real.* "There have been counterfeits of this manifestation, but the counterfeit only proves the genuine coin."—F.E. Marsh[542]

*Mixture of Real Blessing, Fancied Blessing, and Sorrow.* "The Promise of the Father and Speaking with Tongues in Chicago. . . has brought much real blessing to many, and possibly only fancied blessing to others, which will yet eventuate in sorrow and discouragement. Like so many widespread movements, it is a mixture of good and evil, for Satan has not been asleep. . . . There is a hunger and thirst after God, a joy in His service, a yearning for the lost, and a delight in Bible study."—William T. MacArthur[543]

***Both Evils and Greater Blessings.*** "The new movement struck us a few months ago with its evils and with its greater blessings. It came with such force and authority as to refuse absolutely to be ignored. We knew not what to do with it, and knew less what it would do with us. We nestled up a little closer to Jesus. . . . He has made us in some little measure a blessing to the movement and has made it a great blessing to us."—C.D. Sawtelle, Northwest District Superintendent[544]

***Much Is Genuine—No Wholesale Criticism or Condemnation.*** "Many of these experiences appear not only to be genuine but accompanied by a spirit of deep humility, earnestness, and soberness, and free from extravagance and error, and it is admitted that in many of the branches and states where this movement has been strongly developed and wisely directed, there has been a marked deepening of the spiritual life of our members and an encouraging increase in their missionary zeal and liberality. It would therefore, be a serious matter for any candid Christian to pass a wholesale criticism or condemnation upon such movements or presume to 'limit the Holy One of Israel.'"—C&MA Annual Report, 1907-1908.

***Praise for Lifting to the Pentecostal Plain.*** "We praise Him for a clearer vision and conception of a Pentecostal plain to which His church is being lifted. . . . Praise God for the 'Latter Rain' Pentecost with signs and wonders following."—S.W. Gerow, C&MA pastor and Tozer's first mentor[545]

***Tozer Both Sympathetic and Critical of Excess.*** "I have known and studied these dear brethren, and have preached to them for a long, long time. I have studied them, and I know them very well, and I am very sympathetic with them. There are some churches that are very sane and beautiful and godly. . . . The movement itself has magnified one single gift above all others, and that one gift is the one Paul said was the least. An unscriptural exhibition of that gift results, and there is a tendency to place personal feeling above the Scriptures, and we must never, never do that!"—A.W. Tozer[546] (Note: Tozer's mother-in-law was a Pentecostal who laid hands on him to be baptized in the Spirit.)

***Against Evidence View But Pro-Tongues.*** "Simpson and the Alliance rejected the evidence view, but were hospitable to the tongues movement."—John Sawin, C&MA historian and archivist[547]

*Avoid Sweeping Criticism, for Great Blessing Has Come.* "We regret, however, that the writer makes such sweeping statements in regard to the modern 'tongue' movement. . . . We believe that to many has come great blessing through this movement."—editor of C&MA missions periodical The India Alliance, responding to criticism of the movement[548]

## HOW DO WE DISCERN WHAT IS NOT OF GOD?

*Make the Proper Tests.* "In some 'gifted' circles today, there is an almost total lack of spiritual discernment and a credulity beyond belief. I certainly am not making a blanket condemnation of individuals or churches. But there are some who say, 'We have the gifts of the Spirit. Come and join us!' Before I join a movement, a school of thought, a theological persuasion or a church denomination, I must make the proper tests."—A.W. Tozer[549]

*Tozer's Seven-fold Test to Discern the Source of Religious Experiences.* "By this seven-fold test we may prove everything religious [new doctrine, new religious habit, new view of truth, new spiritual experience] and know beyond a doubt whether it is of God or not. How does it affect:

- Our relation to God, our concept of God and our attitude toward Him?
- If it has made me love God more, has magnified Him in my eyes, has purified my concept of His being and caused Him to appear more wonderful than before, then I may conclude I have not wandered astray . . . into error.
- Our attitude toward the Lord Jesus Christ? . . . He must stand at the center of all true doctrine, all acceptable practice and all genuine Christian experience.
- Our attitude toward the Holy Scriptures? . . . Did this new experience . . . spring out of the Word of God itself or was it the result of some stimulus that lay outside the Bible?
- The self-life? . . . If this experience has served to humble me, . . . it is of God.
- Our relation to and our attitude toward our fellow Christians? . . . Whatever tends to separate us in person or in heart from fellow Christians is not of God, but is of the flesh or the devil.
- Our relation and our attitude toward the world? . . . Any spirit that permits compromise with the world is a false spirit.
- Our attitude toward sin? . . . Anything that weakens hatred of sin may be identified immediately as false to the Scriptures, to the Saviour, and to our own soul."[550]

*Tests of the Word of God and Righteousness.* "The simple test of all these things [miracle workers, divine healers, inward visions and revelations, etc.] is the Word of God [1 John 4:1-3], and the practical test of righteousness and holiness. Let us be prepared for false spirits and let us not fear to try them, for if God is giving us any message or revelation, He will always give us ample time to be quite sure that it is God."—A.B. Simpson[551]

*Does It Bear Witness of Christ?* "The apostle John gives us the supreme test [1 John 4:1-3], and that is the witness these spirits bear to the Lord Jesus Christ. When any spiritual influence makes an end of itself and does not directly lead us forward to the Lord Jesus Christ and to glorify and vivify Him, we have good reason to be doubtful of it. Any spiritual experience that rests chiefly in the experience and in its delightfulness or significance, is very apt to prove another spirit. The Holy Spirit always witnesses to Christ."—A.B. Simpson[552]

*Passivity Opens the Door to Enemy Influence.* "The most deadly enemy of the devout believer is spiritual passivity.... Told that all he has to do is to 'let go and let God,' he becomes quite passive, and takes all that comes to him as the working of the divine will. As a result, he may either lose his faith, or, as many in these days have done, become the victim of false impressions and satanic delusions."—John A. MacMillan[553]

*Danger in Abandonment—The Enemy Will Fill a Vacuum.* "There is a kind of 'abandonment' urged by certain spiritual leaders that would throw our whole being open to any powerful influence and hypnotic control which the enemy might wish to exercise. It is a law of the spiritual world as well as the natural that whenever there is a vacuum there is always some powerful current ready to sweep in and possess it. If, therefore, we leave our mind and will vacant and abandoned without any hand upon the helm it is almost certain that the adversary will take advantage. There are good men and women that have been literally hypnotized by Satan or some of his agents, and with the best intentions in the world have become deceived and deceivers. God has nowhere told us that we are to surrender our personal responsibility and self-control even to the Holy Spirit. When He comes into a human heart He does no violence to the nature which He Himself has given. It works in beautiful harmony with all our faculties; possessing, suggesting, inspiring, enabling and elevating all our being, and yet not dethroning the reason or the will."—A.B. Simpson[554]

*Harsh or Strained Manifestations.* "Someone may speak with tongues in your meeting, and you will feel at once that is not of God. It will be harsh and repelling; your spiritual nature will revolt. Just quietly place your hand upon him and ask God to rebuke the evil spirit, and you will have very little trouble. By this procedure you will keep out all fanaticism, and yet you will not interfere with the genuine gift of the Holy Spirit."—Dr. T. J. McCrossan [555]

"This voice was so gruff and different from the gentle voice of the Holy Spirit that I soon understood it was a temptation from the evil one, and He gave the victory."—Mary B. Mullen[556]

*Inconsistent with the Word of God and Sound Interpretation.* "Never did a soul drift into fanaticism or wildfire who did not, at first, either accept a strained or a perverted interpretation of scripture, or read into certain passages a meaning made impossible by an intelligent comparison with other passages."—May Mabette Anderson[557]

"The only limiting condition is conformity to the Word of God."—A.B. Simpson[558]

*What Is Its Fruit? Does It Bring a Person Closer to God and Encourage Christ-likeness?* ". . . deep humility, earnestness and soberness and free from extravagance and error. . . . marked deepening of the spiritual life . . . and an encouraging increase in their missionary zeal and liberality. . . . The Spirit of Pentecost is the spirit of peace and love and holy unity" —A.B. Simpson[559]

"There is a true and holy supernaturalism which will always be recognized by its humility, self-control, holiness, love and good fruits."—A.B. Simpson[560]

"When any man or set of men draw attention to themselves and their own extraordinary gifts we have good reason to question. The best evidence that any movement is of God is the spirit of modesty and humility."—A.B. Simpson[561]

*Does It Bear Witness with Your Spirit? "Let the peace of God rule your heart" (Col. 3:17).* "You will feel at once that is not of God. It will be harsh and repelling; your spiritual nature will revolt."—Dr. T. J. McCrossan [562]

*Is Jesus Christ being continually confessed as Lord and His Deity and Humanity Upheld (1 Cor. 12:3; 1 John 4:1-3)?* "The saints should test the spirits. Here is God's written method of testing—1 John 4:1, 2, 3. . . . Men and women filled with the Holy Spirit will testify and talk of Christ coming in the flesh, filled with other spirits a damper will fall on the enthusiasm or emotions when His coming in the flesh is spoken of. There is certain safety for this is God's own acid test given to us by Him. This is the proper test to use to find if the spirit is speaking in any person or through any person, is the Holy Spirit or some other speaking spirit."—Paul Rader[563]

"The New Testament warns against the acceptance of what is supernatural without conclusive proof of its authenticity. . . . When some unusual manifestation is seen, it is not to be received without question on the supposition that it must be of the Spirit of God. The Holy Spirit Himself commands that it be definitely tested [1 John 4:1]; to fail to do so is disobedience, and is the source of much disorder in many groups of even sincere servants of the Lord."—John A. MacMillan[564]

**Unconfessed Sin Opens the Door for False Manifestations.** "If people desire to be filled with the Spirit of God, they must first confess their sins and be cleansed by the blood of Jesus. They must confess to other Christians if they have touched any of these abominations which God has forbidden, and they must ask believing ones to set them free before then can invite the Holy Spirit to possess the temple."—Carrie Judd Montgomery[565]

**Exposure to Psychic or Occult Practices, Cults, or Eastern Religions.** "I have noticed that when people who have touched these occult things are in a meeting, the devil will bring forth strange manifestations from them, and then people who have no discernment come in a say, 'If that is Pentecostal power, I do not want it.' Beloved, it is not the power of the Holy Spirit, but it is the evil one trying to counterfeit and seeking to turn people away from the blessed baptism of the Holy Spirit. . . . They must confess to other Christians if they have touched any of these abominations which God has forbidden, and they must ask believing ones to set them free before then can invite the Holy Spirit to possess the temple."—Carrie Judd Montgomery[566]

**Impure Motives—Seeking after an Experience.** "Our own experience in this matter leads us to the conclusion that, wherever people really believe they must speak in tongues to be baptized with the Holy Spirit, a large percentage of all such either speak mere 'gibberish' or a real language, which, however, the Holy Spirit has nothing whatever to do with."—T.J. McCrossan[567]

"There have been many instances where [seeking for] the gift of tongues led the subjects and the audiences in to the wildest excesses and were accompanied with voices and actions more closely resembling wild animals than rational beings, impressing the unprejudiced observers that it was the work of the devil."—A.B. Simpson[568]

*Uncontrollable or Peculiar Manifestations (1 Cor. 14:32-33).* "We discovered that the same manifestations take place in the meetings of spiritualist, were prevailing among us . . . the peculiarity as witnessed in some was their imitations of animal sounds as the dog, coyote, cat and fowl." —Joseph Smale, Baptist pastor writing for the C&MA[569]

"Many of the unintelligible utterances resemble the crowing of roosters and the voices of other animals. The door is thus thrown wide open to fanaticism, and weak minds have been known to break down utterly under the strain."—William T. MacArthur[570]

"Once in a large religious gathering I noticed a quiet, gentle looking lady who seemed to have strange power upon her, and she would go through peculiar motions. I did not know her personally, but God laid her upon my heart, and I felt that she must be delivered from the power of the enemy. . . . We found that she was a Christian, and she seemed to have a very sweet spirit. I said, 'Did you ever touch Spiritualism in any form?'. . . After a little she said, 'Oh, I remember, I had a Spiritual doctor once when I was a young girl.' I replied, 'He had some power over you although you did not know it at the time.'"—Carrie Judd Montgomery[571]

"One night a fellow came down the aisle barking like a dog. . . . That fellow was bound by the devil and barked like a dog."—Paul Rader, C&MA president[572]

*Pain, Depression, a Bad Habit, Temptation or Sin after Manifestation or Laying on Hands.* "I do not hesitate to warn every Christian to beware, and not to receive anointing from every man or woman whom you may meet with; but only from those who are really sanctified. I believe in the transmission of spirits through the laying on of hands, and I believe, from real and sad experience. There is such a thing as the transmission carnal spirits. I have seen and heard of cases in which the evil spirits, instead of being cast out, have come into the persons on whom hands were laid, and subjected them to their influence."—Pastor Schrenck, friend of A.B. Simpson[573]

## How Do We Maintain Balance in Discernment?

*Be Careful about What Manifestations You Criticize.* "Any criticism of the fleshly and Satan workings that obtrude themselves into religious meetings must be well guarded and carefully defined, or the things done by the Holy Spirit may be condemned. . . . Where the power of the Holy Spirit produces demonstrations, they will produce conviction on those who witness them. On the other hand, demonstrations which fail to produce this result are not from God."—W.W. Newberry[574]

***Avoid the Ditches.*** "Let us not fear or ignore any of the gifts and manifestations of the Holy Spirit. . . . At the same time let us not fear to exercise the spirit of discernment. . . ." "Exercise at once a wise conservatism and a readiness of mind to receive whatever God is truly sending. . . . guard . . . against the two extremes of danger. . . . the danger of credulity and fanaticism. . . . the extreme of refusing to recognize any added blessing which the Holy Spirit is bringing to His people in these last days."—A.B. Simpson[575]

"Between the ditches is a broad, safe, and direct route. . . . If one avoids the ditch on either side of the road he can make good time in getting to his destination."—Paris Reidhead[576]

***Maintain Both Openness and Caution.*** "We must have the spirit of candor [openness] as well as the spirit of caution."[577] ". . . the spirit of entire openness to the Holy Spirit, and yet of spiritual sanity and practical holiness and wholesomeness."[578]—A.B. Simpson

***Overcome Misuse by Proper Use, Not Disuse.*** "The best remedy for the abuse of anything is its wise and proper use."—A.B. Simpson[579]

"Never allow the abuse of a doctrine to cancel out its use."—A.W. Tozer[580]

## ADDITIONAL RESOURCES

Anderson, Neil. *Walking in the Light: Discerning God's Guidance in an Age of Spiritual Counterfeits.* Nashville: Thomas Nelson, 1992.

## FOR REFLECTION AND DISCUSSION

1.  Read 1 Thess. 5:19-22. How can you examine everything carefully without quenching the Spirit?
2.  Read 1 John 4:1-3. How can you try the spirits?
3.  How can we discern between the flesh and the Spirit?
4.  How can we discern between flesh and demonic?
5.  How can we discern between what is of the Spirit and what is demonic?

# CHAPTER 12

Spiritual Warfare in the
Spirit-Empowered Life

*For we do not wrestle against flesh and blood, but against principalities,
against powers, against the rulers of the darkness of this age, against spiritual hosts of wickedness in the heavenly places. (Eph. 6:12 NKJV)*

*The nearer we get to the heavenlies, the fiercer the foes. . . .
A life of victory is not a life of freedom from the attacks of the enemy.
He is always ready to spring upon us, and there is no victory without
conflict.*—A.B. Simpson[581]

## DOES THE ALLIANCE BELIEVE AND PRACTICE THE AUTHORITY OF THE BELIEVER?

The Christian and Missionary Alliance actually was on the forefront of pioneer-
ing teaching and practice of the authority of the believer, initially through A.B.
Simpson, George Watson, and other early Alliance leaders C&MA missionary
John MacMillan wrote the original book *The Authority of the Believer*, beginning
with a series of articles in *The Alliance Weekly* in 1932, then compiled with other
material and published as a book.

*Believers Have the Authority of Faith—Luke 10:19.* "He did not promise the
disciples power first, but the authority first; and as they used the authority, the
power would be made manifest, and the results would follow. Faith steps out
to act with the authority of God's Word, seeing no sign of the promised power,
but believing and acting as if it were real. As it speaks the word of authority and
command, and puts its foot without fear upon the head of its conquered foes,
lo, their power is disarmed, and all the forces of the heavenly world are there to
make the victory complete."—A.B. Simpson[582]

*Believers Are God's Law Enforcement Officers.* "'I give you authority.' This is the policeman's badge which makes him mightier than a whole crowd of ruffians because, standing upon his rights, the whole power of the state is behind him. . . . Are we using the authority of the name of Jesus and the faith of God?"—A.B. Simpson[583]

"It is not power that He gives us. We do not have the power. He has the power. But He gives us authority to act as if we had the power, and then He backs it up with His power. It is like the officer of the law stepping out before a mob and acting in the name of the government. His single word is stronger than a thousand men because he has authority, and all the power of the government is behind him. So faith steps out in the name of heaven and expects God to stand by it."—A.B. Simpson[584]

*Believers Have Throne Life Sitting with Christ on the Throne of God.* "This is much more than resurrection. It is ascension. It is taking the place of accomplished victory and conceded right, and sitting down in an attitude of completed repose, from henceforth expecting with Him until all our enemies be made our footstool. . . . It is throne life. It is dwelling with Christ on high, your head in the heaven even while your feet still walk the paths of the lower world of sense and time. This is our high privilege."—A.B. Simpson[585]

*Believers Have Throne Rights Through Throne Union.* ". . . asserting in prayer the power of the Ascended Lord, and the believer's throne union with Him. . . . Where in faith the obedient saint claims his throne-rights in Christ, and boldly asserts his authority, the powers of the air will recognize and obey."—John MacMillan[586]

*Like Moses, Our Hands (with Christ's Hands) Are on the Throne.* "Because of the hand that was on the throne, that is, because the hands of Moses were held up in prayer [Exodus 17], and those hands were laid on the throne of Jehovah and prevailed with God in getting the victory. . . . It is because the hands of the man Christ Jesus are on the throne that His prayer prevails, and through Him we lift up our hands and place them on the same throne, that we may prevail against all our enemies. . . . And when we, like Moses, lift up our hands and through Jesus lay them on the throne of grace, it is then we gain the day, . . . the Amalekites were conquered because the hands of a man were upon the throne."—George Watson, Simpson associate, C&MA convention speaker[587]

*When Our Hand of Faith Is on the Throne, It Is God's Battle, Not Ours.* "Remember in that marvelous story how Joshua fought in the plain below and

Moses stood with uplifted hands on the mount, and while the hands of Moses were uplifted, Israel prevailed. When the hands of Moses fell, Amalek prevailed. And when it was all over, we read, 'Because the hand is upon the throne of the Lord, therefore the Lord will have war with Amalek from generation to generation.' The hand of Moses on the throne puts the battle in the hands of God and not on Joshua. Moses is touching the button; Moses is communicating with the sources of infinite power; Moses is using the throne of God; Moses is using the omnipotence of heaven, and Israel must prevail. As long as the hand of faith is on the throne of the Lord, it will be the Lord's battle and not ours. The Lord will do the fighting, power will come, and from generation to generation it will be His victory, and you will just have to stand at attention and obedience and see Him triumph."—A.B. Simpson[588]

*Reigning with Christ, We Wield the Rod of Authority.* "The rod [of Moses] symbolizes the authority of God committed to human hands [Exodus 17]. By it the holder is made a co-ruler with his Lord, sharing His throne-power and reigning with Him. . . . So today, every consecrated hand that lifts the rod of the authority of the Lord against the unseen powers of darkness is directing the throne-power of Christ against Satan and his hosts in a battle that will last until 'the going down of the sun.'"—John MacMillan[589]

*All Things Are Under Our Feet as Christ's Body (Eph. 1:20-23).* "'He has put all things under his feet.' The feet are members of the Body. How wonderful to think that the least and lowest members of the Body of the Lord, those who in a sense are the very soles of the feet, are far above all the mighty forces."—John MacMillan[590]

*Throne Life Overcomes, Rather Than Escapes, Satan's Power.* "'Throne Life'. . . implies a position of advantage over enemies. . . a Scriptural view authorizes the belief that such a victorious position is provided for the Christian over his spiritual enemies. . . . by our authorized faith, triumphing over principalities and powers. . . . The adventuring believer . . . fully estimates the difference between *escaping* from Satan's power, and *overcoming* his power."—George B. Peck, early Alliance Vice President[591]

*We Lack More Power Because We Do Not Claim Our Authority.* "This was the secret of Christ's power that He spoke with authority, prayed with authority, commanded with authority, and the power followed. The reason we do not see more power is because we do not claim the authority Christ has given us. The adversary has no power over us if we do not fear him, but the moment we acknowledge his power, he becomes all that we believe him to be. He is only a braggart if we will dare to defy him, but our unbelief clothes him with an omnipotence he does not rightly possess. God has given us the right to claim deliverance over all his attacks, but we must step out and put our foot upon his neck as Joshua taught the children of Israel to put their feet upon the necks of the conquered Canaanites, and faith will find our adversaries as weak as we believe them to be. Let us claim the authority and the victory of faith for all that Christ has purchased and promised for our bodies, our spirits, or His work."—A.B. Simpson[592]

## How Do We Exercise the Authority of the Believer?

*Speak to the Mountain with Commanding Faith.* "The command of faith is the divine means of removing [mountains] out of the way: 'Ye shall say to this mountain, Be thou removed and be thou cast into the sea; and it shall obey you.' The question involved is not that of an imposing faith, but that of an all-sufficient Name. . . . As he speaks to the mountain in the name of Christ, he puts his hand on the dynamic force that controls the universe. Heavenly energy is released, and his behest is obeyed."—John MacMillan[593]

"It is a good exercise to '*say*' aloud to our difficulties, as we kneel in prayer, 'Be thou removed.' The *saying*, if in faith in the name of the Lord, will cause a stirring at the roots; and as we keep steadfastly holding to God and *saying*, the time will come when the tree which has been opposing, or the mountain which has been hindering, will quietly more into the sea of oblivion."—John MacMillan[594]

## Is Binding and Loosing a Valid Practice for Believers Today?

*The Church Can Bind and Loose and Hasten the Kingdom of God.* "Grant especially, blessed Lord, that your Church might believe that it is by the power of united prayer that she can bind and loose in heaven, cast out Satan, save souls, remove mountains, and hasten the coming of the kingdom."—Andrew Murray[595]

*We Can Bind and Loose Like Elijah.* "Men, as God's mouthpieces, vary in value; not according to their ability, but according to the measure of their entire surrender. There are times, even today, when, like Elijah, we may say: 'There shall not . . . according to my word'—when our hearts, in full comprehension of God, bind and loose in definite power."—John MacMillan[596]

*Bind the Strong Man or He Will Bind Us.* "The way out is blocked—is it not a gracious call to prayer, lest the great adversary block our efforts and shut us up in a small place? We have prayed for the binding of the strongman—we must watch and pray that the strong man does not bind us."—John MacMillan[597]

**Bind Spiritual Forces, Not People.** "The authority committed to the believer is over the powers of the air and never over his fellowmen or their wills. He is called to bind the unseen forces, but to deliver his brethren."—John Mac-Millan[598]

## Who Can Exercise the Authority of the Believer?

**Available as the Right of Every Believer.** "Such authority is not the property only of a few elect souls. On the contrary, it is the possession of every true child of God. It is one of the 'all things' received in Christ."—John A. MacMillan[599]

"The weakest and the most unlettered saint is able by the cross and its conquest of the powers of hell to drive the fiercest 'bulls of Bashan' (Ps. 22:12) in headlong flight."—John A. MacMillan[600]

**Effective Only When Consecrated.** "The authority of Jesus' name cannot be efficacious in the mouth of an unspiritual disciple."—John MacMillan[601]

"Every *consecrated hand* that lifts up the rod of authority of the Lord against the unseen powers of darkness is directing the throne power of Christ against Satan and his hosts."—John MacMillan[602]

**Those Who Exercise It Humbly as Servants of God.** "So Jesus says, when you as servants have done all those things which are commanded you; when you have uprooted trees, removed mountains, healed the sick, led multitudes to salvation—remember that you are still servants of God. What you have done is simply what He has endued you with power to do, and what you have engaged to do for Him. You have not done aught of yourselves—all has been of His working."—John A. MacMillan[603]

**Those Who Abide under the Shadow of the Almighty.** "In this supreme ministry of the son of God for lost men there was secured for those who believe Him and abide in Him a sharing in the fulness which He received as Son of man (Col. 2:9), and which makes them partakers of His authority and sharers in His kingdom. Before such overcomers the hosts of hell give way, and the utmost energy of the unseen world cannot harm them as they dwell 'in the secret place of the Most High,' and 'abide under the shadow of the Almighty.'. . . In the case of every obedient believer who today fulfils the conditions, God stands waiting to show him His victory."—John A. MacMillan[604]

## WHAT DOES THE ALLIANCE BELIEVE ABOUT GENERATIONAL SIN AND CURSES?

*Sin May Bring a "Hereditary Cloud" of Sickness and Death.* "Reuben's shameful crime . . . had left an hereditary cloud upon the tribe. . . in the brief history of the wilderness the numbers of the tribe greatly diminished, so that it may have seemed to many of them that there was a serious danger of their extinction."—A.B. Simpson[605]

*A Principle of Heredity.* "'*Visiting the iniquities of the fathers upon the children*' [Exod. 20:5]. The principle of heredity is involved here. . . . Because of sin, the sinner entails to his offspring sometimes a weakened body, always a tendency to worldliness and departure from God. . . . Grace is shown in that the curse runs out in the third and fourth generation, unless persisted in."—John MacMillan[606]

*Inheriting the Craving.* "Desire for drink may be hereditary. A young man once confessed to me that he had inherited the craving from his father."—John MacMillan[607]

*Transmission of Generational Vulnerabilities—An Inexorable Law of Return and Increase.* "He that sows shall reap. . . . It is true of both the natural and spiritual harvests—it is an eternal principle of the nature of God . . . . an inexorable law of return and of increase."—John MacMillan[608]

*Our Sins Do Not Die with Ourselves.* "Nor does it end with himself; the drunkard transmits a poisoned frame to his offspring; the loose woman has a daughter who is hurrying in the ways of shame. Our sins do not die with ourselves; they scatter themselves over the society about us like the winged seeds of the thistle and the dandelion, impossible to catch, settling down in choice places to reproduce their kind."—John MacMillan[609]

*The Law of Sowing and Reaping Continues Down the Chain.* "Sin may be forgiven but the law of sowing and reaping is not canceled. Cause and effect follow and the link in the chain may not run out for years."—Harold J. Sutton, C&MA pastor[610]

"Suffering, no doubt, in a great many cases is hereditary. God gave Moses the words of the Decalogue, He added the following clause to the second commandment: 'I the Lord thy God am a jealous God, visiting the iniquity of the fathers upon the children unto the third and fourth generation of them that hate me.' As a warning, this statement is repeated frequently in the Scriptures. There is an organic bond between a parent and child through which the offspring often reaps the terrible harvest of the sins of parents and even remote ancestors, as well as in other cases they inherit the temporal and eternal blessings of godly, praying ancestors."—C.H. Brunner, C&MA pastor[611]

**Demonic Holds Have Roots in Family History.** "Breaking family curses was not a concept articulated in those words in the 1950s; but John MacMillan felt strongly that demonic hold on some had its roots in family history, in spiritism, occult, drugs, etc, and referenced the Old Testament Scripture that speaks to the iniquity of the fathers being visited on the children."—Chaplain Jay Smith, on John MacMillan' ministry[612]

## How Can Generational Bondages Be Broken?

**Surrender All to God.** "God is not concerned about your appetite for drink. He can take that away in an instant. What He seeks is the surrender of your life to Him. If you will do that, He will give you the victory."—John MacMillan[613]

**Speak Forth a Blessing.** "The blessing of Moses seems to suggest this danger and to answer this fear. 'Let Reuben live and not die, and let not his men be few' (Exod. 30:6)."—A.B. Simpson[614]

**Declare That We are Redeemed from the Curse of the Law—Galatians 3:13.** "In Gal. 3:13 we read: 'Christ has redeemed us from the curse of the law, being made a curse for us.'. . . Tell me the name of your disease and I will tell you one from which you have been redeemed and can be healed."—F.F. Bosworth[615]

"Of course we know that it was a far-reaching and eternal curse, but it was also a temporal curse. . . . Therefore, it is perfectly scriptural to say Christ has redeemed us from consumption, fever, inflammation, having been made curse for us."—A.B. Simpson[616]

**Actively Refuse and Take Back Ground, Not Passively Acquiescing.** "We must also cooperate with Him—against the things and the forces which assail our individual lives with a faithful and firm refusal of their right to control our bodies or our circumstances. Too often the Christian passively accepts whatever comes to him as being the will of the Lord, yielding without resistance at times to the wiles of the enemy himself. . . . That 'God hath spoken' is the ground upon which every forward step in the spiritual life must be taken."—John A. MacMillan[617]

"Positively resisting the devil and refusing what comes to us from him."—John A. MacMillan[618]

*Rebuke the Enemy Yourself.* "God throws upon man the responsibility for the continuation of the conditions we question. . . . We realize they are the working of the enemy. We cry to God to rebuke the enemy and to alter things. Through the teaching of the Word, He replies, 'My children, rebuke the enemy yourselves. The authority over him is yours. Its responsibility I have committed to you."—John A. MacMillan[619]

## What Does the Alliance Believe about Demons and Deliverance Ministry?

*Deliverance from Demons and Healing Go Hand-in Hand.* "Deliverance from demons stands right along side divine healing and stands or falls with it."—A.B. Simpson[620]

"This intimate association of the exorcism of evil spirits and of the healing of sicknesses is likewise the outstanding feature of apostolic ministry."—William C. Stevens[621]

*The Alliance Was on the Forefront.* "The C&MA was on the forefront of dealing with the demonic because of John MacMillan."—Dr. John Ellenberger, Alliance Theological Seminary professor and C&MA missionary[622]

*Worship and Emotion May Be of the Holy Spirit, the Human Spirit, or an Evil Spirit.* "The heart of man is like a musical instrument and may be played upon by the Holy Spirit, by an evil spirit or by the spirit of man himself. Religious emotions are very much the same, no matter who the player may be. Many enjoyable feelings may be aroused within the soul by low or even idolatrous worship."—A.W. Tozer[623]

## What Does the Alliance Believe about Territorial Spirits?

The spiritual warfare movement of the last decade of the 20th century and early 21st century in the charismatic and Third Wave movements has emphasized doing warfare with principalities and powers, spirits that exercise power over a geographical region or territory. The C&MA became pioneers in teaching an embryonic form of the concept of territorial spirits, especially through the Alliance missions in China in the 1920s.

*There Are Princes over Many Lands and Cultures Today.* "There are veritable princes of darkness who, under Satan, hold dominion over these lands of earth where the Gospel message has never been given. The missionary who goes 'over the top' and enters them will surely meet with these princes of darkness who are appointed by Satan. There was a 'Prince of Persia' and a 'Prince of Greece' in Daniel's day, against whom 'God's chief princes' fought (Dan. 10). There is today a Prince of Tibet, of Afghanistan, of Cambodia, of Arabia, of Mohammedanism, of Bolshevism, who are prepared to defend their lands and the people who are under their dominion against the message of the Gospel. But thank God, we go forth at the command of One who is infinitely greater than all the princes of darkness."—Robert Jaffray[624]

"The "principalities" [of Ephesians 6:12] are satanic princes, angels whose principalities cover the countries of this world."—John MacMillan[625]

*The Prince of the Kingdom of China Must Be Overcome.* "We felt that the principalities and powers in the air and the prince of the kingdom of China himself, were hindering [revival], and must be overcome.... We gave ourselves to prayer and through prayer we overcame.... On the tenth day, ... the Spirit manifested Himself in power in our midst all over the house, reaching the hearts of the men as well as the women. There was quiet weeping and confessing of sins all through the audience... Over 700 people ... [were] inquiring more fully about the way of salvation.... The forces of evil were scattered."[626]—Mrs. L. L. Hess, Alliance missionary in South China

*Roll Back the Powers of the Air.* "We need prayer helpers ... to roll back the powers of the air, and make it possible to bring the Truth to bear on these regions where the devil is blocking the way."—John MacMillan[627]

*Every God Is Confined to Territorial Limits.* "Every god is confined to definite territorial limits, outside of which his influence does not extend."—John MacMillan[628]

*Pray Geographically—Breaking Down Satanic Barriers.* "There is among the saints of the Most High a chosen group—perhaps larger than we think—whose divinely appointed ministry is that of the prayer closet. There, on their knees with a world map before them, its members individually and methodically pray out the problems of the advance of the kingdom. They precede missionaries into areas where Christ has not been named; they observe them as they attack firmly-placed barriers, breaking down by the high explosive of authoritative prayer the Satanic opposition that continues impedes the forward progress of the gospel. Because the working of the Spirit of God is everywhere, working through some mysterious law, dependent on intercession, these unseen workers are the real pioneers of Christian missions. Unknown to themselves their word in the heavenlies is mighty through God to the overthrowing of principalities and powers. National boundaries are melting down before the faith and fervor of their supplications."—John MacMillan[629]

## WHAT ARE THE DANGERS OF WARFARE WITH TERRITORIAL SPIRITS?

*It Is Perilous without Close Abiding with God.* "It is also a service of peculiar peril to those involved. For the enemy strikes with malignant vigor and keen knowledge at every opportunity. True geographic prayer ministry needs close abiding in God."—John A. MacMillan[630]

*Keen Spiritual Discernment Is Crucial.* "The watcher, whose heart and mind are trained in spiritual observation, can discern constant shifting of the lines of combat, which is not obvious to others."—John A. MacMillan[631]

*Beware of Presumption and Overstepping Your Authority.* "In the world's long history, one Man only, with the unmeasured unction of the Holy Spirit upon Him, has been able to say, 'All authority hath been given unto me in heaven and in earth.'"[632]

Note: Alliance leaders advocated *praying against* territorial powers, but *not commanding* them directly as do some today in the strategic spiritual warfare movement. That would be considered in the realm of presumption and over-stepping our authority as a believer. On the dangers of inappropriately battling territorial spirits, see John Paul Jackson, *Needless Casualties of War* (North Sutton, NH: Streams Publications, 1999); Clinton E. Arnold, *3 Crucial Questions about Spiritual Warfare* (Grand Rapids: Baker Books, 1997), pp. 143-199; K. Neill Foster with Paul L. King, *Binding and Loosing* (Camp Hill, PA: Christian Publications, 1998), pp. 249-264.

## CAN A CHRISTIAN BE DEMONIZED?

*Soul or Body May Be Occupied By Demons—But Not a Believer's Human Spirit.* "Being born again of the Spirit means that the Holy Spirit dwells in the human spirit. This does not guarantee that a child of God may not be attacked and indwelt by an evil spirit in soul or body. . . . According to Scripture the believer is the temple of the Holy Spirit (2 Cor. 6:16). The Holy Spirit inhabits the holy of holies, which no evil spirit can enter. The holy place, which corresponds to the soul, and the outer court, to the body, are subject to occupation by a foreign spirit."—Dr. V. Raymond Edman, editor, *The Alliance Witness*, president of Wheaton College[633]

*But Christians Cannot Be "Possessed," i.e., " Owned" by Demons.* "It is a serious mistake to say that Satan possesses any child of God."—William T. MacArthur[634]

Note: Some early Alliance leaders used the ancient and archaic language of "possession" as used in the King James Version of the Bible, but they did not mean that a Christian can be owned by a demon, only controlled by a demon.

*Varying Degrees of Demon Presence and Power.* "Demon presence and power in a person's life and being is by no means confined to the actual and entire surrender of the inmost personality to the demon's abode and sway.... More generally demonism in a life does not preclude salvation, although sometimes exorcism is necessary before salvation can take place, and often demonism is found in the experiences of saved one without the loss of fellowship with Christ. There is a very wide range of demon presence and power which, in manifold ways and degrees, involves the brain, the senses, and the bodily members and functions. Very many conditions commonly viewed as disease are not such and cannot be dealt with as such, at least without first casting out the spirit directly producing and lodged in those symptoms."—William C. Stevens[635]

*Early Alliance Leader Attacked by Demons.* Significantly, a major Alliance leader found himself attacked by demons. Dr. George Peck, one of the Vice Presidents of the Alliance, and his fellow C&MA friend and colleague, C. W. Morehouse, both had earlier been praying for greater power to heal and cast out demons. Being relatively new in the art of spiritual warfare and not realizing the scope of what they were taking on, Peck himself was attacked by demonic forces. In January 1890, he became severely ill with pneumonia, accompanied by insanity and demonic manifestations. Morehouse prayed for his healing and cast out the demons. As a result, Peck launched into a greater ministry, devoting most of his time to healing and deliverance.[636]

*Christian Woman Afflicted with Demons at Nyack Convention.* During the July 1903 Nyack Convention. Toward the end of the altar ministry led by Minnie Draper, "suddenly the working of demons appeared in a dear and devoted sister." She had a partial deliverance earlier, but this session took about four hours for total deliverance and full victory.[637]

*Demonization of a Christian Through Occult Involvement.* "Contact with Spiritism, often in entire ignorance of the danger, is a frequent cause of possession. In one instance a Christian girl, whose mother to whom she was greatly attached had passed away, was told that it was possible to contact the spirit of the mother by means of a medium. Not aware of the evil of such approach, she was soon entangled in the mysteries of the séance. Before long the medium, realizing that the young woman had an unusual degree of psychic attainment, invited her to join her in the work of benefiting humanity in which she was herself engaged. The invitation was accepted, and soon the young woman became, unwittingly to herself, quite under the power of the spirits.

Still unconscious of the fact that they controlled her, she entered a well-known Bible school. There, under spiritual influences, she began to realize that something was wrong with her. She confided in the wife of one of the faculty, and it was not long until her condition became known. At once steps were taken for her deliverance. Over a period of three months some thirty-three demons were expelled, and she was delivered."—John MacMillan [638]

*Transmission of Unclean Spirits.* "About the laying on of hands by those who are not themselves sanctified. I see great danger in this; and in faithfulness to my Lord and to the Church of God, I do not hesitate to warn every Christian to beware, and to not receive anointing from every man or woman whom you may meet with, but only from those who are really sanctified.

I believe in the transmission of spirits through the laying on of hands, and I believe, from real and sad experience. There is such a thing as the transmission of carnal spirits. I have seen and heard of cases in which the evil spirits, instead of being cast out, have come into the persons on whom hands were laid, and subjected them to their influence. We should be very careful, dear friends, ands to whom we choose to lay on hands, and let us be careful how we do it ourselves. Let each ask the Lord 'Am I sanctified, am I the person who is the fit instrument in Thy hands? Am I a channel though whom the Holy Spirit can convey a real, lasting, eternal blessing to others, so that those whom I anoint with oil, and upon whom I lay hands in Thy name, may receive the Holy Spirit?'"—Pastor Schrenck, friend of A.B. Simpson[639]

## BUT ISN'T SUPPOSED DEMONIZATION REALLY JUST INSANITY?

*Some Appearances of Insanity Are Really Demonic.* "Having met the insane frequently, . . . I can detect the symptoms [of insanity or demons] more quickly that most people, and I do hereby testify that I found no trace of insanity, or lack of mental poise in either of these cases [of demonization]."—William T. MacArthur[640]

*Torments of Body and Mind Need the Gift of Discernment.* "Very common are vexing conditions of body and of mind, and torments of body and mind; and it is noticeable that just such conditions are attributed in Scripture to demoniacal presence and afflictions. Yet such explicit rules of diagnosis are not given as to dispense with the need of the Spirit's gifts of discernment."—William C. Stevens[641]

## How Should We Regard the Demonic?

*Be Christ-Conscious, Not Devil-Conscious.* "I know Christians so engrossed with the fight against evil spirits that they are in a state of constant turmoil. Their touching effort to hold the devil at bay exhausts them nervously and physically, and they manage to stay alive only by frantically calling on God and rebuking the devil in the name of Christ. These are innocent spiritists in reverse and are devil-conscious to a point of being borderline neurotics. They grow sensitive and suspicious and always manage to locate an evil spirit as the cause back of everything that irritates them; then their hackles stand straight up and they begin to order the devil about in a loud voice, but their nervous gestures tell how deeply frightened they are. . . .

The scriptural way to see things is to set the Lord always before us, put Christ in the center of our vision, and if Satan is lurking around he will appear on the margin only and be seen as but a shadow on the edge of the brightness. . . .The best way to keep the enemy out is to keep Christ in. The sheep need not be terrified by the wolf; they have but to stay close to the shepherd. It is not the praying sheep Satan fears but the presence of the shepherd.

The instructed Christian whose faculties have been developed by the Word and the Spirit will not fear the devil. When necessary he will stand against the powers of darkness and overcome them by the blood of the Lamb and the word of his testimony. He will recognize the peril in which he lives and will know what to do about it, but he will practice the presence of God and never allow himself to become devil-conscious."—A.W. Tozer[642]

## What Are Some Examples of Deliverance Ministry in the Alliance?

*Ethan O. Allen—Pioneer of Alliance Deliverance Ministry.* Referring to Genesis 3:15 and Luke 10:19, Allen wrote a tract entitled "Satan Under Your Feet." He operated in the gift of discernment of spirits, and often practiced rebuking, binding the strong man, or "words of castin' out" evil spirits before praying for the sick. He followed what he called the "Old Commission," the words of Jesus in Mark 16:17-18. A.B. Simpson held him in high respect and called him the "Father of Divine Healing" in America.[643]

"Ethan Allen once encountered difficulty in casting a demon out of a person. At last he said the demon might go into his pig if it would leave. When he reached home his wife told him that his pig was acting very strangely. Mr. Allen said,

'Oh, I told that demon that he could go into my pig, but I did not say he could stay there.' And going to the pen, he delivered the pig from its oppressor."—recounted by William T. MacArthur and John MacMillan[644]

***Deliverance Ministry by William T. MacArthur.*** Ethan O. Allen prophesied to MacArthur in the 1890s, "Young man, you look like somebody the Lord could use in castin' out devils." [645] His prophecy came true, as MacArthur did indeed engage in deliverance ministry through the years, on at least one occasion teaming up with Simpson in 1912.[646] Here is one example:

"The child was, to all appearance, in constant pain, especially at night. For months the mother had been broken of her rest and deprived of the means of grace, for the child would cry constantly in church. It had not grown nor increased in weight for fully eight months. The mother, now a believer, had called for the elders and requested that the child be anointed according James 5. I therefore took another brother with me, but had just kneeled to pray when the conviction seized me that there was no disease present, but simply an evil spirit. I told the mother how I felt, and suggested that we exorcise the demon instead of anointing. . . . She consented and we all three united in rebuking, while the child began to scream and struggle desperately. . . . Demons will make a desperate resistance when they are rebuked with authority. . . . The child had been . . . doing well ever since."—William T. MacArthur [647]

***Deliverance Ministry by A.B. Simpson for a Christian Woman.*** "The fire fairly flashed from Mr. Simpson's eyes as he said, 'Salvation for devils? Oh, no, hell is the place for him, let us pray.' We three kneeled, while Mr. Simpson led in prayer. . . . He became more and more intense until he burst out in a verbatim quotation from Genesis 19 where the destroying angels said to Lot, 'Escape for thy life, look not behind the, neither stay thou in all the plain.' When he had reached these words the young woman leaped to her feet and sprang like a frightened doe in to a corner of the room."—William T. MacArthur[648]

***Deliverance Ministry by Carrie Judd Montgomery.*** "As I cried to God He showed me that I had sinned, and opened the way for the enemy to have power over my body. . . . I asked [Mrs. Montgomery] to cast out the demons which were tormenting me, and to pray to God to heal me. . . . There was a conflict in my body as if another being was struggling within, but after a definite command in the almighty Name of Jesus, I was delivered. I heard heavenly anthems . . . with a conscious presence of the Holy Spirit. Perfect healing came to my pain-racked body."—recounted by Mrs. Frances Kies[649]

*Deliverance Ministry by Paul Rader.* "One night a fellow came down the aisle barking like a dog. 'What do you do in a case like this?' I was asked. 'Prayer,' I answered, 'It is the same old dose.' That fellow was bound by the devil and barked like a dog. He is now filled with the joy of Jesus and has a hallelujah on his lips, living for Jesus, and walking with Jesus."—Paul Rader, C&MA president, 1919-1924[650]

*Deliverance Ministry by John A. MacMillan.* "At the age of 78, John MacMillan, with the aid of others, engaged in intensive multiple deliverance session, over a three-month period expelling 171 demons from a young woman. The woman had become infested by the dark powers through living with an aunt who had practiced spiritualism. The spirits manifested violently, trying to harm her or others. Procuring her freedom entailed a long and arduous process, but step-by-step through the name and blood of Jesus, she gained total victory. On one occasion, when he walked into the room, an evil spirit manifested, addressing MacMillan in a male voice through the woman's lips, 'I know you from the Philippines.' The demon recognized MacMillan from an encounter about 25 years earlier thousands of miles away on the other side of the globe. Evidently, he had gained a reputation in the spirit world for his exercise of spiritual authority. On this occasion, MacMillan, in his characteristic quiet manner, commanded the spirit to be silent, and in the name of Jesus expelled it from the woman immediately."—from the book *Moving Mountains*[651]

## ADDITIONAL RESOURCES

Arnold, Clinton E. *3 Crucial Questions about Spiritual Warfare.* Grand Rapids: Baker Books, 1997.

Foster K. Neill, with Paul L. King. *Binding and Loosing.* Camp Hill, PA: Christian Publications/ Wingspread, 1998).

King, Paul L. *A Believer with Authority: The Life and Message of John A. MacMillan.* Camp Hill, PA: Christian Publications, 2001.

MacMillan, John. *The Authority of the Believer.* Camp Hill, PA: Christian Publications, 1997.

## FOR REFLECTION AND DISCUSSION

1. Read Ephesians 1:19-23; 2:5-6. What is throne life and throne power?

2. Read John 1:12; Luke 10:19, Ephesians 1:19-23; 2:5-6. How can you exercise the authority of the believer?

3. Read Matthew 12:28-29; 16:18-19; 18:18-20. What does it mean to bind and loose? When is it appropriate?

4. Have you experienced excessive fear, depression, anger, addictions or hindrances to ministry? Do you think evil spirits may be harassing you? How can you overcome?

5. Read Exodus 20:5. What does it mean for the iniquities of the parents to be visited upon the generations? Are you aware of any generational bondage in your family? How can you or your family members be set free?

6. How can you be alert to the realities of spiritual warfare and the demonic without becoming devil conscious?

# CHAPTER 13

# Is There Something More? The Heights and Depths of the Spirit-Empowered Life

## I HAVE ALREADY BEEN FILLED WITH THE SPIRIT— WHY DO I NEED SOMETHING MORE?

*Our Past Filling Is a Foretaste of More to Come.* "When a young girl . . . a power to testify came into my soul, and the Word of God was wonderfully opened to me. . . . This experience I have always referred to as the baptism of the Holy Spirit until a few months ago, when I began to watch what God was doing in pouring out His Pentecostal fulness upon some of His little ones. At first I was perplexed. I knew my experience, above referred to, was real and lasting in its effects. How could I cast it away? Then I came to understand that I was not to depreciate His precious work in the past, but to follow on to receive the fulness of the same Spirit. Before Pentecost, Jesus 'breathed' on His disciples and said unto them 'Receive ye the Holy Spirit' (John 20:22). I believe they then received a foretaste, or earnest, of what they afterwards received in fulness, at Pentecost."—Carrie Judd Montgomery[652]

*There Are Deeper and Higher Chambers in God's House.* "When you enter a house you enter the several rooms in order, and you must pass from chamber to chamber. It is so in the deeper experiences of the Christian life. You come into the vestibule then you pass on to all the apartments until at last you reach the observatory at the top, but you don't get there the first step."—A.B. Simpson[653]

*We Need a Total Immersion—Including Our Head.* "Every time I would get alone in prayer . . . the showers would come down and all my being was filled with God, excepting that the top of my brain didn't get under. What was the matter? I thought I had to superintend the job. . . . Although God has blessed me all these years, I have been deprived for many years of the fullness of blessing through that very thing. . . . I said . . . 'if God ever gives it to me again I will be sure it is baptism by immersion. I will be sure my head goes under.'. . when Mr. Simpson literally baptized me in the Atlantic Ocean . . . I said, 'If my head begins to pop up, stick it under,' and that was the way I felt about the Spirit's baptism. . . One day I was praising Him and . . . my head went under. It was delightful! It was wonderful! The cry in my heart became satisfied, and I have been satisfied ever since."—Carrie Judd Montgomery[654]

*Greater Authentication of Earlier Empowerment.* "Sometime afterwards I asked my precious Lord what the difference was between the unction on my head and the remarkable power manifested at Beulah Park, Ohio [speaking in tongues]. He graciously replied: 'The power was your enduement; the latter I authenticated it.' I said, 'All right, Lord; I am satisfied.' Yes, I am satisfied—not with myself—but with my exalted and glorified and condescending Master, the Lord Jesus Christ, and can exclaim with Thomas, 'My Lord and My God.'"—John Salmon, C&MA Vice President[655]

*Go On to Receive the Rest of the Oil (Anointing).* "This [Pentecostal baptism] was like the 'residue of the oil' (Leviticus 14:18, 25) that flowed down upon the hem of Aaron's robe, and that God was doing this thing for all who would receive."—Mrs. William T. MacArthur[656]

*God Has More to Give—The Experience of Rev. & Mrs. Daniel W. Kerr.* "But," mother parried with her [Mrs. William T. MacArthur], "we have had the Holy Spirit, God has used us all these years, and I don't know why we should expect to receive anything more."

Just then someone came running into the hotel parlor, and said, "Mrs. Kerr, do you know your husband has gone into the prayer room? And God is filling him with the Holy Spirit!" . . . . So now she arose to the occasion, and ran over to the place of prayer, as she put it, "to see that my husband is not going to receive something he should not have."

Into the prayer room she went, with a somewhat belligerent spirit, but feeling the presence of God, she at least got down on her knees, and spreading her fingers over her face, she "watched and prayed." Rev. Whiteside . . . was in charge of the prayer room that night. Noticing my mother, he came to her and said, "Sister Kerr, this is holy ground. You are filled with fear. Get down to real prayer or get out."

In a moment, as she tells it, she felt as though she were handcuffed and held by a force stronger than herself, and she began to cry out to God to forgive her, and to seek Him with all her heart. By two o'clock in the morning, both father and mother side by side, came through to a beautiful baptism of the Holy Spirit, speaking and singing in other languages, as the Spirit gave them utterance.[657]—the experience of Rev. and Mrs. D.W. Kerr, C&MA pastor and wife, as recounted by the Kerr's daughter.

*After Baptism Comes Fullness.* "Glorious, however, as is the reception of the Spirit, it is not the climax of spiritual life. It is only a unique crisis, which marks a new beginning in Christian experience. After the baptism comes the fullness of the Spirit. . . . The fullness of the Spirit marks an advance upon the baptism of the Spirit. . . . It is not an act, but a process. It is not a transaction, but a habit. Having received Christ (act), we grow up into Him in all things (process). Having received the Holy Spirit (transaction), we drink, and keep drinking of His fullness (habit)."—George P. Pardington[658]

*Some Receive Incomplete Effusions.* "Who dare say that the possibilities are exhausted, where miracles are ignored, even deplored? Will anyone assume to say that 'the precious fruit of the earth,' for which 'the gardener waits' in these last days, will be ripened by incomplete effusions of the Holy Spirit, namely, by effusions that leave out of sight those demonstrations which marked 'the early rain,' demonstrations of gifts and powers in the Spirit, which belong to Him in the church permanently?"—William C. Stevens[659]

*Latter Rain Fullness—Enlarging and Expanding Our Enduement.* "We do not need to discredit our past spiritual experiences because we have not yet entered into God's deeper revelations and manifestations. . . . Let us next carefully inquire what is the distinction between this next experience and the baptism of the Spirit. In a very important sense it is simply the enlarging, expanding and completing of that which has already begun. The later experience may be called an enduement, or clothing upon, with divine power. The Spirit on us describes the yet higher manifestation of God in clothing us with power from on high for special ministry in the kingdom."—A.B. Simpson[660]

*There Are Second Pentecosts Lifting Us to a Higher Plane.* "It is not so much a perpetual fullness as a perpetual filling. There are periodic experiences of spiritual elevation that are part of God's plan for our life in Christ and are designed, no doubt, to lift us to a higher plane of abiding in Him. There are the Pentecosts and the second Pentecosts."—A.B. Simpson[661]

*Jesus Promised We Would Do Greater Works.* "Truly, Truly, I say unto you, he that believes on me, the works that I do shall he do also, and greater works than these shall he do because I go to the Father (John 14:12)."

"This is perhaps the most encouraging promise of all the promises of our Lord as regards works of power. This is a promise of, let it be noted, of works, the *same* works. We must understand this to mean the same kind of works that Jesus did, only greater than those which He performed. . . . We have such power manifested in the person of Peter that the sick were carried to the streets in order that His shadow might fall across them, and heal their diseases. Wonderful works of power were manifested in Jesus Christ Himself, but nothing so great as this is recorded." —William T. MacArthur[662]

***Don't Let Abuse of the Spectacular Keep You from the Greater Works.*** "What a striking contrast is presented by the charlatans and pretenders of our own day, who, like the sons of Sceva, have attempted to perform theses 'greater works' of Jesus! . . . God deliver us from these shallow pretenses which only emphasize the pretender himself and serve to gratify his love for admiration, or in some case, his love for money. . . . But let none of these things deter us in our pursuit of the greater works. Let not the unbelief of the indifferent or the pretensions of the ignorant or designing keep us from claiming the exceeding great and precious promises and realizing their fulfillment." —William T. MacArthur[663]

***Don't Settle for the Higher Christian Life, Seek the Highest.*** "Your desire, though pure, may be sluggish and inefficient. You are more content to rest in a 'higher' Christian life than to seek the highest."—George B. Peck[664]

## IS THERE MORE AFTER THE BAPTISM IN THE SPIRIT?

***A Deeper and Fuller Baptism.*** "I pressed upon Him a new claim for a Mighty Baptism of the Holy Spirit in His complete Pentecostal fullness embracing all the gifts and graces of the Spirit. . . . I knew that I had been baptized with the Holy Spirit before but I was made to understand that God had a deeper and fuller baptism for me."—A.B. Simpson, Diary, August 9, 1907

***Beware of Retreating.*** "There is [a] danger of retreating from the baptism of Pentecost and the deepest and highest experiences of the Holy Spirit."—A.B. Simpson[665]

***Follow On to Know.*** "It is here that so many of God's children come short. They receive the baptism of the Spirit, but they do not 'follow on to know the Lord.'"—A.B. Simpson, "The Ministry of the Spirit"[666]

***Something Greater.*** "However wonderful the crisis experience of being filled with the Spirit, we should remember that it is only a means toward something greater: that greater thing is the life-long walk in the Spirit, indwelt, directed, taught and empowered by His mighty Person." –A.W. Tozer[667]

***Larger Capacities and Dormant Powers.*** "We need a larger baptism of the Holy Spirit. . . . There are capacities in the human spirit none of us has ever yet begun to realize! . . . New baptisms awaken the dormant powers that we did not know we possessed."—A.B. Simpson, *A Larger Christian Life*[668]

***Enlargement to All the Heights, Depths, Length and Breadth of God's Fullness.*** "God is calling us to enlargement. He is bringing us out of the narrow channels and shallow currents into a place of broad rivers and streams, where we shall get out of our littleness, our straitened self-life, our narrow thoughts, views, aims, joys, ambitions and affections, and rise to the length and breadth, height and depth of all the fullness of God."—A.B. Simpson[669]

***Launch Out into the Deep!***

> But many, alas, only stand on the shore
> And gaze on the ocean so wide;
> They never have ventured its depths to explore,
> Or to launch on the fathomless tide.
>
> Launch out into the deep, oh let the shoreline go;
> Launch out, launch out in the ocean divine,
> out where the full tides flow.
> —A.B. Simpson

## ADDITIONAL RESOURCES

Boardman, William E. *The Higher Christian Life*. Ft. Washington, PA: CLC Publications, 2007.

Simpson, A.B. *In Heavenly Places*. Harrisburg, PA: Christian Publications, 1968 reprint.

Simpson, A.B. *A Larger Christian Life*. Camp Hill, PA: Christian Publications, 1988

Simpson, A.B. *The Land of Promise*. Harrisburg, PA: Christian Publications, 1969 reprint.

Simpson, A.B. *The Highest Christian Life*. Harrisburg, PA: Christian Publications, 1966 reprint.

## FOR REFLECTION AND DISCUSSION

1. Read John 14:16. What are some of the greater works Jesus was talking about?

2. Read Philippians 3:1-14. Notice that Paul, who already knew Christ and the power of His resurrection and the fellowship of His suffering, was desiring to know Christ, His resurrection power and fellowship of His sufferings even more. What more could he mean? What more does God want for your life?

3. Read Joshua 13:1. What promised land have you not yet possessed? How can you take the promised land God has for you?

4. Read Colossians 1:29; Galatians 2:20. What does it mean to have Christ in you, the hope of glory?

5. Read Isaiah 54:2-3. How does God want to enlarge you?

6. Read Ephesians 3:14-20. What is the Highest Christian Life? How can you experience it?

# About the Author

Dr. Paul L. King is an ordained minister and historian of The Christian and Missionary Alliance and a professor at Oral Roberts University. He has served as Moderator of the Licensing, Ordination, and Consecration Council of the Southwestern District of the C&MA and teaches seminars on Alliance Distinctives, the Holy Spirit, healing, and elder and leadership training. He holds two earned doctorates, a Doctor of Ministry from Oral Roberts University and a Doctor of Theology from the University of South Africa. Author, compiler, or contributor of eleven books, he was selected as Oral Roberts University Scholar of the Year in 2006. He specializes in studies of the 19th and early 20th century faith, healing, Higher Life, holiness and Pentecostal movements and theology, including The Christian and Missionary Alliance.

# Notes

1   A.B. Simpson, "Aggressive Christianity," *The Christian and Missionary Alliance Weekly* (CMAW), Sept. 23, 1899, 260.
2   A. B. Simpson, "Our Trust," CMAW, May 28, 1910, 145.
3   A.T. Pierson, *The Acts of the Holy Spirit* (Harrisburg, PA: Christian Publications, 1980), 92.
4   A. B. Simpson, Editorial, CMAW, July 9, 1910, 240.
5   J. Hudson Taylor, "The Source of Power," CMAW, June 23, 1900, 416.
6   A.B. Simpson, Editorial, *The Alliance Weekly* (AW), Oct. 12, 1907, 211
7   W.T. MacArthur, "Watching the Father Work," AW, July 15, 1916, 244.
8   A.B. Simpson, "Kept and Crowned," AW, Feb. 19, 1916, 322-323.
9   A.W. Tozer, *I Call It Heresy* (Camp Hill, PA: Christian Publications, 1991), 36.
10  MacArthur, "Watching the Father Work," 244.
11  A.W. Tozer, *I Talk Back to the Devil* (Camp Hill, PA: Christian Publications, 1990), 143.
12  A.B. Simpson, *Present Truths or the Supernatural* (Harrisburg, PA: Christian Publications, reprint 1967), 66-67.
13  Simpson, *The Gospel of Healing* (Harrisburg, PA: Christian Publications, 1915), 57.
14  A.B. Simpson, Editorial, *Living Truths*, Apr. 1906, 198.
15  A.B. Simpson, Editorial, CMAW, July 6, 1907, 313.
16  A.W. Tozer, *Tragedy in the Church: The Missing Gifts* (Camp Hill, PA: Wingspread Publishers, 1990), 33, 42.
17  Simpson, *Present Truths*, 45.
18  Simpson, *The Gospel of Healing*, 19-20.
19  A.B. Simpson, "The Son of Man and Sickness, CMAW, Jan. 13, 1906, 22.
20  A.J. Gordon, *The Ministry of Healing* in *Healing: The Three Great Classics of Healing*, ed. Jonathan Graf (Camp Hill, PA: Christian Publications, 1992), 210.
21  William C. Stevens, "Jesus Our Healer," *Christian Alliance and Missionary Weekly* (CAMW), Mar. 30, 1891, 183.
22  Armin R. Gesswein, "Dispensationalism," AW, Mar. 1, 1941, 135, 138.
23  A.B. Simpson, *The Holy Spirit or Power from on High: New Testament* (Harrisburg, PA: Christian Publications, n.d. [1894]), 2:82.
24  Paris W. Reidhead, Jr., "That I May Know Him (Phil. 3:7-15): A Testimony," July 14, 1953, 33.
25  A.B. Simpson, *Missionary Messages* (Harrisburg, PA: Christian Publications, n.d.), 29-30.
26  W.C. Stevens, "The Cross and Sickness," *The Pentecostal Evangel*, Aug. 23, 1924, 6.
27  E.O. Jago, "A Great Crisis!," *Latter Rain Evangel*, Oct. 1913, 2.
28  Laura G. Beecroft, "The Day of His Power—The Spirit's Working in Palestine," AW, Apr. 11, 1925, 248-249.
29  *The Pioneer*, V, No. 21 (Nov. 1934), 7; cited in Louise Green, "Robert Jaffray: Man of Spirit, Man of Power," *His Dominion*, Vol. 16, No. 1 (March 1990), 6.
30  Paris W. Reidhead, Jr., "That I May Know Him (Phil. 3:7-15): A Testimony," July 14, 1953, 5, 16.

31    A.B. Simpson, Editoral, AW, May 26, 1917, 114.
32    A.B. Simpson, Editorial, CMAW, Feb. 11, 1905, 81.
33    *The Pioneer*, V, No. 19 (May 1934), 24; cited in Louise Green, "Robert Jaffray: Man of Spirit, Man of Power," 5.
34    Stevens, "Jesus Our Healer," 183.
35    William E. Boardman, *The Higher Christian Life* (Boston: Henry Hoyt; New York: Sheldon & Co., 1858), accessed online at http://online.ambrose.edu/alliancestudies
36    A.B. Simpson, "The Gospel Its Own Witness, *The Word, the Work, and the World* (WWW), Feb. 1, 1887, 66.
37    A.B. Simpson, "The Highest Christian Life," AW, Dec. 23, 1911, 179.
38    Simpson, *The Holy Spirit*, 1:204.
39    A.B. Simpson, "The Four-fold Gospel, or the Fullness of Jesus," AW July 28, 1911, 228.
40    Walter Turnbull and C. H. Chrisman, "The Message of the Christian and Missionary Alliance," 1927, accessed at http://online.ambrose.edu/alliancestudies/ahtreadings/ahtr_s2.html
41    A.B. Simpson, "A New Missionary Alliance," WWW, June 1, 1887, 365, 367.
42    A.B. Simpson, Editorial, CAMW, Oct. 31, 1890, 257-258.
43    W.C. Stevens, "The Closing Days," CMAW, May 1, 1899, 174.
44    A.B. Simpson, "What Is Meant by the Latter Rain?," CMAW, Oct. 19, 1907, 38.
45    Gesswein, "Dispensationalism," 135, 138.
46    W.C. Stevens, "The Latter Rain," *Living Truths*, Sept. 1907, 530.
47    Simpson, "What Is Meant by the Latter Rain?," 38, 50.
48    D. Wesley Myland, *The Latter Rain Covenant* (Springfield, MO: Temple Press, [1910]), 178.
49    "Notes from the Home Field: Beulah Park Convention," CMAW, Sept. 14, 1907, 128.
50    "Convention of the Eastern District, Rocky Springs Park, Lancaster, Pa.," CMAW, Aug. 31, 1907, 116.
51    "Notes from the Home Field: New York State Convention," CMAW, Aug. 10, 1907, 70.
52    F.E. Marsh, "The Gift of Tongues," *Living Truths*, May 1907, 262.
53    A.C. Snead, "Gleanings from Nyack: India," CMAW, May 16, 1908, 116. See also in report "Fires Are Being Kindled," *The Apostolic Faith*, Vol. II, No. 12, May 1908, 1.
54    "Notes from the Home Field," CMAW, Apr. 11, 1908, 33.
55    A.B. Simpson, "Living Under the Powers of the World to Come," AW, Feb. 21, 1914, 324.
56    A.B. Simpson, "Earnests of the Coming Age," AW, June 23, 1917, 178, 180.
57    A.B. Simpson, "Divine Healing and the Lord's Coming," AW, Sept. 22, 1917, 386.
58    Simpson, *The Holy Spirit*, 1:204.
59    A.B. Simpson, *The Love Life of the Lord* (Harrisburg, PA: Christian Publication, n.d.), 195.
60    A.B. Simpson, *Christ in the Bible* (CITB) (Camp Hill, PA: Christian Publications, 1993), 3:351.
61    A.B. Simpson, *In Heavenly Places* (Harrisburg, PA: Christian Publications, reprint 1968), 114, 116-118, 125.

62    George B. Peck, *Throne Life: The Highest Christian Life* (Boston: The Watchword Publishing Co., 1888), 110.

63    Simpson, "Divine Healing and the Lord's Coming," 386-387.

64    Simpson, "Divine Healing and the Lord's Coming," 387.

65    W.A. Cramer, "A Testimony," AW, Aug. 20, 1938, 544.

66    "The Message of The Christian and Missionary Alliance," June 25, 1932, 402-403. Excerpted from W.M. Turnbull and C.H. Chrisman, "The Message of The Christian and Missionary Alliance," accessed online at http://online.ambrose.edu/alliancestudies/

67    Edgar E. Sellow, "Baptism with the Holy Spirit," AW, June 19, 1920, 181.

68    A.B. Simpson, "The Crisis of the Deeper Life," *Living Truths*, Sept., 1906, 523.

69    A.B. Simpson, "The Baptism of the Holy Spirit: A Crisis or an Evolution?," *Living Truths*, Dec. 1905, 710.

70    A.W. Tozer, *The Divine Conquest* (Camp Hill, PA: Christian Publications, 1950), 121.

71    F.F. Bosworth, in the "Introduction" of Oswald J. Smith, *The Baptism with the Holy Spirit* (New York: Christian Alliance Publishing Co., 1925), 7.

72    Some later Alliance leaders believed that the baptism in the Spirit was received at salvation, but that there is a "filling of the Spirit" that is subsequent to conversion. Regarding of the difference in terminology, the sanctifying reception of the Spirit in power, by whatever term, was considered distinct from conversion.

73    J. Hudson Ballard, "The Spiritual Clinic," AW, Jan. 16, 1915, 254.

74    Smith, *The Baptism With the Holy Spirit*, 19.

75    Jasper W. Smoak, "The Spirit-filled Life: Optional or Imperative?," *Alliance Witness*, Aug. 21, 1963, 7.

76    Simpson, *The Holy Spirit*, 2:119-120.

77    Ira E. David, "A Glimpse at the Lesson," AW, Feb. 14, 1948, 112.

78    T.J. McCrossan, *The Bible and Its Eternal Facts* (Youngstown, OH: Clement Humbard, 1947), 175.

79    Simpson, *The Holy Spirit*, 2:120.

80    George P. Pardington, *The Crisis of the Deeper Life* (New York: Christian Alliance Publishing Co., 1925), 131-132; accessed at http://www.cmalliance.org/resources/archives/downloads/miscellaneous/the-crisis-of-the-deeper-life.pdf

81    A.B. Simpson, "Baptism and the Baptism of the Holy Spirit," accessed at http://online.ambrose.edu/alliancestudies/ahtreadings/ahtr_s2.html

82    Cited by Bertha Pinkham Dixon, *A Romance of Faith* (n.p., 193-?), 129.

83    McCrossan, *Christ's Paralyzed Church X-Rayed* (Youngstown, OH: C.E. Humbard, 1937), 118.

84    Simpson, *Present Truths*, 86.

85    Simpson, *Present Truths*, 86.

86    Simpson, *Present Truths*, 65.

87    Simpson, *Missionary Messages*, 27.

88    A.B. Simpson, *Wholly Sanctified* (Harrisburg, PA: Christian Publications, 1925), 11, 16.

89    Ira E. David, "Sunday School Lesson: The Gift of the Holy Spirit," AW, June 20, 1931, 406, 408.

90    Bosworth, in the "Introduction" of Smith, *The Baptism with the Holy Spirit*, 7.

91   A.B. Simpson, "The Dynamite of God," AW, Oct. 20, 1917, 36
92   Pardington, *The Crisis of the Deeper Life*, 35.
93   Simpson, *The Holy Spirit*, 2:281-282.
94   "Three R's of the Holy Spirit," AW, Feb. 8, 1919, 300.
95   A.W. Tozer, *Keys to the Deeper Life* (Grand Rapids, MI: Zondervan, 1957, 1984), 57.
96   David E. Schroeder, *Walking in Your Anointing* (Bloomington, IN: Author House, 2007), 3.
97   Watchman Nee, *The Normal Christian Life* (Ft. Washington, PA: Christian Literature Crusade, 1957, 1963), 89-90.
98   Smith, *The Baptism with the Holy Spirit*, 45.
99   Smith, *The Baptism with the Holy Spirit*, 46.
100  Fred F. Bosworth, cited in Eunice Perkins, *Joybringer Bosworth* (Dayton, OH: John J. Scruby, 1921), 67.
101  A.B. Simpson, Editorial, *Living Truths*, Apr. 1906, 198.
102  Robert Jaffray, "Speaking in Tongues—Some Words of Kindly Counsel," AW, Mar. 13, 1909, 395.
103  Bosworth, in Perkins, *Joybringer Bosworth*, 53, 57.
104  T.J. McCrossan, *Speaking with Other Tongues: Sign or Gift Which?* (Harrisburg: Christian Alliance Publishing Co., 1927), 26.
105  A.B. Simpson "Gifts and Grace," CMAW, June 29, 1907, 303.
106  A.W. Tozer, *The Tozer Pulpit: Ten Sermons on the Ministry of the Spirit* (Camp Hill, PA: Christian Publications, 1968), 104.
107  Bosworth, cited in *Joybringer Bosworth*, 53, 57.
108  F.F. Bosworth, *Do All Speak with Tongues?* (Christian Alliance Publishing Co., n.d.), 16.
109  Etta Wurmser, "Chosen in the Furnace of Affliction," *Latter Rain Evangel*, Jan. 1917, 21.
110  Simpson, "The Dynamite of God," 36.
111  L.H. Ziemer, *The Story of My Conversion and Relative Experiences* (Toledo, OH: Toledo Gospel Tabernacle, n.d.), 23.
112  A.B. Simpson, "The Call and the Consecration," WWW, Jan. 1, 1882, 19.
113  Simpson, *The Holy Spirit*, 2:24-26.
114  A.B. Simpson, "The Baptism of Fire," AW, Apr. 19, 1919, 52.
115  William Franklin, "Work at Mukti," *The India Alliance*, Feb. 1906, 89.
116  Edward Armstrong, "A Fire Baptism," AW, Aug. 19, 1922, 359.
117  Andrew Murray, *Absolute Surrender* (New Kensington, PA: Whitaker House, 1981), 37.
118  Sellow, "Baptism with the Holy Spirit," 181.
119  Simpson, *Wholly Sanctified*, 21.
120  Turnbull and Chrisman, "The Message of The Christian and Missionary Alliance," accessed online at http://online.ambrose.edu/alliancestudies
121  Pardington, *The Crisis of the Deeper Life*, 109.
122  A.B. Simpson, "The Four-fold Gospel, or the Fullness of Jesus," July 28, 1911, 228.
123  A.J. Gordon, *The Ministry of the Spirit* (Minneapolis, MN: Bethany Fellowship, 1964), 116.
124  A.B. Simpson, *The Holy Spirit*, 2:25.

125  W.T. MacArthur, "Sparks from the Anvil—The Sanctifier," AW, Aug. 2, 1930, 493.

126  Nee, *The Normal Christian Life*, 137, 176.

127  Simpson, *Wholly Sanctified*, 27.

128  A.B. Simpson, *The Land of Promise* (Harrisburg, PA: Christian Publications, reprint 1969), 37.

129  Simpson, *Wholly Sanctified*, 64, 89, 114.

130  Murray, *Absolute Surrender*, 24.

131  A.B. Simpson, *The Four-Fold Gospel* (Harrisburg, PA: Christian Publications, n.d.), 39-40.

132  MacArthur, "Sparks from the Anvil—The Sanctifier," 493.

133  J. Hudson Ballard, "The Spiritual Clinic," AW, Nov. 11, 1911, 87.

134  Pardington, *The Crisis of the Deeper Life*, 62.

135  Pardington, *The Crisis of the Deeper Life*, 62.

136  Simpson, *The Holy Spirit*, 2:81-83.

137  Simpson, "Baptism and the Baptism of the Holy Spirit."

138  Cited in Perkins, *Joybringer Bosworth*, 74.

139  A. B. Simpson, "Fire-Touched Lips," CMAW, Sept. 12, 1908, 404.

140  I.E. David, "The Gift of the Spirit," AW, June 20, 1931, 406.

141  A.B. Simpson, Editorial, CMAW, Sept. 26, 1908, 430.

142  Smith, *The Baptism with the Holy Spirit*, 47.

143  Carrie Judd Montgomery, "A Year with the Comforter," *Confidence*, Nov. 15, 1909, 229.

144  A.B. Simpson, "How to Receive Divine Healing," WWW, July-Aug., 1885, 203.

145  Tozer, *Tragedy in the Church*, 29, 30.

146  A.B. Simpson, Editorial, CMAW, Feb. 11, 1905, 81.

147  Richard H. Harvey, *70 Years of Miracles* (Beaverlodge, Alberta: Horizon House, 1977), 87.

148  May Mabette Anderson, "The 'Latter Rain,' and Its Counterfeit," *Signs of the Times* (New York, NY: Alliance Press Co., 1907), 136.

149  Editorial, *The India Alliance*, Aug. 1907, 19.

150  Mary B. Mullen, "Some Danger Lines," CMAW, Nov. 2, 1907, 75.

151  William T. MacArthur, "The Promise of the Father and Speaking with Tongues in Chicago," CMAW, Feb. 16, 1907, 76.

152  C. J. Moon, "The Receiving of the Holy Spirit," CMAW, Feb. 22, 1908, 344.

153  MacArthur, "The Promise of the Father and Speaking with Tongues in Chicago," CMAW, Feb. 16, 1907, 76.

154  Ira E. David, "Spiritual Gifts," AW, Sept. 29, 1928, 638.

155  R.S. Roseberry, "The Need of Spiritual Gifts," AW, Sept. 18, 1948, 695.

156  J. Hudson Ballard, "The Spiritual Clinic," AW, Nov. 21, 1914, 126.

157  A.B. Simpson, "Members of One Another," AW, Dec. 8, 1917, 148; "Christian Altruism," CMAW, Aug. 7, 1909, 322.

158  John A. MacMillan, "Love's Divine Overflow," AW, May 18, 1940, 306.

159  A.B. Simpson, Editorial, *Living Truths*, Apr. 1906, 198.

160  A.E. Thompson, *A.B. Simpson: His Life and Work* (Camp Hill, PA: Christian Publications, 1960) 195.

161  Stevens, "Jesus Our Healer," 183.

162   A.W. Tozer, *God Tells the Man Who Cares* (Camp Hill, PA: Wingspread Publishers, 1993), 56.

163   Dr. H.M. Shuman, "Dr. A.B. Simpson—Our Founder," AW, Dec. 11, 1943, 789.

164   Tozer, *Keys to the Deeper Life*, 45.

165   Thompson, *A.B. Simpson: His Life and Work*, 195, 199.

166   Editorial, AW, Oct. 30, 1920, 481.

167   David J. Fant, *A.W. Tozer: A Twentieth Century Prophet* (Harrisburg, PA: Christian Publications, 1964).

168   Simpson, "The Holy Spirit," CMAW, Apr. 24, 1909, 61.

169   Thompson, *A.B. Simpson: His Life and Work*, 53.

170   C.H. Chrisman, "Notes from the Home Field," CMAW, Dec. 24, 1910, 205.

171   A.B. Simpson, Editorial, CMAW, Jan. 11, 1902, 24.

172   A.W. Tozer, *Born After Midnight* (Camp Hill, PA: Wingspread Publishers, 1959, 1987 renewal by the Children of A.W. Tozer), 8.

173   James L. Snyder, *In Pursuit of God: The Life of A.W. Tozer* (Camp Hill, PA: Christian Publications, 1991), 58.

174   Tozer, *I Talk Back to the Devil*, 56.

175   Simpson, *Missionary Messages*, 31.

176   A.B. Simpson, "Spiritual Sanity," *Living Truths*, Apr. 1907, 196.

177   Tozer, *The Tozer Pulpit*, 99.

178   A.B. Simpson, Editorial, CMAW, Mar. 2, 1907, 97.

179   Carrie Judd Montgomery, "The Promise of the Father," *Triumphs of Faith*, July 1908, 1-2. See also Carrie Judd Montgomery, *Under His Wings* (Oakland, CA: Triumphs of Faith, 1936), 166.

180   Montgomery, *Under His Wings*, 170.

181   A.B. Simpson, Editorial, *Living Truths*, Aug. 1907, 435.

182   Mullen, "Some Danger Lines," 75.

183   A.B. Simpson, "The Ministry of the Spirit," *Living Truths*, Aug. 1907, 442.

184   A.W. Tozer, *I Talk Back to the Devil*, 24-25.

185   J. Hudson Ballard, "The Spiritual Clinic," AW, Mar. 2, 1912, 343.

186   A.B. Simpson, Editorial, CAMW, Nov. 2, 1894, 410.

187   Ira E. David, "Spiritual Gifts," 638.

188   Carrie Judd Montgomery, "Miraculously Healed by the Lord Thirty Years Ago, Baptized in the Holy Spirit One Year Ago," *The Latter Rain Evangel*, Oct. 1909, 9-10.

189   Montgomery, "The Promise of the Father," *Confidence*, Nov. 15, 1908, 1-2.

190   Bosworth, cited in Perkins, *Joybringer Bosworth*, 70.

191   Paul Rader, *Harnessing God* (New York: George H. Doran Co., 1926), 96-97.

192   Simpson, "Gifts and Grace," 303.

193   William F. MacArthur, "The Phenomenon of Supernatural Utterance," CMAW, Oct. 31, 1908, 73.

194   A.B. Simpson, "The Ministry of the Spirit," cited in Richard Gilbertson, *The Baptism of the Holy Spirit* (Camp Hill, PA: Christian Publications, Inc., 1993), 337.

195   A. B. Simpson, "The Anointing," CMAW, May 23, 1908, 130.

196   A.B. Simpson, *Days of Heaven on Earth* (Camp Hill, PA: Wingspread Publishers, 1897, revised edition 1984), March 31.

197   George D. Watson, *Holiness Manual* (Boston: McDonald, Gall, and Co., 1882), 97.

198 A.B. Simpson, "The Worship and Fellowship of the Church," CMAW, Feb. 2, 1898, 126; reprinted in the *Alliance Witness*, Feb. 1, 1967; see also Simpson, CITB (1994), 5:236.
199 "The Gift of Tongues," *Signs of the Times*, quoted in AW, Nov. 3, 1934, 678.
200 Thompson, *A.B. Simpson: His Life and Work*, 195.
201 A. B. Simpson, "The Double Portion: Striking Lessons from the Life of Elisha," *The Latter Rain Evangel*, Nov. 1909, 12.
202 Ora Woodberry, "John Woodbury," AW, Oct. 22, 1938, 677. For another example of such prophetic direction see CAMW, Dec. 9, 1892, 370-371.
203 Mary G. Davies, "The Ninety-first Psalm," CMAW, Aug. 17, 1907, 78; see also "Notes from the Home Field: The Old Orchard Convention," CMAW, Aug. 31, 1907, 116.
204 May Mabette Anderson, "The Prayer of Faith," CMAW, Feb. 17, 1906, 98.
205 May Mabette Anderson, "The Prayer of Faith: Part II," CMAW, Feb. 24, 1906, 106-107.
206 MacArthur, "The Phenomenon of Supernatural Utterance," 73.
207 John A. MacMillan, "Spiritual Balance," AW, Apr. 24, 1937, 258.
208 A.E. Adams, "Diversities of Gifts," AW, Dec. 4, 1948, 772.
209 John A. MacMillan, *The Full Gospel Adult Sunday School Quarterly* (SSQ), Nov. 30, 1941, 28.
210 John A. MacMillan, "Discrimination," AW, Mar. 14, 1936, 163.
211 A.B. Simpson, "Annual Report of the President and General Superintendent of the Christian and Missionary Alliance," *Annual Report of the Christian and Missionary Alliance* (1907-08), 12-13.
212 Gilbertson, *The Baptism of the Holy Spirit*, 343.
213 Frank S. Weston, "The Gift of Prophecy," AW, Apr. 22, 1935, 247.
214 Bosworth, *Do All Speak with Tongues?*, 16.
215 Montgomery, *Under His Wings*, 160-161.
216 John A. MacMillan, Inquirer's Corner," AW, Aug. 18, 1934, 523.
217 A.B. Simpson, Editorial, AW, May 10, 1913, 82.
218 A.B. Simpson, *The Gentle Love of the Holy Spirit* (Camp Hill, PA: Christian Publications, 1983), 48; see also *CITB*, 4:581, where Simpson expounds on this further.
219 Simpson, *Days of Heaven on Earth*, Nov. 17.
220 Simpson, *Days of Heaven on Earth*, Nov. 17.
221 Simpson, *Gospel of Healing*, 90.
222 A.B. Simpson, Editorial, AW, Aug. 24, 1912, 321.
223 A.B. Simpson, Editorial, AW, Sept. 30, 1916, 417.
224 Simpson, *Days of Heaven on Earth*, Dec. 3.
225 Simpson, "The Worship and Fellowship of the Church," 126.
226 Simpson, CITB (1992), 4:190.
227 A.B. Simpson, "Jeremiah, an Example of Faith and Courage," AW, Nov. 14, 1914, 98.
228 Simpson, "Gifts and Grace," 303.
229 Simpson, "Gifts and Grace," 303.
230 A.B. Simpson, Editorial, AW, Feb. 14, 1914, 305.
231 Montgomery, *Under His Wings*, 168-170.
232 Simpson, "The Worship and Fellowship of the Church," 126.

233   For Kenning's lengthy testimony, see Henry Kenning, "After He Has Come . . . Ye Shall Be Witnesses," *Word and Work*, Jan. 1910, 10-13.

234   Mary B. Mullen, "A New Experience," CMAW, Oct. 5, 1907, 17.

235   O. Lapp, "Akola Orphanage," *The India Alliance*, June 1908, 136.

236   Rev. and Mrs. J. Woodberry, "Report of Beulah Chapel," CMAW, May 22, 1909, 134.

237   Stanley H. Frodsham, *With Signs Following* (Springfield, MO: Gospel Publishing House, 1941), 56-57.

238   Wayne Warner, *Revival! Touched by Pentecostal Fire* (Tulsa, OK: Harrison House, 1978), 33-35; Alice Reynolds Flower, "My Day of Pentecost," *Assemblies of God Heritage*, Winter 1997-98, 17.

239   "A Remarkable Testimony," CMAW, Nov. 9, 1907, 98; see also T.B. Barratt, *The Work of T. B. Barratt* (New York and London: Garland Publishing, 1985), 170.

240   Frodsham, *With Signs Following*, 234-237; Montgomery, *Under His Wings*, 168-170.

241   Kenning, "After He Has Come . . . Ye Shall Be Witnesses," 10-13.

242   Wurmser, "Chosen in the Furnace of Affliction," 21.

243   Frodsham, *With Signs Following*, 57-58.

244   Stanley H. Frodsham, *Jesus is Victor: A Story of Grace, Gladness and Glory in the Life of Alice M. Frodsham* (Springfield, MO: Gospel Publishing House, 1930), 40; Frodsham, *With Signs Following*, 47; Carl Brumback, *Suddenly. . . from Heaven* (Springfield MO: Gospel Publishing House, [1961]), 89-90; Simpson, Editorial, CMAW, June 8, 1907, 205.

245   Joy Boese, *Adventures in Learning to Trust God* (West Conshohocken, PA: Infinity Publishing, 2005), 49-55.

246   Simpson, "Gifts and Grace," 303.

247   Simpson, "The Worship and Fellowship of the Church," 126.

248   Paris W. Reidhead, Jr., "That I May Know Him (Phil. 3:7-15): A Testimony," July 14, 1953, 34.

249   Simpson, "Gifts and Grace," 303.

250   W.T. Dixon, "About Tongues: A Word in Season," *Confidence*, Feb. 1914, 27.

251   Boese, *Adventures in Learning to Trust God*, 49-55.

252   Marsh, "The Gift of Tongues," 262-263.

253   MacArthur, "The Phenomenon of Supernatural Utterance," 73.

254   A.W. Tozer, *The Purpose of Man* (Ventura, CA: Regal, 2009), 30.

255   Jaffray, "Speaking in Tongues," 395.

256   Jaffray, "Speaking in Tongues," 395.

257   Jaffray, "Speaking in Tongues," 395.

258   Bosworth, cited in Perkins, *Joybringer Bosworth*, 73-74.

259   A.E. Thompson, "The Corinthian Epistles: Spiritual Gifts and Graces," AW, Feb. 12, 1916, 315-316.

260   MacArthur, "The Phenomenon of Supernatural Utterance," 73.

261   MacArthur, "The Phenomenon of Supernatural Utterance," 73.

262   MacArthur, "The Phenomenon of Supernatural Utterance," 73.

263   Bertha Pinkham Dixon, *A Romance of Faith*, 73.

264   H.L. Blake, "A Minnesota Preacher's Testimony," *The Apostolic Faith*, Vol. I, No. 6, Feb.-Mar. 1907, 5.

265   A.B. Simpson, "Golden Censers," AW, Jan. 4, 1908, 234.

266  Mullen, "A New Experience," 17.

267  Montgomery, "The Promise of the Father," *Confidence*, Nov. 15, 1908, 4.

268  Mattie E. Perry, *Christ and Answered Prayer: Autobiography of Mattie E. Perry* (Nashville, TN: Benson, 1939), 72.

269  Brumback, *Suddenly . . . from Heaven*, 79-80.

270  McCrossan, *Christ's Paralyzed Church X-Rayed*, 197.

271  McCrossan, *Speaking with Other Tongues*, 34-35; see also Charles S. Price, *The Story of My Life* (Pasadena, CA: Charles S. Price Publishing Co., 1935).

272  Mary Gainforth, *The Life and Healing of Mrs. Mary Gainforth* (Trenton, Ontario: Jarrett Printing and Publishing Co., [1924?]), 42.

273  Frank Bartleman, *Azusa Street* (New Kensington, PA: Whitaker House, 1982), 111-112; Harvey Cox, *Fire from Heaven* (Reading, MA: Addison-Wesley Publishing Co., 1995), 68; Charles W. Nienkirchen, *A.B. Simpson and the Pentecostal Movement* (Peabody, MA: Hendrickson, 1992), 52.

84-85; "Notes from the New York Convention," CMAW, Oct. 19, 1907, 48.

274  MacArthur, "The Phenomenon of Supernatural Utterance," 73.

275  McCrossan, *Speaking with Other Tongues*, 4.

276  Wayne Warner, *Revival! Touched by Pentecostal Fire* (Tulsa, OK: Harrison House, 1978), 35. Alice Reynolds Flower, "Pentecostal Recollections," Jim Corum Interview with Alice Reynolds Flower, Flower Pentecostal Heritage Center, Springfield, MO.

277  Kenning, "After He Has Come . . . Ye Shall Be Witnesses," 10-13.

278  Myland, *The Latter Rain Covenant*, 174-177.

279  Myland, *The Latter Rain Covenant*, 178.

280  Myland, *The Latter Rain Covenant*, 178.

281  Mrs. May Evans, "Healed of Cancer," AW, July 10, 1915, 231.

282  Marsh, "The Gift of Tongues," 262-263.

283  J. Hudson Ballard, "Spiritual Gifts with Special Reference to the Gift of Tongues," *Living Truths*, Jan. 1907, 24.

284  Rader, *Harnessing God*, 95-96, 99.

285  J. Hudson Ballard, "Spiritual Gifts with Special Reference to the Gift of Tongues," 24.

286  Cited in Elizabeth V. Baker, *Chronicles of a Faith Life* (New York and London: Garland Publishing Co., 1984), 142.

287  Jaffray, "Speaking in Tongues," 395.

288  Montgomery, "The Promise of the Father," *Confidence*, Nov. 15, 1908, 1-2.

289  MacArthur, "The Phenomenon of Supernatural Utterance," 73.

290  Thompson, "The Corinthian Epistles: Spiritual Gifts and Graces," A.E. Thompson, "The Corinthian Epistles: The Use, Abuse and Value of Gifts," AW, Feb. 26, 1916, 341.

291  Simpson, "Worship and Fellowship of the Church," 126.

292  Simpson, *Gifts and Grace*, 302.

293  Simpson, *Gifts and Grace*, 302.

294  McCrossan, *Christ's Paralyzed Church X-Rayed*, 320-321.

295  Simpson, *Gifts and Grace*, 302.

296  "Healing of Mrs. Williams," CAMW, May 9, 1890, 295-296.

297  Jean Ratan Cole, "Getting Telegrams from God," *Latter Rain Evangel*, Aug. 1920, 11.

298   Irene E. Lewis, *Life Sketch of Rev. Mary C. Norton: Remarkable Healings on Mission Fields* (Los Angeles: Pilgrim's Mission, Inc., 1954), 30-32.

299   Judith Adams, *Against the Gates of Hell: The Story of Glenn V. Tingley* (Harrisburg, PA: Christian Publications, 1977), 111-112. For other incidents of prophetic words or what is sometimes called word of knowledge in Tingley's life, see pp. 83-84, 111.

300   William Wisdom Newberry, *Untangling Live Wires: Light on Some of the Problems of Divine Guidance* (New York: Christian Alliance Publishing Co., 1914), 35.

301   Simpson, *Gifts and Grace*, 302.

302   W.C. Stevens, cited in F.F. Bosworth, *Christ the Healer* (Grand Rapids: Fleming H. Revell, 1973), 76.

303   Simpson, *Gifts and Grace*, 302.

304   A.B. Simpson, *The Lord for the Body* (Camp Hill, PA: Christian Publications, 1996), 132-133.

305   Simpson, *Gifts and Grace*, 302.

306   Simpson, *Gifts and Grace*, 302.

307   Stevens, cited in Bosworth, *Christ the Healer*, 77.

308   Bosworth, *Christ the Healer*, 77.

309   A.B. Simpson, cited in Gainforth, *The Life and Healing of Mrs. Mary Gainforth*, 38-39.

310   Stevens, "Jesus Our Healer," 183.

311   A.B. Simpson, *The Gospel of Healing*, 178.

312   A. B. Simpson, Editorial, CAMW, Dec. 4, 1896, 517.

313   Simpson, *The Lord for the Body*, 133.

314   Simpson, *The Gospel of Healing*, 178.

315   Simpson, *The Gospel of Healing*, 90.

316   Tozer, *God Tells the Man Who Cares*, 3.

317   A.B. Simpson, Editorial, WWW, Feb. 1883, 17.

318   Cited in Lindsay Reynolds, *Footprints* (Beaverlodge, Alberta: Buena Book Services, 1981), 387.

319   McCrossan, *Bodily Healing and the Atonement* (Youngstown, OH: Clement Humbard, 1930), 111-112.

320   Simpson, *Days of Heaven on Earth*, June 27.

321   Ziemer, *The Story of My Conversion*, 23.

322   A.W. Tozer, *Worship: The Missing Jewel* (Camp Hill, PA: Christian Publications, 1992), 20-21.

323   Ira David, "The Presence of God," AW, July 16, 1927, 468.

324   Mullen, "A New Experience," 17.

325   Dr. Thomas Moseley, "Revival at Nyack," AW, Oct. 10, 1942, 643.

326   A.B. Simpson, cited by a reporter in "Healing by Faith: Sick Persons Miraculously Cured," Simpson Scrapbook, p. 200, C&MA Archives.

327   McCrossan, *Speaking with Other Tongues*, 46.

328   Lewis, *Life Sketch of Rev. Mary C. Norton*, 27.

329   Kenning, "After He Has Come . . . Ye Shall Be Witnesses," 10-13.

330   Montgomery, *Under His Wings*, 168-170.

331   McCrossan, *Bodily Healing and the Atonement*, 109-110.

332   Lewis, *Life Sketch of Rev. Mary C. Norton*, 27.

333   *Stevens' History of U. S. A. Methodism*, Vol. 4, p. 16; cited in McCrossan, *Bodily Healing and the Atonement*, 111-112

334  *Stevens' History of U. S. A. Methodism,* Vol. 4, p. 372; cited in McCrossan, *Bodily Healing and the Atonement,*111-112.

335  Wilbur F. Meminger, "Touring New York," CMAW, Dec. 7, 1907, 168.

336  Mullen, "A New Experience," 17.

337  Jaffray, "Speaking in Tongues," 396.

338  Gainforth, *The Life and Healing of Mrs. Mary Gainforth,* 41.

339  McCrossan, *Bodily Healing and the Atonement,* 111-112.

340  McCrossan, *The Bible and Its Eternal Facts,* 192-194; McCrossan, *Christ's Paralyzed Church X-Rayed,* 258-260.

341  McCrossan, *Bodily Healing and the Atonement,* 111-112.

342  McCrossan, *Bodily Healing and the Atonement,* 111-112.

343  McCrossan, *Bodily Healing and the Atonement,* 111-112.

344  Newberry, *Untangling Live Wires,* 9.

345  A.B. Simpson, *CITB: Matthew* (Harrisburg, PA: Christian Publications, n.d.), Vol. XIII, 163.

346  A.W. Tozer, *Wingspread* (Camp Hill, PA: Christian Publications, 1943), 62.

347  Emma Beere, comp., "Simpson Anecdotes," as found in C. Donald McKaig's unpublished *Simpson Scrapbook* (Colorado Springs, CO: A.B. Simpson Historical Library, n.d.), 231; cited in Gary Keisling, *Relentless Spirituality: Embracing the Spiritual Disciplines of A. B. Simpson* (Camp Hill, PA: Christian Publications, 2004), 128-129.

348  A.B. Simpson, "Jesus in the Psalms," CAMW, Jan. 8, 1892, 20.

349  Simpson, *CITB: Matthew* (n.d.), 163.

350  Newberry, *Untangling Live Wires,* 10.

351  Newberry, *Untangling Live Wires,* 14.

352  Newberry, *Untangling Live Wires,* 48.

353  Newberry, *Untangling Live Wires,* 52-53.

354  Simpson, Editorial, *Living Truths,* Dec. 1906, 708-709.

355  Newberry, *Untangling Live Wires,* 12-13.

356  Newberry, *Untangling Live Wire,* 13.

357  Simpson, *CITB: Luke* (Harrisburg, PA.: Christian Publications, n.d.), Vol. XIVB, 178.

358  A.B. Simpson, *Friday Meeting Talks, Series 3: Divine Prescriptions for the Sick and Suffering* (New York: Christian Alliance Publishing Co., 1900), 30-31.

359  A.B. Simpson, "Jesus in the Psalms: The Priest-King Psalm," CAMW, Feb. 5, 1892, 86.

360  Andrew Murray, *Divine Healing* (Springdale, PA: Whitaker House, 1982), 13.

361  A.B. Simpson, "Jesus in the Psalms: The Missionary Psalm," CAMW, Apr. 8, 1892, 228.

362  A.B. Simpson, "The Master Workman in Relation to Sickness and Divine Healing, CMAW, Nov. 27, 1909, 138.

363  Andrew Murray, *The Prayer Life* (Basingstoke, Hanks, UK: Marshall, Morgan and Scott, 1968), 18.

364  A.B. Simpson, "Jesus in the Psalms: The Pivot Psalm," Mar. 25, 1892, 197.

365  Simpson, "Jesus in the Psalms: The Priest-King Psalm," 86.

366  Simpson, CITB (1992), 1:44.

367  W.C. Stevens, "The Cross and Sickness," 6.

368  Murray, *Divine Healing,* 73-74.

369 Simpson, *CITB: Luke* (n.d.), 178.

370 A.B. Simpson, "Divine Healing in the Atonement," CMAW, Aug. 1890, 122, 124.

371 Simpson, "Divine Healing in the Atonement," 123.

372 Simpson, *The Gospel of Healing*, 15.

373 R. Kelso Carter, cited in Keith M. Bailey, *Divine Healing: The Children's Bread* (Harrisburg, PA: Christian Publications, 1977), 44.

374 Stevens, "The Cross and Sickness," 6.

375 Simpson, *The Lord for the Body*, 79.

376 A.J. Gordon, cited in Keith M. Bailey, *Divine Healing*, 45.

377 T.J. McCrossan, *Bodily Healing*, 25, 28.

378 F.F. Bosworth, *For This Cause* (New York: Christian Alliance Publishing Co., n.d.), 19-20.

379 Simpson, "Divine Healing in the Atonement," 123-124.

380 A.B. Simpson, "Editorial," CAMW, Nov. 1890, 274.

381 Simpson, *The Four-fold Gospel*, 62.

382 Simpson, *The Gospel of Healing*, 54, 127.

383 Simpson, "How to Receive Divine Healing," 205.

384 A.B. Simpson, *A Larger Christian Life* (Camp Hill, PA: Christian Publications, 1988), 19.

385 Montgomery, *The Prayer of Faith* (Chicago: Fleming H. Revell, 1880), 50.

386 A.W. Tozer, *Of God and Men* (Harrisburg, PA: Christian Publications, 1960), 57.

387 A.W. Tozer, *Faith Beyond Reason* (Camp Hill, PA: Christian Publications, 1989), 34, 42.

388 Simpson, *The Gospel of Healing*, 89.

389 Simpson, *The Life of Prayer*, 70.

390 Simpson, *The Gospel of Healing*, 88-89.

391 Simpson, *The Gentle Love of the Holy Spirit*, 135.

392 Montgomery, *The Secrets of Victory* (Oakland, CA: Triumphs of Faith, 1921), 28.

393 Simpson, *The Four-fold Gospel*, 62.

394 Simpson, *The Gospel of Healing*, 90.

395 A.B. Simpson, "According to Your Faith," CMAW, Sept. 8, 1906, 146.

396 Simpson, CITB (1992), 4:247.

397 Simpson, CITB (1992), 4:207.

398 Murray, *Divine Healing*, 133.

399 A.B. Simpson, "The Embosomed Miracles," AW, Jan. 15, 1910, 250.

400 Andrew Murray, *The Blood of the Cross* (Springdale, PA: Whitaker House, 1981), 78.

401 Simpson, "The Embosomed Miracles," 250.

402 W.T. MacArthur, "Fabrics Filled with Power," AW, Sept. 14, 1912, 390.

403 Paul L. King, *A Believer with Authority* (Camp Hill, PA: Christian Publications, 2001), 63.

404 King, *A Believer with Authority*, 89.

405 A.E. Funk, "Pittsburgh Convention," AW, Apr. 9, 1921, 57.

406 Simpson, "How to Receive Divine Healing," 205.

407 Simpson, *Gifts and Grace*, 302.

408  Simpson, *The Four-fold Gospel*, 51.
409  MacArthur, "Fabrics Filled with Power," 390.
410  MacArthur, "Fabrics Filled with Power," 390.
411  Simpson, CITB (1993), 3:472.
412  See Paul L. King, "Holy Laughter and Other Phenomena in Evangelical and Holiness Revival Movements." *Alliance Academic Review 1996*, Elio Cuccaro, ed. (Camp Hill, PA.: Christian Publications, 1998), 107-122.
413  Montgomery, *Secrets of Victory*, 65.
414  Simpson, CITB (1992), 2:34-35.
415  A.B. Simpson, *Triumphs of Faith*, Nov. 1921, 253.
416  A.B. Simpson, *Christ for the Body* (Nyack, NY: The Christian and Missionary Alliance, n.d.).
417  Simpson, CITB (1992), 3:241.
418  A.B. Simpson, "The Obedience of Faith," CAMW, June 6, 1895, 410.
419  Simpson, *The Gospel of Healing*, 128.
420  John A. MacMillan, SSQ, Nov. 22, 1942, 25.
421  John A. MacMillan, "The Cooperating Spirit," AW, May 4, 1936, 275.
422  Simpson, *How To Receive Divine Healing*, 12.
423  Bosworth, *For This Cause*, 17-18.
424  Simpson, *Lord for the Body*, 102, 103, 110-111.
425  Simpson, CITB (1993), 5:209, 212.
426  Kilgour, "Ordained a Preacher," 292.
427  Bosworth, *For This Cause*, 7.
428  Bosworth, *For This Cause*, 8-9.
429  Mrs. N. S. Dean, "Testimony," CMAW, Jan. 26, 1901, 56.
430  Simpson, *Days of Heaven on Earth*, June 18.
431  A.B. Simpson, *The Old Faith and the New Gospels* (Harrisburg, PA: Christian Publications, 1966), 60.
432  A.B. Simpson, "How to Keep It," AW, Apr. 27, 1940, 263.
433  Simpson, *The Old Faith and the New Gospels*, 59.
434  A.B. Simpson, "Editorial," CAMW, Nov. 1890, 274
435  Kenneth MacKenzie, "Healing or Helping?," *Triumphs of Faith,* Jan. 1903, 11.
436  A.B. Simpson, "Editorial," CAMW, Nov. 1890, 274.
437  A.B. Simpson, "Editorial," CAMW, Nov. 1890, 274
438  Simpson, *The Four-fold Gospel*, 48.
439  Simpson, *The Gospel of Healing*, 68.
440  Russell Kelso Carter, *Faith Healing Reviewed After Twenty Years* (Boston, Chicago: The Christian Witness Co., 1897), 110, 112.
441  Carter, *Faith Healing Reviewed*, 112-114.
442  S.D. Gordon, *The Healing Christ* (New York: Fleming H. Revell; Ann Arbor, MI: Vine Books, [1924] 1985), xi.
443  S.D. Gordon, *The Healing Christ*, 65-66.
444  A.B. Simpson, *Triumphs of Faith*, Nov. 1922, 252.
445  A.B. Simpson, "Inquiries and Answers," WWW, Nov. 1886, 294; "Inquiries and Answers" was published later in A.B. Simpson's book, *The Lord for the Body* (New York: Christian Alliance Publishing Co., n.d.), accessed at http://online.ambrose.edu/alliancestudies/ahtreadings/ahtr_s2.html.
446  Simpson, "Inquiries and Answers," WWW, Nov. 1886, 294.

447   Bailey, *Divine Healing*, 55.

448   J. Hudson Ballard, cited in Bailey, *Divine Healing*, 56.

449   R.A. Torrey, cited in Bailey, *Divine Healing*, 49.

450   G.P. Pardington, *Twenty-five Wonderful Years* (New York: Christian Alliance Publishing Co., 1912; New York: Garland, 1984), 59-60.

451   A.B. Simpson, "Two Stages of Divine Healing," AW, Jan. 28, 1953, 5.

452   Simpson, "Inquiries and Answers," WWW, Nov. 1886, 292-293.

453   Carter, *The Atonement for Sin and Sickness*, 126; see also pp. 124-133.

454   Torrey, *Divine Healing*, 19.

455   S.D. Gordon, *The Healing Christ*, 90.

456   Simpson, *The Gospel of Healing*, 64.

457   Simpson, "Inquiries and Answers," *Word, Work and World*, Nov. 1886, 291.

458   Carter, *Faith Healing Reviewed*, 91.

459   Simpson, *Seeing the Invisible*, 177.

460   A.W. Tozer, *Worship: The Missing Jewel* (Camp Hill, PA: Christian Publications, 1992), 8, 10.

461   A.B. Simpson, "Hindering the Holy Spirit," AW, Mar. 13, 1915, 370.

462   A.B. Simpson, "Spiritual Worship," *Living Truths*, May 1907, 242.

463   A.W. Tozer, *The Purpose of Man* (Ventura, CA: Regal, 2009), 71.

464   Tozer, *The Purpose of Man*, 30.

465   Tozer, *The Purpose of Man*, 8.

466   A.W. Tozer, *The Root of the Righteous* (Camp Hill, PA: Christian Publications, 1955, 1986), 92, 94.

467   A.B. Simpson, "Our New Hymn Book," CAMW, June 5, 1891, 354.

468   A.B. Simpson, "Side Issues and Essentials," AW, Jan. 1, 1910, 217-218.

469   A.B. Simpson, cited in MacMillan "Our Alliance Message," AW, Dec. 27, 1941, 826.

470   Simpson, *Present Truths*, 9-10.

471   Wilbur F. Meminger, "Touring the Pacific Northwest, CMAW, May 15, 1909, 116.

472   John MacMillan, "Modern Hymns," AW, Feb. 24, 1940, 115.

473   Tozer, *Worship: The Missing Jewel*, 20-21.

474   Tozer, *God Tells the Man Who Cares*, 4.

475   John MacMillan, "With Heart and Voice," AW, May 13, 1939, 290.

476   John Salmon, "My Enduement," CMAW, Oct. 26, 1907, 54-55.

477   F. E. Marsh, "Revival in the Missionary Institute at South Nyack on Hudson," CMAW, Nov. 17, 1906, 316; Fred R. Bullen, "Among the Nyack Students," CMAW, Dec. 8, 1906, 363.

478   Simpson, "The Worship and Fellowship of the Church," 126.

479   Ballard, "The Spiritual Clinic," AW, Nov. 21, 1914, 126.

480   A.B. Simpson, Editorial, CMAW, Mar. 16, 1907, 121.

481   Simpson, "Spiritual Sanity," 195.

482   William T. MacArthur, "Excerpts from Annual Reports," May 25, 1909.

483   Dr. Keith Bailey, Vice President of Church Ministries, paper to C&MA District Superintendents, 1977.

484   Mullen, "A New Experience," 17.

485   McCrossan, *Speaking in Other Tongues*, 33.

486   A. B. Simpson, "Editorial Correspondence," CAMW, Apr. 17, 1895, 248.

487   Madele Wilson, "Children's Page," AW, Oct. 28, 1911, 61.

488   John MacMillan, "With Heart and Voice," AW, May 13, 1939, 290.

489   A.W. Tozer, *The Warfare of the Spirit* (Camp Hill, PA: Christian Publications, 1993), 37.

490   W.W. Newberry, "David Brings the Ark to Jerusalem," AW, July 17, 1920, 252.

491   Newberry, "David Brings the Ark to Jerusalem," 252.

492   Newberry, "David Brings the Ark to Jerusalem," 252.

493   Madele Wilson, "Children's Page," AW, Oct. 28, 1911, 61.

494   A.B. Simpson, "The Lord's Supper, AW, Sept. 8, 1934, 567.

495   Tozer, *Tragedy in the Church*, 120-121.

496   A.B. Simpson, "The Lord's Supper," 567.

497   Tozer, *Tragedy in the Church*, 121.

498   Tozer, *Tragedy in the Church*, 129.

499   Kilgour, "Ordained a Preacher, 292.

500   Edith L. Blumhofer, *The Assemblies of God: A Chapter in the Story of American Pentecostalism, Volume 1 — To 1941* (Springfield, MO: Gospel Publishing House, 1989), 185.

501   A.B. Simpson, Editorial, *Living Truths*, May 1906, 257-258; A.B. Simpson, "Fervor and Fanaticism," CMAW, Dec. 22, 1906, 390

502   McCrossan, *Speaking with Other Tongues*, 3-4.

503   Jaffray, "Speaking in Tongues," 395.

504   W.T. Dixon, "About Tongues: A Word in Season," 28.

505   A.B. Simpson, Editorial, AW, Feb. 2, 1907, 49.

506   Simpson, "Gifts & Graces," 303.

507   Simpson, "Gifts and Grace," 303.

508   W.C. Stevens, "The Recovery of the Sick," AW, Aug. 17, 1929, 535.

509   Jaffray, "Speaking in Tongues," 396.

510   Simpson's Diary, May 1907.

511   Montgomery, *Under His Wings*, 165.

512   McCrossan, *Speaking with Other Tongues*, 42-43.

513   MacArthur, "Healing from Deafness and Deliverance from Demons," AW, Jan. 26, 1924, 770.

514   *Word and Work*, Aug. 13, 1921, 5.

515   Simpson, Editorial, AW, Feb. 24, 1912, 322; MacArthur, "Healing from Deafness and Deliverance from Demons," AW, Jan. 26, 1924, 770.

516   William T. MacArthur, "A Reminiscence of Rev. A.B. Simpson," AW, Aug. 21, 1920, 325-326.

517   Carrie Judd Montgomery, "Witchcraft and Kindred Errors," AW, Oct. 15, 1938, 661.

518   A.B. Simpson, AW, Feb. 24, 1912, 321.

519   Simpson, "Editorial," CMAW, Jan. 23, 1909, 280.

520   Simpson, "Editorial," CMAW, Jan. 23, 1909, 280.

521   A. B. Simpson, "A Week of Prayer," CMAW, Feb. 6, 1909, 314.

522   A.B. Simpson, Editorial, AW, Feb. 24, 1912, 321.

523   Jaffray, "Speaking in Tongues," 395.

524   A.W. Tozer, *The Counselor* (Camp Hill, PA: Christian Publications, 1993), 63-64.

525   A.B. Simpson, Editorial, CMAW, Sept. 19, 1908, 414.

526  A.B. Simpson, Editorial, CMAW, Jan. 21, 1911, 264.

527  A.B. Simpson, Editorial, CMAW, May 4, 1907, 205.

528  McCrossan, *Speaking with Other Tongues*, 42.

529  Rader, *Harnessing God*, 95-96, 99.

530  Ballard, "Spiritual Gifts with Special Reference to the Gift of Tongues," 24.

531  Montgomery, "Miraculously Healed by the Lord Thirty Years Ago," 9.

532  Rev. N. H. Harriman, "'War on the Saints': An Analytical Study, Part III," AW, Jan. 10, 1914, 230-231.

533  Mary E. McDonough, "The Harvest Rain," CMAW, Feb. 5, 1910, 305.

534  John A. MacMillan, SSQ, Dec. 25, 1938, 39.

535  May Mabette Anderson, "The 'Latter Rain,' and Its Counterfeit, Part IV" *Living Truths*, Sept. 1907, 535.

536  Burton K. Jones, *The Lady Who Came* (St. John's, Newfoundland, Canada: Good Tidings Press, 1982), 103.

537  W.A. Cramer, "Pentecost at Cleveland," CMAW, Apr. 27, 1907, 201.

538  Jaffray, "Speaking in Tongues," 395.

539  "An Influential Endorsement," *The New Acts*, April 1907, 3, cited by Gary B. McGee, "Levi Lupton: A Forgotten Pioneer of Early Pentecostalism," *Faces of Renewal*, ed. Paul Ebert (Peabody, MA: Hendrickson, 1988), 207n41.

540  A.W. Tozer, *Wingspread* (Harrisburg, PA: Christian Publications, 1943), 133.

541  Bertha Pinkham Dixon, *A Romance of Faith*, 128.

542  Marsh, "The Gift of Tongues," 259-264.

543  William T. MacArthur, "The Promise of the Father and Speaking with Tongues in Chicago," CMAW, Jan 26, 1907, 40.

544  A. B. Simpson, Annual Report of the Christian and Missionary Alliance, 1907-1908, 75.

545  "Notes from the Home Field," CMAW, Apr. 11, 1908, 33; S.M. Gerow, "Report of Annual Convention of Akron, O. Branch of the C&MA," CMAW, Apr. 17, 1909, 48.

546  Tozer, *The Tozer Pulpit*, 99.

547  John S. Sawin, "The Response and Attitude of Dr. A.B. Simpson and the Christian and Missionary Alliance to the Tongues Movement of 1906-1920," 29. Paper presented at the Society of Pentecostal Studies Conference, September 1986, Fort Myers, Florida.

548  Editorial, *The India Alliance*, August 1907, 19.

549  Tozer, *Tragedy in the Church*, 20.

550  A.W. Tozer, *Man: The Dwelling Place of God* (Camp Hill, PA: Christian Publications, 1966), 121-132.

551  Simpson, CITB (1994), 6:375.

552  Simpson, *The Holy Spirit*, 2:546.

553  John A. MacMillan, "Spiritual Energy," AW, June 22, 1940, 386.

554  A.B. Simpson, Editorial, CMAW, Mar. 16, 1907, 121.

555  McCrossan, *Speaking with Other Tongues*, 42-43.

556  Mullen, "A New Experience," 17.

557  Mae Mabette Anderson, "The Latter Rain and Its Counterfeit, A Message for the Hour: Part I," *Living Truth*, July 1907, 383.

558  A.B. Simpson, Editorial, AW, Jan. 13, 1917, 225.

559  Simpson, 1907-1908 C&MA Annual Report, 10.

560   A.B. Simpson, "The Church," AW, June 21, 1919, 195.
561   A.B. Simpson, Editorial, CMAW, July 30, 1910, 288.
562   McCrossan, *Speaking with Other Tongues*, 42-43.
563   Rader, *Harnessing God*, 99-101.
564   John A. MacMillan, SSQ, Dec. 6, 1942, 30.
565   Carrie Judd Montgomery, "Witchcraft and Kindred Errors," 661.
566   Montgomery, "Witchcraft and Kindred Errors," 661.
567   McCrossan, *Speaking with Other Tongues*, 3-4.
568   A.B. Simpson, Editorial, AW, Feb. 2, 1907, 49.
569   Joseph Smale, "The Gift of Tongues," *Living Truths*, Jan. 1907, 39.
570   MacArthur, "The Promise of the Father and Speaking with Tongues in Chicago," CMAW, Feb. 9, 1907, 64.
571   Montgomery, "Witchcraft and Kindred Errors," 661.
572   Paul Rader, "At Thy Word—A Farewell Message," AW, Nov. 20, 1920, 532.
573   Pastor Schrenck, "Dangers and Warnings," WWW, July-Aug. 1885, 211-212.
574   Newberry, *Untangling Live Wires*, 99.
575   Simpson, "Gifts and Grace," 303; Simpson, "All the Blessings of the Spirit," 198.
576   Paris W. Reidhead, Jr., "That I May Know Him (Phil. 3:7-15): A Testimony," July 14, 1953, 36.
577   A.B. Simpson, Editorial, *Living Truths*, Dec. 1906, 706-710.
578   A.B. Simpson, Editorial, CMAW, Apr. 6, 1907, 157.
579   A.B. Simpson, "Ministry of Women," CAMW, Mar. 27, 1891, 195.
580   A.W. Tozer, cited in "Minutes of General Council 1995 and Annual Report 1994," The Christian and Missionary Alliance, 142.
581   Simpson, *The Land of Promise*, 69-70.
582   A.B. Simpson, "The Authority of Faith," *AW*, Apr. 23, 1938, 263.
583   A.B. Simpson, "Spiritual Talismans," *AW*, June 14, 1919, 178.
584   A.B. Simpson, *CITB: Luke* (n.d.), 183.
585   Simpson, CITB (1992), 5:413-414.
586   J.A. MacMillan "The Authority of the Believer in the Ephesian Epistle, Part VI," AW, Feb. 20, 1932, 116.
587   George D. Watson, *Bridehood Saints* (Cincinnati: God's Revivalist, n.d.), 117-118, 120-122.
588   A.B. Simpson, "Motors, Or the Secret of Spiritual Power," AW, Sept. 20, 1913, 387.
589   J.A. MacMillan, "The Authority of the Rod," AW, May 18, 1940, 311, 314.
590   J.A. MacMillan "The Authority of the Believer in the Ephesian Epistle," AW, Jan. 23, 1932, 61.
591   Peck, *Throne Life*, 37, 50, 76.
592   A.B. Simpson, "The Authority of Faith," *AW*, Apr. 23, 1938, 263.
593   J.A. MacMillan, "The Authority of the Intercessor," AW, May 23, 1936, 327.
594   John MacMillan, SSQ, May 3, 1936, 17.
595   Andrew Murray, *With Christ in the School of Prayer*, 117.
596   John MacMillan's Diary, cited in King, *A Believer with Authority*, 66.
597   John MacMillan's Diary, cited in King, *A Believer with Authority*, 90.
598   J.A. MacMillan "The Authority of the Believer in the Ephesian Epistle," AW, Feb. 13, 1932, 108.
599   J.A. MacMillan "The Authority of the Believer in the Ephesian Epistle" AW, Jan. 9, 1932, 22.

600  "Heavenly Quickening," AW, Sept. 21, 1946, 594.

601  "Fasting as an Aid to Prayer," AW, Mar. 4, 1950, 130

602  J.A. MacMillan, "The Authority of the Rod," AW, May 18, 1940, 314.

603  John A. MacMillan, SSQ, May 3, 1936, 17.

604  "The Victory of God," AW, Apr. 22, 1944, 210.

605  Simpson, CITB (1992), 1:371.

606  SSQ, Oct. 10, 1943, 6.

607  SSQ, Feb. 2, 1941, 14-15.

608  SSQ, Aug. 16, 1936, 22; SSQ, Feb. 2, 1941, 14-15.

609  SSQ, Aug. 16, 1936, 22; SSQ, Feb. 2, 1941, 14-15.

610  Harold J. Sutton, "The Teacher," Alliance Witness, May 12, 1965, 18.

611  Pastor C.H. Brunner, "The Afflictions of the People of God," AW, Oct. 10, 1942, 642.

612  Chaplain Jay Smith comments on MacMillan's teaching, cited in King, A Believer with Authority, 170.

613  SSQ, Feb. 2, 1941, 14-15.

614  Simpson, CITB (1992), 1:371.

615  Bosworth, For This Cause, 19-20.

616  Simpson, "Divine Healing in the Atonement," 123-124.

617  John A. MacMillan, "The Cooperating Spirit," AW, May 4, 1936, 275.

618  SSQ, Nov. 28, 1941, 24.

619  J.A. MacMillan "The Authority of the Believer in the Ephesian Epistle," AW, Feb. 27, 1932, 133, 142.

620  A.B. Simpson, "The Casting Out of Devils," CAMW, Nov. 13, 1895, 311.

621  W.C. Stevens, "The Recovery of the Sick," 535.

622  Conversation with Dr. John Ellenberger.

623  Tozer, Man: The Dwelling Place of God, 122.

624  R.A. Jaffray, "Our Great Unfinished Task," AW, July 9, 1927, 456.

625  SSQ, Aug. 9, 1953, 18.

626  Mrs. L.L. Hess, Preaching and Prayer or Special Services at Wuchow," AW, Apr. 24, 1920, 56.

627  John A. MacMillan, "Our Mohammedan Problem in the Philippines," AW, June 22, 1929, 404.

628  "Our Most Stubborn Foe," AW, June 27, 1942, 402.

629  "Praying Geographically," AW, Sept. 14, 1946, 579.

630  "Praying Geographically," 579.

631  "Praying Geographically," 579.

632  "A United World," AW, Sept. 14, 1946, 578.

633  V. Raymond Edman, "Questions You Have Asked," The Alliance Witness, Sept. 14, 1966, 18.

634  MacArthur, "The Phenomenon of Supernatural Utterance," 73.

635  Stevens, "The Recovery of the Sick," 533, 535.

636  "Substance of Dr. Peck's Account of His Healing of Acute Mania," CAMW, Mar. 21-28, 1890, 192ff.; George B. Peck, "In His Name," CAMW, Aug. 14, 1895, 102.

637  "Nyack Convention," CMAW, July 25, 1903, 109.

638  John A. MacMillan, Encounter with Darkness (Harrisburg, PA: Christian Publications, 1980), 82-83.

639  Pastor Schrenck, "Dangers and Warnings," WWW, July-Aug. 1885, 211-212.

640  MacArthur, "A Reminiscence of Rev. A.B. Simpson," AW, Aug. 21, 1920, 325-326.

641  Stevens, "The Recovery of the Sick," 535.

642  Tozer, *Born After Midnight*, 43.

643  William T. MacArthur, *Ethan O. Allen* (Philadelphia, PA: The Parlor Evangelist, c. 1924), 1-14.

644  John A. MacMillan, SSQ, Feb. 27, 1938, 28.

645  MacArthur, *Ethan O. Allen*, 11.

646  MacArthur, "A Reminiscence of Rev. A. B. Simpson," 325-326.

647  William T. MacArthur, "Healing from Deafness and Deliverance from Demons," AW, Jan. 26, 1924, 770.

648  MacArthur, "A Reminiscence of Rev. A.B. Simpson," 325-326.

649  Montgomery, *Under His Wings*, 200-201.

650  Paul Rader, "At Thy Word—A Farewell Message," AW, Nov. 20, 1920, 532.

651  Paul L. King, *Moving Mountains: Lessons in Bold Faith from Great Evangelical Leaders* (Grand Rapids: Chosen Books, 2004), 187-188.

652  Montgomery, "The Promise of the Father," *Confidence*, Nov. 15, 1908, 1-2.

653  Simpson, "The Baptism of the Holy Spirit: A Crisis or an Evolution?," 710.

654  Montgomery, "Miraculously Healed by the Lord Thirty Years Ago," 9-10.

655  John Salmon, "My Enduement," CMAW, Oct. 26, 1907, 54-55.

656  Brumback, *Suddenly . . . from Heaven*, 79-80.

657  Brumback, *Suddenly . . . from Heaven*, 79-80.

658  Pardington, *The Crisis of the Deeper Life*, 177-178.

659  William C. Stevens, "Divine Healing in Relation to Revivals," CMAW, Feb. 28, 1903, 124.

660  Simpson, "What Is Meant by the Latter Rain?," 38.

661  Simpson, *A Larger Christian Life*, 42.

662  MacArthur, "Fabrics Filled with Power," 390.

663  MacArthur, "Fabrics Filled with Power," 390.

664  Peck, *Throne Life*, 217.

665  A.B. Simpson, *Danger Lines in the Deeper Life* (Camp Hill, PA: Christian Publications, 1991), 2.

666  Simpson, "The Ministry of the Spirit," 438.

667  Tozer, *The Divine Conquest*, 127.

668  Simpson, *A Larger Christian Life*, 57, 64.

669  Simpson, *In Heavenly Places*, 114, 116-118, 125.

CPSIA information can be obtained at www.ICGtesting.com
228343LV00002B/3/P

9 780981 952666